Plains
Country
Towns

The John K. Fesler Memorial Fund
provided assistance in the publication of
this volume, for which the University of
Minnesota Press is grateful.

Plains Country Towns

John C. Hudson

University of Minnesota Press
Minneapolis

Published by the University of Minnesota Press,
2037 University Avenue Southeast, Minneapolis, MN 55414
Printed in the United States of America

Library of Congress Cataloging in Publication Data
Hudson, John C.
Plains country towns.
Bibliography: p.
Includes index.
1. Cities and towns—North Dakota—History.
2. Railroads—North Dakota—History. I. Title.
HT123.5.N9H82   1985   307.7'62'09784   84-13049
ISBN 0-8166-1347-8
ISBN 0-8166-1348-6 (pbk.)
The University of Minnesota
is an equal-opportunity
educator and employer.

Contents

Tables

Preface

The aim of this book is to explain the processes of town development in the Great Plains, from their origins at the beginning of white settlement up to the time when retrenchments and adjustments began around 1920. Understanding how a system becomes established requires studying that system in its relevant context, examining not only the parts but also their connections with one another. We need to consider towns jointly and simultaneously to understand why they were founded and why they grew as they did. Settlements grow for reasons of their own — internal character — but also because they gain at the expense of others, usually those close at hand. Selecting a random sample of places for study removes the geographical context of trade relations and market formation.

All towns start out small, but this obvious fact is ignored in studies of urbanization that start by studying the communities successful enough to survive. Understanding success also requires an understanding of failure, and to accomplish that one must approach the subject developmentally by examining what was attempted, not just what succeeded. An after-the-fact analysis of urbanization based on comparative population growth rates not only invites circular reasoning, but it also removes towns from their real origins as ideas in the minds of their creators.

A regional case-study approach overcomes some of these problems because it allows examination of the totality of factors in a manageable geographical setting. Case studies, of course, raise difficult methodological problems as well. If the case chosen is claimed as truly representative and treated as though it were an unbiased sample, it becomes a tacit claim to greater knowledge than is justified; otherwise the whole could be presented rather than the part. If the case study makes no claim to represent events beyond its own, self-imposed limits, it is open to questions of bias if any attempt is made to extrapolate the findings. I respectfully lay these questions aside at this point with the hope that they will be addressed meaningfully after comparably detailed studies have been done elsewhere.

The north-central portion of the state of North Dakota, an area of about 20,000 square miles covering fourteen counties, was chosen for study. I made the choice after a survey of available data sources showed that this area was particularly well represented. No common regional label is attached to the area. It is simply a slice of territory, large enough to admit diversity yet small enough to have been shaped by a limited number of outside influences. Stretching roughly from Devils Lake to Minot, it is bordered to the south and west by the rougher land of the Coteau du Missouri and to the north by the boundary with Canada. Commercial grain farming, notably spring wheat culture, has characterized the area's economy since the 1880s.

It is a region of many small towns, few cities and no metropolitan centers. More than two hundred towns were platted here and about twice that many rural post offices or inland towns made their appearance, totaling some five hundred locations that, at one time or another, qualified for the geographers' term "central place." Not all the places are shown on the maps in this book because some had life spans of only a few months. This ample supply of towns in a region that has always been known as sparsely settled suggests a measure of the interest that attached to town-making activities in the settlement process.

The scope and content of this book obviously reflect my own combination of interests and biases. It is not a regional monograph, yet I have allowed more details of the study area to creep in than would be the preference of those who view town formation as a complex of economic and social processes. Statistical concepts are used where they seem advantageous, and the style of reasoning peculiar to geographical location theory is important in several sections; however, I have tried not to force the subject away from the context of people and place. I believe that these separate traditions of scholarship are more valuable as complements to one another than they are as competing strategies, each aimed at a "true" explanation.

Many people and organizations helped me, directly or indirectly, during the research. I am indebted to the National Science Foundation and to program directors Howard Hines, Patricia McWethy, and Barry Moriarty for the support that allowed me to make several lengthy visits to the study area and to have extended contact with relevant archival materials.

I would like to thank Robert W. Lovett, Baker Library, Harvard University; the Department of Geography, Boston University; Kenneth Smemo, History Department, Moorhead State University; Ruby J. Shields and John Wickre, Division of Archives and Manuscripts, Minnesota Historical Society;

John Bergene, Soo Line Railroad Company; and the helpful people I found at the Iowa Historical Society, Des Moines; the State Historical Society of North Dakota and the State of North Dakota Library, Bismarck; the Minnesota Historical Society Library, St. Paul; the Transportation Library and the Map Library, Northwestern University, Evanston; and the Newberry Library, Chicago, for the courtesies they extended. More than a score of county recorders of deeds in North Dakota helped me find plat maps and accompanying documentation for hundreds of towns in the study area.

Brief portions of the present volume appeared earlier in several articles. I am indebted to the State Historical Society of North Dakota for permission to use parts of my article "North Dakota's Railway War of 1905," *North Dakota History*, Winter 1981. Some of the argument in chapter 3 draws upon "The Plains Country Town," which appeared in *The Great Plains: Environment and Culture*, edited by Brian W. Blouet and Frederick C. Luebke, University of Nebraska Press, 1979. Portions of chapters 1 and 7 (including fig. 21) are based on "Towns of the Western Railroads," *Great Plains Quarterly*, Winter 1982. I am grateful to the University of Nebraska Press for permission to draw upon these earlier papers. I would also like to thank Fred Luebke, Center for Great Plains Studies, University of Nebraska, and Brian Blouet, former director of the Center, now at Texas A&M University, for inviting me to participate in the symposia that let to those two papers. Richard Abel and, later, William Wood of the University of Minnesota Press provided friendly support of this project from its early stages through to final publication.

Thomas Harvey of the University of Minnesota Geography Departments, whose study of Red River Valley towns somewhat parallels the approach taken here, freely shared his ideas and his data. Michael Conzen, University of Chicago, helped me organize my thoughts in the early stages and also directed me to several valuable sources of information. I am extremely indebted to Frank Vyzralek, former State Archivist of North Dakota, who not only suggested sources of information but also shared with me his amazingly comprehensive knowledge of North Dakota's development. This book never would have emerged had it not been for Frank's assistance and encouragement.

Less tangible, but equally important, has been the inspiration I have received from fellow geographers, especially John Fraser Hart, in whose company I have visited countless "country towns" in both hemispheres; and Leslie Hewes, Walter Kollmorgen, and Cotton Mather, whose writings years ago showed me what a geographer might contribute to the study of the Great Plains region. Finally, I would like to express my appreciation to Barbara, who has more than repaid her former editor by forcing me to express my ideas more clearly.

John C. Hudson

Plains
Country
Towns

Chapter 1

Introduction

The summer of 1886 was uncommonly dry in northern Dakota Territory. Cold winds came late in September that year, and they fanned the inevitable fires that burned across the dry prairies toward the flanks of the Turtle Mountains just south of the Canadian border. The country was new to the few dozen homesteaders and their families; none had wintered there more than once, and most had filed their land claims just months before. O. W. Burnham, a civil engineer employed by the Northwest Land Company, was trying to finish a townsite plat as he braced against the wind and squinted through smoke from the prairie fires that threatened nearby.

There was already a town in place, just a mile north of the tract Burnham was surveying. Known as Bottineau, it had begun as a lone store building in 1883; in 1885, it had been platted as a twenty-four block townsite by John and Michael Ohmer of Dayton, Ohio, on land that Michael had taken as a homestead along one of the small creeks that flowed out of the wooded "mountains" just to the north. By the spring of 1886 Bottineau had two stores, a hotel, and a school to serve the surrounding population that was beginning to grow just as the Ohmers had predicted in their promotional newsletter. John Ohmer did his part by directing potential settlers to the Turtle Mountains from among the patrons of the railroad hotel he operated at Barnesville, Minn. Michael Ohmer's titles included presidency of the Turtle Mountain Coal and Land Co., whose chief business was the sale of lots in their other new town, Dunseith, east of Bottineau.[1]

The Ohmers' Turtle Mountain venture reached a crucial stage in the spring of 1886: they needed a railroad. James J. Hill's St. Paul, Minneapolis & Manitoba had missed Bottineau, thirty miles to the south, as it stretched 3 west from Devils lake toward Montana. A branch of Hill's road would secure Bottineau's future. Without a railroad, the Turtle Mountain country would never experience a farming boom and grow much beyond what it already was; and unless the branch were extended to Bottineau soon, investors would shift their attention elsewhere. A town could be promoted on faith as long as it remained ahead of the general course of development; but when the pace quickened, as it always did when a railroad appeared ready to build further, that promise had to be redeemed by the imminent arrival of rails or the town could collapse overnight.

There was little surprise when Hill decided to build a branch line to the Turtle Mountains, since the course of settlement there was already well established. The news that Hill's railroad would bypass the existing town of Bottineau, however, terminating at a new townsite barely a mile south of the older one, was hard for John Ohmer to believe. He begged Hill to reconsider, arguing that it was not too much to ask, given the business he had brought Hill's company by attracting settlers. Hill's response was characteristic: "I know nothing of the matter," he wrote across Ohmer's letter, and forwarded it to his townsite agents.

Hill knew plenty about the matter, of course. The railroad's town at the foot of the Turtle Mountains was being platted by the Northwest Land Company on a site purchased by the company's partners, Solomon G. Comstock and Almond A. White, prominent businessmen of Moorhead, Minn. Comstock and White had developed nearly two dozen townsites for Hill's Manitoba road in the Red River Valley and had reorganized their business in May 1886, to develop towns for Hill west of Devils Lake. Engineer Burnham shuttled between the various new townsites on the line, surveying plats for Comstock and White. Burnham finished his work near Bottineau and headed south to Rugby Junction on the main line to await the train back to Moorhead. There he chanced to meet an undaunted John Ohmer, who claimed he had persuaded the railroad company to run its line through his town, not the one that Burnham and his assistant had just finished demarcating by driving some 600 wooden stakes. When Burnham arrived back in Moorhead, he immediately checked out Ohmer's story with Solomon Comstock.[2]

Neither Burnham nor Ohmer, let alone the local residents, knew the railroad's plans for sure. Even Comstock and White, who received numerous inquiries during 1886 and early 1887 from parties interested in business possibilities at the new townsite, had to deflect attention from their venture because they did not yet know what the town was to be named. On 13 April 1887, Hill's general manager, Allen Manvel, finally told Comstock that "the terminal station we shall have to, as a matter of advertising and choice, call Bottineau." Comstock set out for Bottineau immediately to take advantage of the real estate boom that was sure to follow. All of the businesses from the older town moved over to the railroad by June, and they were joined by more than a dozen entrepreneurs before the end of 1887. When Comstock later filed his plat at the county courthouse, he identified it as "South Bottineau." The "South" was soon dropped, but it did not matter anymore: the old town was already deserted, and the Ohmers had quietly retreated.[3]

The rise of one Bottineau and the fall of another was not a remarkable event in the settlement of the American West. By changing the characters, time, and place, the same scenario could be used to describe a sequence that took place hundreds, perhaps thousands, of times in the late nineteenth and early twentieth centuries: small-time investors like the Ohmers, enthusiastically promoting schemes they hoped would make them rich; railroad presidents, no one of them more successful than James J. Hill, ruling from oak-paneled offices hundreds of miles away over developments that would forever shape a region's economy and settlement pattern; Comstock and White, the townsite agents, who did their best to make money for themselves while following the whims of the railroad men who decided where towns should be placed and for whom they should be named; business people eager to establish themselves in a new town that was "sure to grow"; surveyors like Burnham, packing along their well-worn tents, cooking gear, and tools as they hunted out the tracts of open prairie on which they would stake out the townsites; the shattered hopes for growth in places like old Bottineau, left deserted when the railroad passed it by; and the excitement of hopes reborn as business people skidded their store buildings across country to be relocated on the new railroad townsite—all of these were part of the process that created what is now known as the "network" of towns that covers the nation's agricultural interior.

Anyone who has traveled across the prairies and plains gathers an impression of the region's settlement fabric. A grain elevator rises predictably against the horizon, followed by a church steeple or school poking up above the canopy of cottonwoods. Up close, a small cluster of false-front store buildings lines Main Street, with perpendicular rows of white frame houses on one side of the highway and a railroad depot on the other. These perceptions mark one's passage through yet another of the villages that look so much alike to the outsider. The geometry is more regular when viewed from the air: individual structures are lost, but the regular spacing of towns along a railroad line that cuts across the rectangular grid of farms and fields is all the more remarkable.[4] It is the dominant settlement pattern in a broad region beginning with the Grand Prairie of Illinois on the east, stretching northwest to the Canadian prairies, south through Texas, and west to the Rocky Mountain front. Few of the towns have been the subject of extensive historic preservation; yet, because of their comparative youthfulness and the lack of sweeping developments that would have replaced them, they remain as living testimony to the ways in which people, money, and resources once were combined in the process of regional development.

The plains country town—what it was and how it got to be that way—touches on many of the traditional themes of western history. The subject is only partially rooted in the interplay of farmers, environment, and federal policy that has been the focus of most scholarly interpretations of agrarian settlement on the Great Plains. Towns depended less directly on the local climate and land resources, and, as entities in their own right, they reproduced with far less adaptation to local conditions the practices carried into the region by new settlers.[5] The perspective of local urban history is also useful, but again only partially so, because the process of town settlement took place on a regional scale. Towns were not independent of one another; rather, they were interdependent components of plans formulated by the largest corporations of the day for extracting value from dependent, colonial hinterlands.

Much can be learned about these towns through systematic study of the individual railroad corporations that created them.[6] This approach is limited, however, because most railroad towns came about as a result of traffic competition between railroads, rather than from the colonization strategies of companies working independently of one another. The locational models of urban and economic geography, which show how business people developed their trade areas, are also useful. But they assume just two classes of people, buyers and sellers; without a third class, the designers of the system, there would have been no framework in which the process could operate.

The theme of town design applies somewhat unevenly to the present study, since it is far more relevant in certain stages of growth than it is in others, but town planning deserves some elaboration at the outset to show how the plains country town resulted from an organic body of ideas about urban settlements that had been growing and changing for hundreds of years before the first plains towns were built. The term *design*, as used here, refers not only to the internal morphology of places but also to the context in which the settlements were deliberately founded—their raison d'être.

Almost all the towns on the plains were founded for the single purpose of serving the trade brought by a surrounding agricultural population. Their reason for being was commerce, which superordinated all other aspects of town life. Streets were invariably arranged in a grid pattern, and each town had clearly defined limits that were marked by a sharp break in building density. Towns were spaced interdependently so as to organize the trade of the hinterlands most efficiently.

The idea of deliberately planting towns in such fashion can be traced to the late medieval *bastide* of western Europe. From the twelfth through the fourteenth centuries, new urban centers appeared in areas where existing settlements had been destroyed or in territory that lacked sufficient towns. The *bastide* was often fortified, its walls containing a compact town laid out with a rectilinear, although not rigidly geometric, pattern of streets. Its strategic function was shared with virtually all other medieval urban settlements; and its internal structure, planned before settlement began, simply revived earlier Greek and Roman ideas about grid-pattern towns. Its preconceived purpose, however — to provide a "small-town" center of economic production and exchange for a surrounding territory — represented a break with the past.

The *bastide* form was widely copied in western Europe. Various aspects of its form and function were brought to North America by the English, the French, and the Spanish, who laid out the towns that would organize economic life in the colonies. Historians of city planning see unmistakable parallels between the European *bastide* and the original plans for New Haven, Philadelphia, and Cambridge, Massachusetts, to name a few.[7]

Many colonial New England towns had a more informal geometry, dictated by the placement of roads and paths that connected the settlements with their wharves and outlying fields, as well as with one another. They grew in piecemeal fashion, adding streets to connect existing ones, as population growth created new demand for building space. The process stood in sharp contrast to that in William Penn's Philadelphia, where population growth filled in the checkerboard design determined by the initial plat. As Vance has noted, "In New England, land utilization seems to have been the main test of the forms of land division; in Philadelphia, land-sale probably determined the form."[8]

If the Philadelphia and New England models can be taken as representative extremes of the choices open to later founders and promoters of towns, it is easy to understand why they followed Penn's example rather than that of New England's. Real estate parcels already existed in the predetermined plat, and they could be purchased and held by speculators who bet their value would increase as the town grew in size. Even in New England, speculation in town lands was commonplace by the first half of the eighteenth century as the tradition of covenanted communities began to give way to market forces. After 1715 in Connecticut and 1727 in Massachusetts, townsites were sold to the highest bidders. It was Ray Billington's thesis that "this desire for profits changed the whole course of new England's westward advance by breaking down the emphasis on groups and preparing the descendants of the Puritans to move into the trans-Appalachian area as individuals."[9]

By the time New Englanders were ready to look west for new economic opportunities, they had largely abandoned the town form they knew best in favor of compact, grid-pattern plats such as Philadelphia's. The migrating Yankees who streamed into central and western New York between 1780 and 1810 thus held in common three important ideas: that towns are the appropriate form of settlement to organize local agricultural trade as well as to act in an intermediary role with larger, distant urban centers (an inheritance from the *bastide*); that towns should be platted in advance of settlement to create a market for land that attracts real estate investment (as demonstrated by the success of Penn and others); and, perhaps as a corollary, that towns not only organize business, they are themselves a business that, if properly conducted, can bring their proprietors substantial wealth. These ideas were accepted not only by those who wished to make money in urban real estate, but also by settlers who came into the new towns seeking opportunities in trade and commerce.

As Turpin C. Bannister observed, the first decades of the nineteenth century were witness to "an orgy of town platting" in New York state.[10] By 1820, the nuclei of most present-day communities of central and western New York had been established. Townsite speculators, never a group to wait for the advancing agricultural frontier to catch up with them, quickly spread their operations into newly opened lands, hard on the heels of the military detachments that were herding the Indians toward reservations in the West. Ohio became the speculator's field after 1785, when the Northwest Territory was opened to settlement. Accompanying each wave of town founding was a subsequent period of rapid investment, followed by an inevitable collapse of real estate values and charges of fraud leveled against the promoters.

The problem of unregulated speculation was so serious that, in 1800, Ohio Territory enacted a law regulating town plats. Similar laws were passed in California, Colorado, Dakota, Florida, Illinois, Indiana, Iowa, Kansas, Michigan, Minnesota, Missouri, Nebraska, Oregon, Virginia, and Wisconsin by 1878.[11] Most made it unlawful to sell lots without first recording the plat at the office of the County Recorder (register of deeds). Other aspects of the town plat laws of various states required full information on the dimensions of streets, alleys, and other public grounds plus a statement by the proprietor conveying such properties to the public. Regulations also governed the mode of making surveys (placing of markers, stakes, etc.), and made provision for the vacation of plats in cases where all or a portion of the land set aside for certain purposes on the townsite was abandoned to other uses.

The list of states enacting town plat laws by 1878 is by no means a random grouping; only two of them were south of the Ohio River, and most were in the region where an extension of Yankee influence, via New York, was the dominant cultural background of town founders. The idea that towns had to be platted to be real was firmly entrenched in the northern mind, along with the idea of selling lots on a checkerboard to optimistic, energetic newcomers who intended to establish themselves in some mercantile venture that would bring them a stable, prosperous future. Wherever this group went, their ideas about towns followed, and hence their constellation of beliefs was embodied in the physical structure and economic life of hundreds of new towns founded in the Middle West.

South of the Ohio River was another story. The Upland South is acknowledged to have two forms of urban, or quasi-urban, settlement. County seat towns were formally platted, often around a central square that copied early southeastern Pennsylvania models and where important public and private business of the county was focused. Informal, unplatted hamlets (sometimes no more than a crossroads general store and one or two houses) occupy road or river junctions, hilltops, or valley bottoms. Spaced no more than a few miles apart, these hamlets grow slowly, in piecemeal fashion, if they grow at all. County seats and hamlets of this sort are found in all parts of the United States, but even a casual inspection of their respective maps of distribution shows an unmistakable alignment with the growth and spread of population south along the grain of the Appalachian Mountains and then west into the interior plateaus of Kentucky and Tennessee.[12] In short, those who were born and raised in this section of the country were not, and still are not, wedded to the idea that all towns must be platted, grow in an orderly fashion, and exhibit sharply defined boundaries.

The significance of this sectional split in ideas about towns bears directly on the experience of settlement in the Middle West and, later, the Great Plains. Until the 1840s, the middle and upper Mississippi Valley was most directly accessible by water transportation. Since the river system of the region is much like a tree, branching away from the trunk of the lower Mississippi, access was afforded most easily from the south, rather than directly overland from the east via a road system that was inferior or nonexistent. The first wave of new settlers to the Middle West came from the upper southern states for this reason, and along with these people inevitably came their ideas about towns. So-called "river towns" of the Missouri and upper Mississippi valleys bear the stamp of their influence, but few towns away from the principal rivers do, largely because these towns came later and hence embodied a different set of ideas held by a different group of people.

The northerners who invaded the middle western prairies and woodlands only slightly preceded the penetration of the interfluves by railroad lines in the 1850s, but their arrival so closely coincided in most areas that "Yankees" and "railroads" were nearly synchronous events. Before the railroads, settlements located away from navigable streams were at a strong disadvantage in terms of transportation cost. With a railroad, however, towns served by water transport possessed few advantages over their dryland counterparts. Logistics thus were inverted between 1850 and 1870, the Middle

West acquired a new population almost simultaneously, and the towns founded by this wave of northerners were located along the new railway lines extending from Milwaukee, Chicago, Kansas City, Omaha, or St. Paul-Minneapolis—the railroad capitals of the region.[13]

The era of railroad towns in the West began in this context in the 1850s; but accompanying the new phase of town building were some important changes in the geographical scale of economic activity. The hundreds of new communities founded along the expanding network of railroad lines were populated by a new migration of northerners, and those responsible for platting the towns came from similar backgrounds. No longer, however, were towns founded on an individual basis. An increasingly larger share of the wealth generated by the Middle West's agricultural surplus was channeled through the region's leading urban centers, which processed or transshipped the commodities and performed manufacturing and wholesaling functions for the smaller towns linked to them by railroads. The wealth accumulated by merchants and manufacturers in the large cities because of this economic role was, in turn, invested in the construction of more railroad lines. As this happened, railroad builders arrogated unto themselves the responsibility for creating the new towns that would connect their lines with the surrounding agricultural countryside. Town platting thus became the function of railroad corporations, or their designated townsite agents, and the opportunities for individual townsite speculators were decreased commensurately.

The first chain of trade center towns was created by the Illinois Central Railroad on its lines north from Centralia toward Chicago and Galena. The Illinois Central, which received a substantial federal land grant, was forbidden to engage in town building itself. But the officers of the company, known as "the Associates," purchased land adjacent to the station grounds located by the railroad and proceeded to lay out a series of symmetric, gridded plats bisected by the tracks. They not only used the same plat for most of the towns, they also used the same street names.[14] Were it not for the vagaries of economic success in the various towns they platted, it would be possible today to stand at the corner of 1st and Chestnut streets and look northeast to the Illinois Central depot in more than a score of Illinois towns.

Townsites along the Burlington & Missouri River Railroad west of Lincoln, Nebraska, were controlled by the Eastern Land Association, again a group of railroad-affiliated entrepreneurs who saw the profits to be made in such a venture. As if to underscore the line-chain nature of the towns, they used an alphabetical sequence (Crete, Dorchester, Exeter, Fairmont, Grafton, Harvard, etc.) of names—many reflecting their own New England heritage.[15] By the 1870s, when the railroad frontier and the population frontier moved westward in synchronous spurts of development, the business of founding new towns was essentially a responsibility for railroad companies to discharge as they saw fit. The profitability of each new line of road depended on the amount of traffic that could be generated, and the traffic volume stood in direct proportion to the tons of freight and the number of passengers each town along the line could produce. The railroads' new communities seldom were "company towns," a practice more characteristic of mining and lumbering corporations; nevertheless, they were an indispensable part of the transportation business.

The Civil War briefly interrupted railroad and townsite activity, but the northern victory indirectly produced another injection of Yankee influence. The war, with its attendant difficulties of supplying and transporting troops, had been a training ground for young men who found themselves possessed of engineering skills that were in great demand by the new railroads in the West. Gen. Grenville M. Dodge, who became chief engineer for the Union Pacific when he left the army in 1866, frankly acknowledged that "construction of the Union Pacific was upon a military basis."[16] The heads of the engineering parties and all the construction chiefs had been officers in the war.

Dodge, who served a term in Congress representing the western district of Iowa while simultaneously directing Union Pacific construction west of North Platte, was also placed in charge of Union Pacific's Town Lot Department in 1867. Born in Massachusetts, Dodge had received engineering training at Norwich Academy in Vermont and had come west to seek a career in railroad building. Employment with several Illinois and Iowa roads eventually took him to Council Bluffs, where, by his own estimation, he conceived the idea that the Pacific railroad should be built westward from that point and then persuaded Abraham Lincoln to favor that route for the nation's first transcontinental line.

He was probably the most colorful of the western railroad-townsite builders. As a recent biographer noted, "Dodge's favorite occupation was anything that made money, irrespective of whether it were ethical or permanent."[17] His influence with army generals, his seat in the Congress, and his simultaneous association with the Union Pacific doubtless helped that company through the earlier crises it experienced. Later, with his son-in-law R. E. Montgomery, Dodge directed townsite operations for the Texas & Pacific and the Forth Worth & Denver City. Cheyenne, Laramie, Midland, and Odessa were some of his more successful creations, although there is little evidence that he had more than passing acquaintance with his towns.[18]

Most of the Union Pacific's Nebraska towns had been built when Dodge assumed control in 1867. It became his duty to supervise railroad construction and to locate and plat towns across the vast, unprotected stretches of Wyoming Territory. He used his influence to obtain army cavalry companies to protect his crews and to enforce his order banning the sale of whiskey near Union Pacific construction. Under General Dodge's command, there was little distinction between railroad and military matters; in his own mind, there was probably no difference. He had the city of Laramie, Wyo., platted on the grounds of a military reservation (Fort Sanders) "for the protection of our property and the people connected with our enterprise," and then he persuaded Gen. William Tecumseh Sherman to approve it.[19]

In December 1867, Dodge sent an assistant to visit the land departments of the Illinois Central and the Cedar Rapids & Missouri River railroads. What he borrowed from their experience is not clear, but at the end of 1870 Dodge reported that his Town Lot Department now had "a perfect system, well established, and after the most approved system used in the country." His department had "brought to the U.P.R.R. Company nearly $200,000 directly in cash or its equivalent and its cost has been nominal as it has been run by the Engineering Dept. without extra help or wages."[20]

His strategy for getting each town off to a good start was one that was adopted by other railroad townsite companies. The Town Lot Department sold alternate lots at nominal prices to the first comers but reserved the rest for future sale at higher prices. Lumber and fuel dealers were given special consideration; without them, Dodge observed, it was difficult to sell any lots on a townsite. Most of all, he stressed the need to coordinate various departments of the railroad to stimulate business.

Grenville Dodge's vision of what the company could do for itself by encouraging on-line settlement summarizes the philosophies of many others who promoted railroad townsites in the West:[21]

> Our Road at no distant future will open a country susceptible of sustaining almost every known branch of trade and traffic, situated as we are midway between two great commercial centers. Towns on our Road can command supplies from the East or the West; with Mining yet in its infancy, with a stock trade that is growing in such proportions as very soon to cover the prairies with herds of cattle and sheep, with a much larger per cent of our land fit for agricultural purposes than is generally supposed, all of which will build up with it the towns on our lines, it seems to me it is our duty to at once place the Department upon a healthy, reliable basis for all time. . . . It will bring income to them who have so often risked and pledged their all to the enterprise.

Dodge's statement that the Union Pacific and its towns would "open" the country to settlement was a common assumption of those in his position. Although the development brought by a railroad marked a sharp break with any settlement system that preceded it, no railroad placed its tracks and towns upon an empty scene.

Ideas brought to the Great Plains about the proper form and function of towns had to be expressed within an ongoing process of development. The plains country town evolved in place, through three phases of regional development: the frontier era of trading posts and military forts, a subsequent phase of inland towns (a regional term referring to settlements not served by a railroad), and a third, that of railroad towns, which became the dominant form thereafter. Each phase "opened" the region for what followed. Accompanying the shifts from one system to the next were parallel changes in economic and social life (table 1).

The sequence is based on time with development interpreted as forward looking rather than functionally necessary on the basis of what followed. Neither was the driving force behind the three-stage sequence some mysterious, Turnerian engine propelling the region through a progression of inexorable stages. The succession of trade- and town-building activities was undertaken by individuals who *anticipated* that their efforts would pave the way for what was to come. The business of the frontier was to establish conditions under which white traders and their settlements could prosper, with the military present during this phase less to meet needs of the time than those of the projected settlement to follow. Trading activity was extended into the hinterlands in the form of inland towns or speculative townsites created in anticipation of a railroad-based settlement system. Centralization of the more important decisions affecting settlement under the auspices of a few agencies (mainly railroads and their townsite affiliates) created a new system that produced towns founded with the single purpose of collecting the region's agricultural surplus for shipment to terminal markets.

My thesis can be comprehended easily by viewing towns not as indivisible entities but rather as a threefold division of variables—*people, activities,* and *structures*—that are set in the relevant *context* of time and place. Activities refer to all forms of human social and economic behavior that make towns function. Structures include plats, buildings, modifications of the natural environment, and other static forms that result from and simultaneously influence human activities. The groups of variables impinge on each other, and all respond to the peculiarity of circumstances (context). We are aided in the comparative study of town systems by systematically varying some components while holding others constant.

The threefold grouping also reflects competing hypotheses about the success of towns: that growth is a function of the skill of leading business people and promoters; that towns grow because of the nature and range of the activities they perform; or that success is a function of the town's location and the structure provided by its designers.[22] Most historians ascribe community success to influential *people* who organized the same mix of structures and activities found elsewhere, only more successfully.[23] Geographers are more inclined to measure success by enumerating town *activities*: the larger the trading area, the larger the number and variety of functions, and hence the greater the volume of business; the role of personal entrepreneurship is all but overlooked in such an approach.[24]

The primacy of structure in this triadic framework is much less common;

Table 1. Phases of Town Development in Northern Dakota

Aspect of Town Life	1870	1880	1890	1900	1910	1920
	----Frontier----		----Inland Towns----		----Railroad Towns----	
People						
Population density		Discontinuous		Fewer than 2 per square mile	2-10 per square mile	
Ethnicity		Aboriginal, French-Canadian, Anglo-American		Anglo-American (towns), North European (rural)	Anglo-American, European	
Family		Tribal structure, individuals (white)		Individuals; nuclear family	Nuclear family	
Structures						
Spatial organization		Linear, strategic	Open, inclusive		Closed, exclusive	
Location of towns		Post stations of fur companies and U.S. government	Entrepreneurial trial-and-error		Determined by railroads	
Town types		Trading posts and military forts		General stores and post offices, scattered	Platted towns, regularly spaced	
Activities						
Agricultural mode		Subsistence; government provision contracts	Stock raising and general farming		Commercial grain farming	
Transport		Steamboat, freight wagon, horseback		Freight and stage lines	Steam railroad	
Business ownership		Appointed agents and factors	Single proprietors		Proprietors, partners, line chains	
Personal mobility		Occasional long-distance trips	Infrequent, mainly long-distance trips		Frequent trips, short distance	
Social life		Post-centered	Undifferentiated local community		Town-country social separation	

its role is preeminent, however, in towns founded by the western railroads, and this priority distinguishes plains country towns from those of similar size in other regions. It is commonly acknowledged that railroads created most of these communities, but how and why they did so can be understood by focusing on their role as designers. *Structure* assumed priority because railroads were interested in creating a total system that would advance their corporate goals. The first consideration lay in placement of railway routes, with townsites created afterward to capture traffic. The regional design was accompanied by a standardization of internal town structure and rules for building that would make these places grow and prosper. Central places did not have to come into being in this manner, as illustrated by the many so-called inland towns and speculative townsites that preceded those created by railroads; but the power of railroad corporations eradicated the prospect for urbanization at any sites that they ignored with prejudice. This influence has also been documented beyond any question, although the purpose of the railroads in exerting the influence has not been given adequate weight.

Most studies of central place systems or of individual towns take settlements — agglomerations of activities providing goods and services — as the starting point, from which interconnections of trade develop. The priority assumes that activity begets structure and that economic transactions give rise to commerce between places. Thus, farmers produce crops that have to be moved to market, so transport routes are provided; division of labor dictates that they do not produce all they consume, and so tradespeople locate centrally to provide the necessary "support" functions. The explanation is demand-driven, and it ignores the design within which such transactions take place. Railroad companies, in contrast, were suppliers not only of transportation but also of *structures*, at the regional, local, and townsite scale, that gave the settled landscape its commercial geometry.

The resemblance between the railroad-created system — nearly equal-sized market areas surrounding regularly spaced, small towns along lines of transport — and the stylized patterns of central place theory requires an explicit, advance warning to geographers and others familiar with this theory who may find confirmation of central place reasoning in this book. The ideas of Walter Christaller and August Lösch are treated here as basic to an understanding of the reciprocal relationships between established trading points and their surrounding consumer hinterlands.[25] That a concatenation of such relationships leads automatically to a Christallerian or Löschian "landscape," however, clearly cannot be argued using this case study as a base. Central place theory assumes no externally imposed design of the town network. The point I make here is that this network was designed, quite deliberately, by those with enough money and influence to make their plans a reality.

Neither should those who argue the inadequacy of central place theory take this disclaimer as evidence for an antithesis, such as Vance's "mercantile model" of town location and growth.[26] I will show that those who designed the town network held in their own minds what might be termed a "folk location theory." That is, they followed optimality principles roughly comparable with those embodied in central place theory, although their reasoning did not follow from a formal body of location rules—"rules of thumb" would be a better description.[27] What can be distilled from this study, in relation to central place theory, is a hypothesis: those who planned town networks, cognitively and deliberately, shared ideas of optimal spacing and function very similar to notions that are deducible from formal location theory in general and central place theory in particular.

The following chapters trace the processes of town formation in the North Dakota study area through the designs and purposes of those who wielded influence, whether before or during the phase of railroad town construction. In the frontier phase (chap. 2), trading activity took place outside the context of trade center towns. Inland towns (chap. 3) were an unsuccessful attempt to anticipate the developments that would attend the coming of the railroads; they were independent entities located in ignorance of the railroads' plans. The same failure characterized speculative townsites (chap. 4), which, although they possessed formal structure in their own right, were nonetheless irrelevant in the plans laid by railroad companies for colonization and traffic capture. Creation of a system for collecting the region's agricultural surplus at a minimum cost, and doing so with an eye for besting similar strategies of competing railroads, determined the system of trade center towns (chap. 5). Specification of external relations was followed by attempts to standardize the internal form and function of towns that collected the traffic moving over the company's lines (chaps. 6 and 7). In time, regional economic activity came into conformity with the hierarchical structure of transportation routes (chap. 8). The social life of commerce reflected the need to inject human activity into the structure that railroad companies had specified (chap. 9). The limits were reached in the early decades of the twentieth century (chap. 10), when railroad plans overreached what was economically viable in a region of sparse settlement.

Chapter 2

Frontier Beginnings

Trade center towns did not exist in the frontier phase of development in northern North Dakota, but the trading function was, nonetheless, an integral part of early settlement. The centers of fur-trading activity were located to provide access to the Indian populations. Military forts, which came later, were built near some of the Indian villages. Their sites were chosen mainly for strategic reasons, though forts also performed an economic role.

Travel by water, or by horseback and wagon following a watercourse, was faster and safer than that afforded by overland trails across unsheltered prairies. Wooded ravines concealed those who preyed upon the traders, messengers, and scouts shuttling between the isolated outposts. Routes commonly consisted of a series of dogleg segments, from a river valley across country to a landmark grove of trees, a butte, or a lake, thence in another direction to some other feature that could be seen and recognized at a distance. Outposts were connected in a zigzag, linear fashion, and the serious business of choosing and maintaining the routes was a time-consuming activity for those who depended on them.

One such trail connected the British forts along the Assiniboine River, in what was to become Manitoba, and the Mandan and Hidatsa villages on the Missouri (fig. 1). It led from the Souris River to the Turtle Mountains, then passed via Dogden Butte to reach the Missouri near the mouth of the Knife River. Many traders used this route, including employees of the Hudson's Bay and North West companies as well as free traders and the Cree and Assiniboin Indians. Access to the south, via the Missouri River, was first accomplished by keelboats. Steamboating on the upper Missouri did not begin until the 1830s.

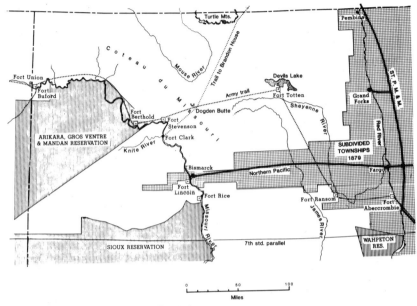

Figure 1. Northern Dakota: frontier to 1879

U.S. interest in the upper Missouri region, which became part of the United States with the Louisiana Purchase in 1803, was quick in coming. When Lewis and Clark returned down the Missouri in 1806 they reported meeting eleven parties totaling twenty boats loaded with trade goods coming upriver.[1] The allegiance of the Indians remained with the British, however, even after the War of 1812, although St. Louis fur traders began to make inroads. By the late 1820s, under the virtual monopoly of John Jacob Astor's American Fur Company, the upper Missouri had become part of St. Louis's fur trade hinterland. The posts Astor and his predecessors built along the river were supplied once or twice each year via steamboats sent upriver by the company. Furs were sent downriver in flat-bottomed boats called mackinaws that could take a fifteen-ton load down to St. Louis in a week.

Astor's forts were stockaded structures that enclosed residences, stables, workshops, and a building for trading. The forts employed clerks, craftsmen, teamsters, interpreters, and laborers of various sorts. Many of the post employees were of French and Indian heritage (métis). Fort Clark, built in 1831 at the Mandan and Hidatsa villages located at the mouth of the Knife River, had a stockade that enclosed nearly 20,000 square feet and employed about twenty men. It was a trading center for beaver pelts (bought from white trappers) plus the buffalo robes and other furs bought from the Indians. The fort was abandoned prior to 1864 when the American Fur Company sold out to the St. Paul-based Northwestern Fur Company.

In 1845, the Hidatsas living near Fort Clark moved some forty miles upriver. Fort Clark trader Francis Chardon followed and, with Indian help, built Fort Berthold next to the village (fig. 2). The Mandans, whose numbers had been decreased more than 90 percent by a smallpox epidemic, and the Arikara later joined the Hidatsas at the new village, named Like-a-Fish-Hook for the bend in the Missouri just below.[2] The first Indian agent was appointed in 1868, and soon a sawmill, gristmill, blacksmith shop, and carpenter shop were constructed. Another smallpox epidemic, scurvy, and crop failures took their toll among these agricultural people, as did occasional raids by the Dacotah (Sioux). A company of infantry troops was stationed there to protect them. Fort Berthold and Like-a-Fish-Hook village, which functioned as a single settlement, for a time served three purposes—that of Indian village (with a population estimated at 2,300 in 1866), trading post, and military camp, with a variety of craftsmen and tradespeople under the employ of the fur company, the army, or the Indian agency.[3]

The presence of army troops marked the beginning of a new era. Discoveries of gold in the Pacific Northwest made northern Dakota a migrant's corridor in the 1860s, just as Nebraska had been during California's gold rush a decade before. News of strikes in Idaho's Clearwater district, followed closely by still larger finds near Virginia City, Mont., spread an epidemic of

Figure 2. Fort Berthold in 1867, as sketched by General de Trobriand. From *Army Life in Dakota.*

gold fever in the eastern states. Thousands of fortune seekers began the journey west, and many came via St. Paul and headed northwest toward the Red River.

Fort Abercrombie on the Red River marked the western edge of territory that could be considered safe for travel, and even that was surrounded by vast stretches of country crossed by Sioux hunting parties. Angry and retreating, the Sioux were fighting back repeated attempts to push them west. Unescorted passage between the Red and the Missouri was discouraged, and the Secretary of War arranged for several wagon trains to be guided west from Fort Abercrombie to Montana. The War Department continued its campaigns against the Sioux, while protecting the passage of white adventurers, but the commitment of men was burdensome in a territory so large and without military installations.

The army soon began construction of a series of forts to secure the land and water routes across the northern Plains. Fort Rice, built in 1864, was followed by Forts Buford, Stevenson, Totten, and Ransom in 1867. The land route that travelers were encouraged to follow led them from Fort Abercrombie straight west to Fort Ransom on the Sheyenne River, north to Fort Totten on Devils Lake, then west to Fort Stevenson on the Missouri (fig. 1). From there, the Missouri was followed past Fort Buford at the mouth of the Yellowstone River to Fort Benton, the head of navigation on the Missouri.

A French aristocrat—Gen. Philippe Regis de Trobriand, the eldest son of one of Napoleon's generals—who had come to the United States and served in the Civil War was placed in command of Fort Stevenson in 1867. The troops he was to command had been removed from Fort Berthold a few months before his arrival, when the army abandoned the old fur trade post in favor of Fort Stevenson. To de Trobriand's surprise the men were infantry, not cavalry, and his thoughts quickly turned to defense of his small garrison.[4] Isolation was broken by the regular passage of steamboats plying the Missouri and by the nearly constant movement of nearby Indians. The most serious problem he faced was maintaining contact with the post at Fort Totten.

The 150 miles of open country across the Coteau du Missouri that separated Fort Totten and Fort Stevenson was the weakest link in the army's chain. Dispatches were exchanged between the posts and, although many of the messages were of little consequence, a high priority was placed on keeping open the lines of communication. The U.S. government had also awarded a mail contract for the route between Fort Abercrombie and Montana that joined the sequence of military posts across northern Dakota. Fort Totten's garrison of three companies received its provisions via contact with the Missouri steamboats at Fort Stevenson, adding a third reason for protecting passage along the trail. A schedule was established whereby, on fixed dates, men would set out from both ends of the route. Five station shacks were built along the way to provide shelter each night. At the middle station, the couriers exchanged dispatches and then returned to their respective forts.[5]

Two months after de Trobriand took command at Fort Stevenson, the mail carriers told of encountering a camp of fifty hostile Uncpapa (Teton Dacotah) near Dogden Butte. Plans were immediately made to avoid Dogden by using a new route to the north via the Mouse River, but this more circuitous route also proved dangerous. In January, a six-day blizzard marooned the Fort Stevenson party at one of the shelters. They were forced to abandon their horses and sacrifice their pack mule as food for the dogs; two of the sled dogs became food for the men. More than a month passed before the party was able to return to Fort Stevenson. In May 1868, two mail carriers were killed by several Uncpapa near Dogden. Three months later, a sergeant and two of his soldiers were ambushed about thirty-five miles west of Fort Totten. Frank Palmer, a mail carrier on that expedition, escaped and returned to the fort with the news.

Whites like Palmer whose frontier presence was not directly attributable to the fur trade or the military nonetheless conducted their business under what protection the army's presence could offer. Woodcutters, who worked the banks of the Missouri selling firewood to steamboats, blacksmiths, teamsters, mail carriers, and an assortment of craftsmen, found a niche in the system not served by the post traders, Indian agents, and army sutlers. Their places of business were bound to the locations where their services were needed or could bring a price. Those whose business did not specifically involve cross-country travel increasingly stayed as close as they could to the safety of the stockades. The Indian villages and the trading or military posts nearby were by no means self-sufficient. Few goods were exchanged between them except those that served ceremonial purposes or relieved emergency shortages. Rather, all of the settlements depended on distant sources of supply for their existence.

The first transportation route across northern Dakota that supplied these early white settlements was the Fort Totten-Fort Stevenson trail. Men from both posts risked their lives to maintain it. In the summer of 1867, Charles Ruffee of Minneapolis won the mail contract on the Fort Abercrombie-Fort Benton route that included this segment. Plans called for frequent service, but they were soon abandoned as impractical. In the first nine months of its operation, not one letter had reached Fort Buford from the east, despite numerous attempts. Ruffee's supervisor at Fort Benton, Montana, trekked east to Fort Stevenson and then to Fort Totten to investigate why the mails had not arrived. At Fort Totten he learned that Ruffee's company had gone bankrupt.[6]

The man who made this trek was Frank Palmer. The command at Fort Totten recognized Palmer's abilities and experience and hired him on the spot. With the title of post guide, Palmer was put in charge of the mail service on the Fort Stevenson route. He escaped with his life in the 1868 ambush, but he soon had the mail service established on a regular basis. Palmer also clerked for Brenner and Terry, the appointed Fort Totten post traders, and, in 1877, received that appointment himself.[7]

An army post trader dealt in such exotic goods as crackers, tea, cheese, and tobacco, and he carried some lines of clothing and hardware; but the function for which he was known best was the sale of liquor to the men of the post. Disputes over the price of whiskey led more than one trader to lose his licensed status, and the rate of turnover was high. Fort Stevenson saw five post traders in its sixteen-year existence.[8]

Credit ratings were especially important to these men who operated businesses hundreds of miles from their nearest source of supply. Without established connections, few wholesalers would risk transactions at such a distance and over territory considered so unsafe for passage. Even as Gen. George Armstrong Custer and two hundred of his men were falling at the Battle of the Little Big Horn in 1876, a field man for R. G. Dun & Co. of New York was visiting posts on the upper Missouri, gathering information for the credit ratings that his company issued.

The most common complaint the Dun man recorded was that all stores — on or off military posts — charged too much for the goods they sold.[9] The $1.50 per pound for tea that trader A. L. Bonnafon, Jr., charged at Fort Stevenson was set by the post's Council of Administration, as were all of his prices. If one considers the route that this pound of tea had to follow to get there from China, and the number of hands through which it passed, the price may not have been unreasonable. Bonnafon sold Kentucky whiskey at $6 per gallon, gin at $8, and brandy at $10, or 15 cents per drink.[10] Any temptation the post council may have felt to reduce prices on those ever-popular beverages no doubt was checked by the vision of what would happen if they did.

Despite their problems, many post traders maintained a good business. Brenner and Terry at Fort Totten impressed the R. G. Dun field man. Terry, a real estate agent, lived in Duluth while Ernest Brenner, an industrious Württemberger, handled the trade. Real estate was also the business of A. C. and James Leighton of Omaha, who operated the post store at Fort Buford. The Leighton brothers owned a half interest in the store at Fort Fetterman, Wyoming, and a third brother had interests at Fort Lincoln, Dakota.[11] They purchased most of their goods in New York, a not uncommon practice of frontier merchants in the West and South, even in the 1870s.

Lewis Atherton provided an excellent account of how these long-distance connections were established.[12] Early nineteenth century merchants in the lower Missouri and Ohio valleys made annual trips that took six weeks or more to complete in order to purchase their goods in wholesale houses on the eastern seaboard. New York, Philadelphia, and Baltimore firms had international connections, and they sold at lower prices than did wholesalers west of the Appalachians. The eastern houses made purchases on credit substantially easier—a strong attraction for western merchants, few of whom were able to offer cash for a year's supply of goods.

Baltimore and Philadelphia initially dominated this trade because of their access to populated areas of the Ohio and Missouri valleys. New York overtook their lead in the 1830s and 1840s when migration from New York and Ohio brought a new population to the upper Middle West. Chicago later assumed a similar role after it was connected by rail to the eastern cities.

The Leightons purchased dry goods, utensils, and other manufactured items in New York and had them shipped to Omaha. They procured foodstuffs in Omaha or Chicago. In this way they were able to fulfill their government contract by buying goods in the cheapest markets, and they took advantage of the fastest means of transportation. As rail service reached Omaha, then Sioux City, Yankton, and, finally, Bismarck, sources of supply shifted to take advantage of the new connections. Frontier logistics were changing so rapidly that orders placed in one season sometimes were shipped the next season along routes that had not existed when the trader placed his order.

The army installations were outposts in every sense of the word; as businessmen, however, the post traders were part of a national system of trading and credit transactions that included them just as it had the fur traders who came before. In fact, many of the old traders became sutlers at military forts. Durfee and Peck, who operated Missouri steamboats in connection with their fur-trading activities, were the first post traders at Fort Rice; they also held the commission at Fort Stevenson from October 1870 through January 1872. The Northwestern Fur Company of St. Paul sent an agent to Fort Totten expecting to receive the appointment as post trader there in 1867, but the bid was unsuccessful.[13] New entrepreneurs, taking advantage of their political connections, in time replaced those remaining from the fur trade. The typical business transaction was no longer one between Indian and white, and thus the intermediary role once occupied so commonly by the métis became outmoded. Anglo-Americans assumed control of the trade, and they were to dominate in that role for the remainder of the settlement period.

With their hunting grounds gone and their movements under close surveillance, the Sioux gradually began to live near the military posts. Herds of beef cattle were being driven from southern Minnesota to Fort Totten by

1870 to feed the increasing number of Sioux who, reported to be starving, were lured from the Mouse River country to the government's fort. By 1872, 725 Indians were on beef rations at Fort Totten. A few of the frontiersmen managed to retain a place in the old system, although conditions were changing rapidly. Frank Palmer's appointment as Indian trader there in 1877 continued well into the era of white agricultural settlement. In 1884 his letterhead read "Frank Palmer—Indian Trader, Freighter, and Dealer in Gen'l Merchandise, Fort Totten."[14]

The freighting Palmer did no longer involved the dangers he had once known. His teamster had only a short haul to James J. Hill's St. Paul, Minneapolis & Manitoba railroad, which had reached Devils Lake in 1883. Palmer shipped to a St. Paul dealer the furs he took in trade from the few Indian trappers who worked near Fort Totten. The army closed the fort as a military post in 1890, but Palmer remained in business there another seventeen years. Born in Ohio in 1847, Palmer had come west to Montana with the army and had worked for several stage lines before the sequence of events that brought him to Fort Totten. His career thus spanned three of the most common frontier occupations: military, transportation, and trade. His pursuit of the three in that order illustrates the priorities of the frontier: a major responsibility of the military was to open and protect the routes of transportation; without transportation, traders could not exist; and without traders, no further development was possible.[15]

Traders and sutlers of the frontier period operated in similar contexts to the extent that both had appointments to a specific location intended to guarantee them a monopoly at that site. The sutler was also a transitional figure between the fur post trader, whose market was one of barter and exchange, and the isolated merchant of the agricultural era that followed, who sold far more goods for cash than he took in trade for commodities. Decisions made by the fur companies or the military determined where the trader or sutler would locate. The early fur traders had to worry about competition from other companies in their trading areas, although in later years the American Fur Company's monopoly of trading posts was as secure as was the U.S. government's over military posts.

Early merchants who operated stores near agricultural settlements enjoyed no such monopoly. Pembina, in the Red River Valley, was part of Lord Selkirk's colony that established a European presence in the northern portion of the valley. Although Pembina was cut off from British territory when the international boundary was established in 1818, it had a population of more than a thousand people by the early 1850s, and three or four times that many lived in the hills just to the west. Most of them were métis, who had come south from Canada and retained strong ties with their sister settlements to the north.

In 1876, Pembina had a general store owned by Nathan Myrick of St. Paul, Minnesota, but managed by a local man. In the Dun man's opinion, Myrick's outpost was doing a good business but "ought to do better if he did not charge too high prices." Some residents bought their supplies from Myrick, but others preferred the cheaper prices in distant centers. Neree and Adaline Ethier lived only six miles west of Pembina, but they did not trade with Myrick. Instead they made annual trips to Winnipeg, seventy miles away, where prices were cheaper. The annual trip was also a social occasion, and that compensated for the inconvenience. Others from Pembina made similar trips up the valley to Grand Forks.[16] What seemed to be a monopoly for Myrick, who had no real competitors at hand and who served a substantial enclave that was separated by many miles from any other, was instead a market in which he had to compete for business. The prices he quoted had to be higher because of the freight charges he paid to get the goods to his store. The Myrick store was just as isolated as its customers.

The transition from appointed monopolies to competitive markets was just one of the changes that accompanied the arrival of agriculture. When merchants began to move out into the new lands opened to white settlement, they also had to decide where to locate their places of business. Many tried to anticipate the course of settlement by establishing themselves ahead of any competition at sites that would prove attractive to other business people whose offerings might complement their own. The overwhelming consideration for all speculative locators was selecting a site that could attract a railroad.

The era of frontier trading patterns ended when the railroads arrived, but the arrival was presaged by an interim phase of speculative activity that produced its own settlement pattern. Isolated country merchants, connected to the railhead by freight and stage lines, kept their distance ahead of the westward push of the railroads. The St. Paul, Minneapolis & Manitoba reached Grand Forks in 1879, Larimore in 1881, and Devils Lake in 1883. Each advance of the railroad marked an expansion of stage routes to the west. A similar process took place as the Northern Pacific built north from Jamestown. "Inland towns," the regional term for settlements located ahead of the railroads, were the hallmark of this interim phase.

Chapter 3

Inland Towns

When Mike Manning rode into the Mouse River country south of present-day Sherwood, N. Dak. in the spring of 1883, he saw an immense grassland broken only by occasional groves of poplar. Manning established his ranch headquarters along a small creek and started bringing in cattle. Within ten years, he was known as one of the largest ranchers in northern North Dakota. Manning boasted of never putting up a ton of hay for his cattle, so lush were the native grasses. Even the blizzards that brought ruin to many cattlemen did not seem to discourage him. The valley flooded every spring, and a small acreage of the rich bottomland was put into grain and feed crops. Prairie fires were a menace, but the benefits to the range from these annual burns clearly outweighed the hazards. Manning was soon bordered by neighboring ranchers who operated in much the same fashion, making little investment except in cattle, running their stock on the public domain, and raising a small crop acreage.[1]

The first cattlemen moved into the Mouse River "loop" in 1882, a development that followed but did not grow out of the extension of the southern plains range cattle industry that had reached north to the Little Missouri Badlands by the 1870s. The Mouse River cattlemen affected many of the styles of the Texas ranching complex, but they kept no Texas cattle and their herds were comparatively small.[2] "Colonel" Oscar Towner, who had been manager of the Elk Valley farm at Larimore, scouted the Mouse River in 1883 and came back with one hundred head of cattle the next year. In 1884, an Englishman who called himself "Lord Thursby" came in with a substantial herd that he grazed near present-day Granville. Two years later, another mysterious Englishman, Coutts Marjoribanks, arrived with one hundred head of Aberdeen Angus, the likes of which Mouse River's cattlemen had never seen. Marjoribanks was known locally as a remittance man, and some of the money he received at regular intervals from England was spent repairing the local saloon, through which he was fond of riding his horse after an evening's patronage.[3]

More than a dozen inland towns appeared in the Mouse River loop country during the 1880s (fig. 3). They drew trade from the cattlemen, but the merchants who located there knew, as did the ranchers, that the days of the "big pasture" were numbered. Soon there would be farmers and railroads, the bases upon which trade centers would prosper. Speculation began in 1881, when the Northern Pacific surveyed a line from Jamestown to the Mouse River. One of the surveys terminated at a location named Villard, after Henry Villard, president of the Northern Pacific. A group of Jamestown investors located another townsite nearby, which they called Scriptown. By 1883, interest in these locations had collapsed because the Northern Pacific decided not to build the line; but settlers started arriving in large numbers because the St. Paul, Minneapolis & Manitoba was headed straight for Mouse River on its way west from Devils Lake.

From 1882, when the first mail service and stage line joined Villard with points south toward Bismarck, until late in 1886, when the St. Paul, Minneapolis & Manitoba set the course for future development by locating its

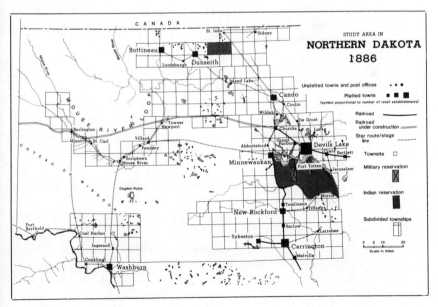

Figure 3

station at Minot, merchants, farmers, and ranchers established themselves at scattered locations in the lower loop. R. H. Copeland, an astute observer of the region, published a newspaper to promote his town of Villard. In March 1886, he was able to boast that "there are now nearly 2,000 people settled on Mouse river, by whom nearly all the timber claims along the river have been taken."[4]

The U.S. Post Office, under steady pressure from Congress, was lenient in extending mail service to sparsely populated areas. Many open-country post offices were known as "farmers' p.o.'s" and amounted to nothing more than a farmhouse designated as a mail delivery point. The postal function was even more eagerly sought by the isolated merchant. As a fourth-class post office, the postmaster-merchant was allowed to keep the box rents and to receive a percentage on all the sales at his office. When local folks came by for their mail, they might also purchase a pound of coffee, a pair of shoes, or some yard goods. The occasion presented an opportunity to remind some people about the bills they were running at the store.

The merchant was trying to achieve, in economic-geographic parlance, "centrality" — the ability of a place to provide goods and services in excess of the needs of its own residents. Generally speaking, the more centrality a place achieves, the wider will be the trading area from which people are drawn and the greater the variety of goods and services it offers. General stores were thus the most likely form of initial business activity. The entrepreneur added lines of goods and services to his business in an attempt to draw more customers. In the abstract, creation of centrality was the life-force behind growth of the trade center.

The dynamics of trade center growth depended on the ability of entrepreneurs to form market areas for the goods they sold. Both the selling price and the consumer's transportation costs figured in the merchant's calculation (fig. 4). If a merchant charged a price, p, for one unit of a good at his store, then the total cost to a consumer living at the merchant's location would also be p. If, however, that consumer had to travel a distance to purchase the good, the cost of the trip would, from the consumer's view, be added to the selling price, thus forcing distant patrons to pay a higher price, p'. If all consumers had identical demands, the ones living close to the store would be able to purchase many units of the good at a given price, q, while distant consumers would be able to afford much less, q'; or, in more realistic terms, the more distant consumers either would patronize the store less frequently or else find a closer supplier. There would thus be some outer limit at which consumer demand would fall to zero — the limit beyond which no consumer would patronize the store. Such a limit, r, is called the *range* of the good.[5]

Distant consumers would be expected to overcome their disadvantage by making fewer trips or by buying in quantity on each visit. By reducing

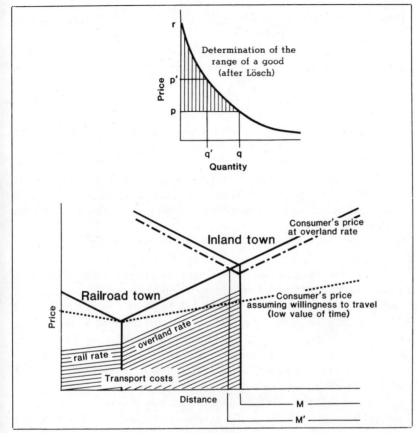

Figure 4. Top, determination of the range of a good; *bottom,* market areas for railroad towns and inland towns.

their transportation costs, they would restore demand nearly to the level of a customer who lived nearby. Such a result did occur, and it remains even today as a characteristic of shopping trips in sparsely settled areas.

The merchant, on the other hand, could increase his trade by decreasing the selling price of his goods, whereby consumers at all locations could afford to purchase more. This also would have the effect of increasing the *range* of the goods. The strategy of price competition was open to all sellers, of course. If a merchant cut his prices enough, he could extend his trading territory beyond that of his nearby competitors, capturing their trade and thereby adding it to his own. In actuality, the process of trade competition was more complex.

A general store owner trying to establish a business in newly settled territory dealt with consumers who had little cash at their disposal. Most of them never had been, and never would be again, as poor as they were in their first years on their farms. Many were not able to afford coffee or sugar; roasted peas or barley substituted for coffee, honey for sugar. The Perry Johnson family, who homesteaded near Sawyer on the Mouse River in 1883, realized less than $30 for their first year's crop, five acres of wheat. There was little local demand, and transportation to a distant market took what little profit there was. Their nearest inland town was Burlington, twenty miles away. Sugar, which sold for $7 cwt. there, was beyond their means. Instead, the Johnsons and their neighbors undertook two-hundred-mile journeys that took a whole week to complete to reach stores in Devils Lake or Bismarck where prices were lower. Such trips were cooperative affairs, usually undertaken by one man or a few, who took along shopping lists from their neighbors as well.[6]

Ole Forde lived in a log house on the banks of the Sheyenne River near the store and post office known as Lee, in Nelson County, in 1880. He got his mail at the Lee store, but he did not trade there because of the high prices. Every fall he made a trip to Fargo where he was able to purchase one hundred pounds of good flour for $3.00 to $3.50; that same barrel would have cost him $6 or more at Lee.[7] The few dollars he saved by making the nearly two-hundred-mile round trip himself, plus what he saved by making other purchases in Fargo, undoubtedly did not equal what he spent on his annual spree in the city; but, figured on that basis, he also received a free vacation away from his normal routine.

The cost difference on one hundred pounds of flour between Devils Lake and Burlington was $1.50 ($2.50 versus $4.00) in 1885. Assuming that the two barrels of flour were of roughly equal quality, the homesteaders near Burlington were willing to travel two hundred miles with team and wagon, on trails that were passable only during dry, summer or autumn weather, for savings of this magnitude. Their behavior illustrates that not only were they short of cash, they also placed a low value on their time. The monetary cost of the long journey was almost negligible, but it took a week to complete a round trip with ox team and wagon. A visit to Devils lake or Bismarck afforded other opportunities that one to an inland store did not, but such journeys probably would not be justified if there were chores to do at home.

The low value the homesteader placed on his time reflected the nature of his enterprise. Farm-making activities were time-consuming, but they did not occupy most homesteaders the year around. Many homesteaders sought wage work elsewhere in the early years in order to survive until their farms produced a living.[8] When it became possible for farmers to make a profit from their investment, their own farm labor greatly increased in value; time spent off the farm, hauling to or from town, meant time lost from more productive activity. In the transition from homesteading to commercial farming, profits appeared at about the same rate as spare time disappeared.

The inland merchant's competitors thus were not the other general stores that had appeared in open country. Price competition among them was as uncommon as it was pointless. Their real competitors were the merchants in towns served by railroads who did not have to bear the expense of overland drayage to procure their stock of goods. The freight charges on one hundred pounds of groceries shipped by rail from St. Paul to Devils Lake in 1885 was $1.35. Teamsters charged that much or more to haul the same quantity less than seventy-five miles from Devils Lake to one of the inland towns.[9] The added transportation cost appeared in the price the inland store patron had to pay, which meant that the *range* of the good was smaller at the inland store.

If potential customers living near the inland merchant's store figured their own travel costs as the teamster did, then the inland merchant could either share a market (M) with the railroad town merchant or, if he absorbed some of the freight charges, could dominate the nearby trade (M') because his freight costs would equal the consumer's cost in time and money to travel an identical distance to the railroad (fig. 4).

Since the inland merchant's potential customers placed such a low value on their time, however, they effectively figured their per-mile "shopping" costs at a much lower rate than did the teamster who sought a profit. Some inland merchants handled their own drayage, although most could not afford to be away from their stores for long periods. They absorbed some freight costs by taking a smaller markup on the goods they sold, although that strategy, obviously, put them in an even weaker position with respect to their railroad town competitors. Price competition always worked to the disadvantage of the smaller trade centers, whether they were served by railroads or not, and that feature remained a restraint on small town viability in later years.

George H. Mackay, who, along with his blacksmith brother, made up the population of the 1886 inland town of Wallace on the Mouse River, sold flour at $4 cwt. Mackay's competitor was Thomas E. Mather, one of four general merchants eighty-five miles away in the Northern Pacific town of Minnewaukan, who sold the same hundred pounds of "best patent flour" for $2.25 or a lower grade for $1.50. R. H. Copeland, for reasons he did not state, published these prices, side by side, in his *Villard Leader*. Mackay was able to offer some items, especially the less bulky, expensive goods, at a price only slightly higher than his Minnewaukan competitor.[10] It was on the bulk commodities, such as flour and sugar, that the inland merchant faced the greatest disadvantage.

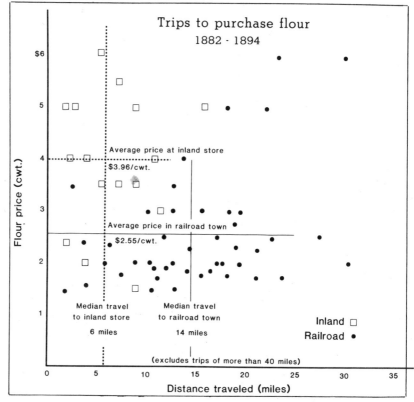

Figure 5. Trips to purchase flour, 1882–94. Computed from Historical Data Project questionnaires for the fourteen-county North Dakota study area.

In the late 1930s, questionnaires administered by the Historical Data Project sponsored by the Works Progress Administration in North Dakota asked pioneer settlers to recall the places where they first shopped and the prices they paid for consumer goods. Although questionable in individual detail, the average prices and median travel distances probably offer a reliable estimate of the true values (fig. 5). In the fourteen-county study area, no more than one settler in every five traveled beyond twenty miles to purchase wheat flour, the commodity most often mentioned in the shopping trip data. Those traversing greater distances than this were families, like the Johnsons on the Mouse River, who were settled well beyond the area then served by railroads. The average price of a barrel of flour was more than half again as much when purchased from an inland merchant, but trips to an inland store required journeys less than half as long as those to a railroad town. Evidently the tradeoff was most often settled in favor of the longer trip to obtain cheaper prices.

In 1886, J. H. Vaughan operated the inland store and post office known as Pendroy; like George Mackay, he took farm produce in trade for groceries to stimulate local business. Inland prices for eggs, butter and hams (all locally produced) were no higher in Pendroy or Wallace than they were in Minnewaukan. Mackay also traded wheat, corn, furs, and hides for merchandise, but the prices he was able to pay farmers for those commodities were, in turn, lower than they could get in Minnewaukan because of the same disadvantage in transport costs.

Buffalo bones, which were many a pioneer homesteader's source of cash, were purchased by P. G. Potter, operator of the lone store at Scriptown in 1886 and 1887. Sugar producers who used the bones in their refining process, paid $15 to $20 per ton in the late 1880s. The tariff posted on bones for rail shipment from Devils Lake to St. Paul was $7.80 per ton.[11] Bones littered the prairies, and there was little expense in selling them other than the cost of transportation. If the bone seller took his load to Devils lake, he had more than twice as much profit than if he sold them to an inland buyer who, in turn, had to pay a teamster to haul them to the railroad.

Potter, Vaughan, Mackay, and other general merchants were determined to succeed in business despite their obvious handicap. Potter advertised aggressively that he sold at "Devils Lake prices," although the dollar amounts were not listed. "Buy your supplies of Potter and save the expenses of a trip to Towner or Devils Lake," he wrote in November 1886. By then, Vaughan had quit his store and moved to Illinois; Pendroy was abandoned. Mackay went out of business at Wallace as soon as the railroad established Minot, where he opened another store. Potter restocked his store at Scriptown for the 1887 season, but by then the move to Minot was overwhelming; he, too, discontinued business in September. Copeland remained for a time at Villard, publishing his newspaper and booming the community in which he was the sole businessman.

None of Mouse River's inland merchants was more determined than the Brunelle brothers of Dunseith. They had operated a general mercantile business in Devils Lake, but they decided to move to the new town of Dunseith in 1886. Dunseith, as it turned out, was not to receive a railroad for another twenty years, but hopes were high in 1886. To extend their business, the Brunelles loaded a large wagon with merchandise and hired a man to drive it down into the Mouse River district where their "store on wheels" called on potential customers. Such an arrangement made for even higher prices, but the novelty of it was enough to make the venture successful for a short time. The Brunelles were not the first or the last to get such an idea, but their attempt to serve a market they knew was there bespeaks the determination of inland merchants to make a success of their business and their town.[12]

Bones, hides, furs, fish, ducks, geese, and snakeroot made up a Dakota harvest unlike what was to follow, but it was a valuable harvest that sustained many homesteaders until their crops and livestock began to pay. It would be a mistake to characterize this phase as a "hunter-gatherer" economy, because few who sold such items envisioned it as a way of life. Nor did this traffic in nature's bounty indicate a tendency toward subsistence-scale living; sale for cash, or its equivalent, was the universal objective.[13] The creation of value was not limited to the common agricultural pursuits. Everyone needed capital to invest in the future, and human ingenuity was thus reflected in a variety of schemes to make money.

The appearance of small-scale manufactories also characterized the inland town period. Few goods were available at towns away from the railroad, and those that were for sale carried prices so high that many had to forgo them. If a good is unavailable, if its price is too dear, or if its only point of sale is so distant as to make its purchase prohibitively expensive, then the obvious solution is to manufacture it yourself. Ole Forde's annual trip to Fargo to purchase flour made him realize the possibilities of beginning his own business. In 1890 he built a flour mill on his property, and he operated it until 1898 when the railroad arrived. Local farmers were able to purchase flour against their own wheat delivered to his mill, benefiting them as well. Forde also helped organize a farmer's cooperative lime kiln on the banks of the Sheyenne River, obviating the need for farmers to haul another bulky product long distances. Lime kilns, brick kilns, and mills of various sorts were found in scattered localities where there was sufficient local demand to make them viable.[14] They served local markets, but providing a service was not the aim of most of them; earning money was.

Blacksmiths were, second to general stores, the most common business in the inland towns. It took little capital to begin a blacksmith shop, and many would-be farmers with training and skill in smithing were able to conduct the business as a sideline. Many of them forged farm tools of various sorts and, if they also possessed woodworking skills, manufactured farm implements. The blacksmith offered a general store of another sort: often a jack-of-all-trades, his skills could be applied to a variety of problems brought to him. The value of time worked to his advantage because farmers never wanted to make a long trip when equipment broke down during use. General store owners welcomed a blacksmith's presence because of the business he drew to the vicinity.

The most valuable boon the inland store proprietor could receive, however, was acquisition of the post office for his area. It paid money, drew customers, and provided a regular link with the outside. Most mail stages also hauled passengers, small amounts of freight, and anything else that could be transported for a fee, including shipments from the railroad depot that were consigned to the inland merchant. All post offices not on a railroad or boat line were served by star routes, a designation that allowed the carrier to choose any method of transportation as long as he made the connection. Star routes were kept as short as possible, usually originating at the railroad station closest to the inland post offices they served.

Federal law required the second assistant postmaster general, who had charge of the transportation of the mails, to advertise star-route contracts for reletting every four years. All routes to be let in a given year were listed in a brochure. This system, begun in 1845, was the mainstay of the rural mail service, the subject of frequent controversy and of occasional fraud.[15]

The star-route service was provided by a local carrier, although he was not generally the person to whom the government awarded the mail contract. Star-route contracts were a commodity. Speculators bid on scores of offerings and were awarded those on which they were low bidder; they then set out to find a local party to carry the mail. One of the most successful bidders for Dakota contracts was Ambrose A. Call, pioneer resident of Algona, Iowa, a newspaperman and wealthy landowner. Call bid on practically every contract in the Devils Lake, Jamestown, Mitchell, and Huron districts, and he had Iowa contracts as well.[16] Many contract buyers had routes in half a dozen states. Once awarded, they were likely to be successful in subsequent bids. Tales of bravery and perseverance in getting the mails through clouded the abuses this system invited.

Bidders awarded star-route contracts were free to make their own financial arrangements with a local carrier who, in turn, had to bid his own services to the contract holder. Local carriers, who did all the work and took most of the risks, were often underpaid. To make some money for themselves, they adopted freight and passenger businesses. This arrangement worked to the advantage of the inland merchant by providing convenient transportation, although the frequency of service was fixed in the mail contract. It also posed a disadvantage, however, because the star route/stage line operator raised his freight and passenger fares to make up for the slim profits from the mail service. Teamsters who hauled freight in larger quantities could operate profitably with or without mail contracts, but a stage line operator without a mail contract was redundant. The star-route contract system, which was designed to guarantee a fair return to the mail hauler, effectively did the opposite by allowing contract holders to skim off the profits.

Passengers who rode the mail stage paid for the privilege. In 1882, the ride to Fort Totten from Larimore cost $6. A trip to Bismarck cost $10 from Burlington, $9 from Fort Berthold. At a time when wheat brought sixty-five cents per bushel, such prices obviously pushed the luxury of stage transportation well beyond the means of most potential riders. The average stage fares in northern North Dakota before 1900 varied from six to eight cents per mile, with a fifty-cent minimum.[17] Rail travel for trips of comparable length averaged between three and four cents per mile. In terms of time, cost, and comfort, railway travel was preferable, and the differential was reflected in the immediate cessation of star route/stage line service between points as soon as a parallel railroad was in place.

An entrepreneur who moved out ahead of settlement with the intention of establishing a general mercantile business generally chose a sparsely populated location, sometimes with only a few dozen families within trading range. His strategy was not to serve a thin, scattered market, of course, but rather to establish a business before the tide of new settlers arrived. The most rudimentary of structures was sufficient to start the business. A log cabin, lean-to, frame shack, or even a tent was enough. Erection of a larger building would come later, perhaps at the initially chosen site or in another location if the first one was missed by the railroad that everyone knew would arrive eventually.

Where to build the store was decided only after much discussion with people who had ideas about how the country would develop. One consideration that weighed heavily, judging from the sites most often selected, was proximity to a wooded area. It was evident by then that railroads did not zigzag across the plains like the early wagon trails, from one wooded grove to another, nor were townsites along the tracks located with any regard for the proximity of wooded land. Most of the inland general stores, however, were built near timbered river valleys or lake margins.[18] The choice was not a poor one in the early years of settlement, because wooded tracts were the ones that attracted homesteaders in most areas; but chances were remote that the railroad would come very near the site, and the merchant knew it. He remained constantly ready to change his location to accommodate the railroad's plans, yet he continued to proclaim the future success of his would-be urban center right up to the day the railroad announced its nearest townsite; thereupon, he packed up his stock and moved. Inland town boosting was more a matter of pragmatism than of pride.

George Smith's 1906 inland town of LaFollette, southwest of Minot, consisted of his newspaper shop, the *LaFollette Forum*; Ericson and Berg's general store; and nothing else. Smith located there in March of that year, anticipating the new Soo Line branch that was being built west from Max. His newspaper mentioned merchants in other self-proclaimed inland towns, who were also awaiting the railroad but clearly did not know precisely where to situate themselves. Smith claimed that his newspaper had five hundred readers in southern Ward County, a matter of particular importance to him because he was seeking election to a county office. Ericson and Berg, typical of inland merchants, advertised in Smith's newspaper: "Don't be afraid of country store prices. We sell as low as anybody." Those who read the *LaFollette Forum* might have assumed the town had a bright future.[19]

When the Soo Line's townsite agent, C. A. Campbell, visited Minot late in June, he promised Smith that the railroad's new town in the LaFollette vicinity would be surveyed in the next few days and that lots would go on sale on 20 July. As for the town's name, Smith had to report that "Mr. Campbell said he did not know what the name would be." By the following week's edition, "Plaza" had been announced as the new town's name, and Smith immediately started to promote it. On 19 July, he renamed his newspaper the *Plaza Pioneer*. By mid-August, Smith's print shop and Ericson and Berg's store had been moved to Plaza. The town of LaFollette was dead at the age of four months.[20]

The railroad's arrival began a process that replaced one settlement system with another (see table 1). Scattered stores, post offices, and other businesses, which had been connected by stage lines under star-route mail contracts in a thinly settled country devoted to stock raising and general farming, gave way to a system of platted towns, evenly spaced along the railroad, whose elevators soon collected the grain that nearby farmers could now profitably raise on a large scale. The first system never would have been established had the second not been anticipated, nor could the railroad-based system have fallen into place so quickly had the prior inland town phase not existed.

The term "inland town" is a misnomer in both its words: the use of "inland" to label only certain towns, when all of them were inland; and the use of "town" to describe what were usually no more than isolated places of business. Stores, post offices, newspapers, blacksmith shops, hotels, and others were scattered about the countryside in the larger interstices not served by the railroad, but they did not attract one another into agglomerations large enough to be recognizable as towns. Each business site was some entrepreneur's statement of hope that a town might grow there. Sites were named for purposes of identification and because many performed a postal function, but few had either defined limits or an official plat of building lots and streets.

This dispersal of townlike activities could have several explanations. Because of the limited range of the goods and services offered, one might expect some dispersal, especially of general stores, so that the settled territory was "covered" with market areas. This explanation is consistent with economic models of trade-area formation, which suggest that other businesses would be attracted to the more viable sites so as to create an eventual coherent network of trade center towns. The failure of this development could be explained by lack of time: most inland towns had very brief life spans before railroad companies imposed a new system that determined business locations.

One might also argue, however, that it was not a tendency to agglomerate that produced trade center towns; rather, the very act of platting a townsite drew business people of various sorts together into one location. Suppose, for the sake of argument, that railroads of the late nineteenth and early twentieth centuries had been much less successful in selling the bonds that financed construction of new lines. There might have been many fewer miles of railroad, thus many fewer railroad towns and a correspondingly longer life for towns in the interstices.

If these interstitial towns actually had been platted, as the railroad towns were, would they have grown in size and in functional complexity? Probably not, because railroad towns, no matter how few, would have maintained a transportation cost advantage. In any case, they would have stored and shipped the produce of the hinterlands, which would have continued to make them far more attractive as business sites. These forces would have been arrayed against the inland town regardless of the overall level of railway construction activity. Inland towns would have remained a loosely defined scatter of business functions, marginally serving a local market.

Successful trade center towns, then, were not the product of some innate tendency to agglomerate, nor did they prosper because of the attractiveness of platted townsites. What caused trade centers to grow, instead, was the obliteration of all other nearby business sites that took place when the railroad announced a new town. That, effectively, drove merchants out of their scattered locations and into the railroad towns. Railroads made the hinterlands repel business activity because their townsites were the only places where merchants could operate profitably.

Chapter 4

Townsite Speculators

The creation of new towns in the American West is a subject often discussed in terms of the boomers, swindlers, robbers, and worse elements who were interested only in selling real estate. Such people somehow acquired possession of a tract of land, gave it a name, had it platted, and then published fanciful descriptions that they hoped would lure unsuspecting investors.[1] What has not been observed is the guileless and unsuspecting way in which some of these people invested their own money in townsites that would soon revert to wheat fields or cow pastures. The creators of these "paper towns" would not have been disappointed had their broadsides turned out to be accurate predictions. Their goal was making money, but many of them also came to believe in their own dreams.

There were cities all over the East with smoking factories, teeming business districts, busy railroad yards, and wharves lined with ships. Philadelphia, Chicago, and plenty of other cities had grown from little or nothing save a plat of streets, blocks, and property lines, and speculators doubtless believed that the same could be true of their "coming metropolis" of the prairies. From the earliest penetrations of settlement in the river-based era of commerce in the 1840s until the depression of the 1890s, there appeared in the trans-Mississippi west a succession of townsite promoters bent on creating the next Emporium of Commerce. Northern North Dakota saw its share of these dreams.

No matter how great or how modest their plans, the people who attempted to create cities and towns simply by anouncement never understood how little influence they had. They differed from the inland merchants, who promoted their location by doing business and thereby setting an exam- 39 ple of the *activity* people associate with towns. Townsite speculators, on the other hand, attempted to manipulate the *structure* people identified with urban places. Usually the speculators had a design or framework into which they hoped, somehow, the businesses and professions of a city would fall. Streets were given names. Public squares and parks were set aside. There were labels of all sorts, but they existed only on a piece of paper or, at best, in a row of wooden stakes driven into some remote corner of the prairie. Promoters expected businesses to come in, and some did; but characteristically they did not wait for evidence of activity before proclaiming that they had a city on their hands.

Dakota townsite promoters were stimulated by the same force that prompted merchants to build stores in remote locations—the promise of a railroad. Sometimes the railroad company actually made a promise, but more often the officials were evasive. The presence of a surveying party was more than enough evidence for many that a new line was going to be constructed. Newspapers faithfully passed along the details—where the surveyors had been, where they were going, and what the railroad's plans were. If railroad officials were guarded in their statements, this only added evidence of their firm intentions. People wanted to believe a railroad was coming, and they were more than willing to fill in the details themselves to make it seem more real. It took some time, but eventually railroad men perceived their influence and began deploying survey crews in various localities just to keep alive talk of their "intentions," whether they had any or not.

The appearance of Northern Pacific railroad surveyors north of their main line through Jamestown in 1881 was not unexpected. The company had already constructed several tributary lines into the area covered by its land grant, and more were likely to follow. The grant had awarded the Northern Pacific ownership of odd-numbered sections of land in a swath eighty miles wide (forty on either side of the line) across the territories, plus alternate sections within fifty miles if any sections of the basic allotment were unavailable.[2] This grant amounted to little less than one-fourth of the land area in what became the state of North Dakota. Not content with colonizing this enormous area, the railroad, under president Henry Villard, began plans for expansion beyond these limits and even into Canada. Villard's plans ran counter to those of James J. Hill for developing the country south of the Canadian border, and in 1882 the two roads entered into an agreement over territory that basically confined future Northern Pacific construction to lines within its grant area.

In 1881, however, the Northern Pacific had surveyed a line from Jamestown to the Mouse River. This was the survey that prompted Villard and Scriptown, neither of which was ever to see the Northern Pacific. Whether or not the railroad was serious about constructing all the way to the Mouse

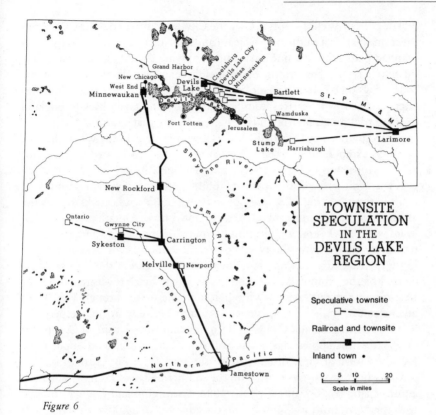

Figure 6

River was a matter of debate. The survey may have been only a test of Hill's determination, but it may also have been a serious plan.

The first survey ran directly northwest from Jamestown (fig. 6). Odd-numbered sections in this territory had been purchased from the Northern Pacific in 1881 by Richard Sykes, a member of an English syndicate interested in Dakota lands. Sykes intended to establish a bonanza wheat farm, a town, and assorted over ventures.[3] In 1882 his operation employed 125 men who, among other accomplishments, broke three thousand acres of land that summer. Sykes had a competitor in the person of J. Gwynne Vaughan, also from England, who saw the Northern Pacific survey and decided that a townsite somewhere within Sykes's bonanza operation would be a money-making proposition. In May 1882, Vaughan platted Gwynne City in one of the even-numbered (public land) sections within Sykes's checkerboard and began to promote it.

The small stream known as Pipestem Creek that flowed through his property was embellished considerably in Vaughan's advertising. The "metropolis of Wells County," Gwynne City, was "situated on the Pipestem River, in the midst of the best Wheat Lands in Northern Dakota." His lithographed plats showed a line of steamboats plying the Pipestem between his bustling city and Jamestown. Spokesfield's generally reliable history of the county says that Vaughan made considerable money on his venture but was later "arrested by detectives from Scotland Yard and taken back to England to stand trial for crimes committed before leaving that country."[4] Whatever success Vaughan may have had with his town was short lived. When the railroad was extended into Sykes's domain in 1883 it terminated on his land, and the town was called Sykeston, not Gwynne City.

The Northern Pacific's plans to build west from Sykeston stimulated another town. Acting in advance of construction, a syndicate known as the Mouse River Land Company platted the townsite of Ontario about fifteen miles west of Sykeston in 1885 and promoted it through a Chicago real estate firm. By the time the Northern Pacific built west of Sykeston, some fourteen years later, nothing remained of Ontario except the lone building erected by the promoters. The forty-eight square block townsite, with east-west running streets labeled Washington on the north through Van Buren on the south, replicated downtown Chicago, but only in that respect.[5]

The Carrington and Casey Land Co. laid out the townsite of Carrington in 1882, with the blessings of the railroad. There was also an opportunity for a new town at some distance down the track, south of Carrington. The townsite of Newport was platted on the southern edge of Foster County, on a public land section, in early June 1882. Carrington and Casey countered with their own townsite, Melville, on the adjacent section that they had purchased from the railroad. Josephine Keepers, the proprietor of Newport, received a quick lesson in townsite strategy when Melville was staked out on the edge of her land. Once the railroad designated Melville as the local station, Newport collapsed, and what little demand there was for town lots there was absorbed by Melville.[6]

Gwynne City, Ontario, and Newport were failures because their promoters lacked an arrangement with the railroad company. They knew nothing of the railroad's construction plans, and even after they learned of them they were powerless to attract the line to their townsites. In these cases, and in many others, independent townsite companies tried to interest railroads in their ventures. Promoters invested money in land, surveys, and sometimes in buildings to demonstrate their seriousness. The more seriousness they demonstrated, the less likely it was that the railroad would come their way. The railroad's interest in a potential townsite was inversely proportional to the amount of investment others had already made, and they characteristically avoided anything that would narrow their options.

Another series of townsite speculations took place along the St. Paul,

Minneapolis & Manitoba as it advanced west from Larimore in 1882 (fig. 6). The line seemed to be aimed toward the north shore of Devils Lake, and a town was sure to be constructed somewhere in that vicinity. Anyone was free to guess its location. If one had a map of the region on which to project the long tangents railroads preferred to follow, enough capital to acquire and plat a townsite, plus some knowledge of local conditions, it was possible to enter the game.

The Devils Lake district had not yet been opened up to public land entry, but there was a ready means of securing rights to land in the form of scrip. Issued by the government to satisfy land claims by individuals (whose names were then used to identify the various issues), scrip was bought, sold, and traded, especially in areas where settlement was advancing ahead of the government surveyors. In 1879, the value of one piece of scrip was established at 160 acres for $1.25 per acre minimum land.[7] The holder could pay for public land selling at the double minimum, or $2.50 per acre, by forfeiting two pieces of scrip or by settling the balance in cash. The piece of property was "covered" by "laying" enough scrip or cash to meet the government's price and by filing a sketch map and description of the tract at the nearest land office. Within three months after the survey had been completed, the buyer had to return to the land office and adjust the scrip he had laid to conform to the nearest government description. With a few hundred acres entitlement in scrip, enough to cover the parcel with room for error, the speculator possessed a hunting license for a townsite.

By 1882, northern Dakota had a small number of business people and promoters who could be counted on to engage in promising ventures. Alexander Griggs and George Walsh of Grand Forks and Judson LaMoure of Pembina were three of the most prominent. Griggs, who platted Grand Forks, had been a partner of James J. Hill in the Red River flatboat days. In March 1882, he asked Hill about townsite possibilities. Griggs, Walsh, and LaMoure were interested in starting a town on the north shore of Stump Lake and sought Hill's advice — in other words, they wanted to know where he was going to put his railroad.[8] Regardless of what Hill may have let them believe, the three partners went ahead with their plans for a town, which they called Harrisburgh (fig. 6).

Their advertising was a casebook example of the boomer's art: "HARRISBURG ON STUMP LAKE" was not only the "COMING METROPOLIS OF NORTH DAKOTA" but also "THE PROSPECTIVE CAPITAL OF NORTH DAKOTA." "The Manitoba Railroad . . . will come straight in the center of the townsite," they claimed. By June 1882, Harrisburgh was alive. Eleven business houses were going up, five of them in operation.[9]

Next to Harrisburgh was another townsite, Wamduska, which was on land scripted by M. I. Mendelson of Grand Forks. By June, Wamduska had a hotel ready to open that measured 54' × 50'. The site received a post office in July, served by the stage line from Larimore to Fort Totten. All it needed, like neighboring Harrisburgh, was the railroad. The same issue of the *Larimore Pioneer* that announced Wamduska's new post office also carried news that the railroad had bypassed Wamduska by six miles. The line, which was also supposed to pass through the center of Harrisburgh, had not even come close.[10]

With the end of track at Bartlett, six miles north of Stump Lake, possibilities for the townsite along Devils Lake were seen in sharper focus. Griggs, Walsh, and LaMoure abandoned Harrisburgh immediately and tried their luck at a site known as "the Narrows" on what was then a much more extensive body of water. This time they made Hill a more pointed offer: "We have over 2,000 acres covered with Valentine scrip . . . and we are prepared to give your company an undivided one-half interest to secure the road"at the Narrows.[11] Hill did not accept the offer but they went ahead with their plans, joined by stockholders William Budge and J. S. Eshelman of Grand Forks, Col. Oscar Towner, and several others. On 11 November 1882, the group proclaimed their townsite "Odessa," a name Colonel Towner suggested, after the "Russian wheat port on the Black Sea." The *Larimore Pioneer* reported more than $50,000 in lot sales at Odessa by January 1883.[12]

Odessa was not, however, the town Hill favored with his railroad. Nor was nearby Minnewaukon (not to be confused with Minnewaukan) that seemed, for a few months, to be *the* place. Creel City was another new townsite, the work of Lt. Heber M. Creel who, after resigning from the army at Fort Totten, began promoting the Devils lake region. In April 1883, Creel City (or Creelsburg, as it was also known) had four or five businesses in operation, moved there from yet another erstwhile townsite, Devils Lake City. James Stewart's plat of Devils Lake City, filed in 1882, showed twenty-five city blocks centered around the intersection of Broadway and Railroad streets, but the railroad did not take Stewart's hint.[13]

The St. Paul, Minneapolis & Manitoba reached the lake on 1 July 1883, and the townsite plat was filed 25 July. Named simply "Devils Lake," it was owned by a syndicate that included none other than James J. Hill and two other officers of the railroad. Although he often told others that his railroad did not engage in the townsite business (which was true at the time), Hill nonetheless had a substantial investment of his own money in townsites.[14]

The meaning of the term "townsite speculator" is made more vivid when applied to those who bet against Hill on the location of towns along his own line. Men like Griggs, Creel, and Towner, who were among the better-known figures of the region at that time, scarcely resembled the class of promoters who, like J. Gwynne Vaughan, appeared from nowhere with a scheme to sell a town and then made off with the proceeds. It was reasonable for Griggs, and perhaps others, to assume that Hill would welcome the investment of outside parties in towns that could not help but build traffic for his railroad, and perhaps that is why they persisted with their plans. Regardless of what they may have thought, Hill had no interest in schemes he did not control.

Plans for a great city on the western edge of Devils Lake were first embodied in a settlement with the hopeful name of "New Chicago" that appeared in the spring of 1883. The townsite was not platted, although six businesses operated there that summer. Transportation from New Chicago to Creelsburg was provided by a small steamboat that had been shipped by rail to Bartlett and then hauled overland to the lake. Capt. Edward E. Heerman purchased the boat line and expanded the operation, offering frequent service connecting settlements around the lake. Heerman was also interested in townsites. In September 1883 he became the proprietor of West End, which was located about two miles southwest of New Chicago (fig. 7). Heer-

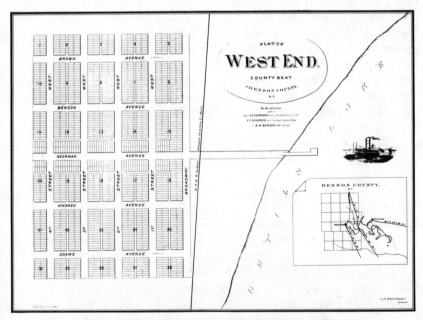

Figure 7. Plat of West End, Dakota Territory, 1883. Capt. Edward E. Heerman platted the town hoping he could lure the Northern Pacific to make West End its station on the western edge of Devils Lake. Seven weeks after he filed the plat, the railroad established its own town of Minnewaukan about a mile south of Heerman's town. Copy of West End plat from Historical Data Project files, Benson County, State Historical Society of North Dakota.

man and his five associates named the streets of the twenty-four block plat for themselves. Soon all of New Chicago's business people had moved to Heerman Street in West End, at the foot of which a new boat dock was constructed. The town had thirteen buildings by March 1884.[15]

Heerman had put New Chicago out of business by shifting his boat line. His reported investment of $1,500 in the West End dock alone indicated his seriousness. He also believed that the Northern Pacific's branch line would pass through his property, which was not an unreasonable assumption: the line from Carrington that had reached New Rockford in 1883 was headed north in such a direction that it would surely pass the western edge of the lake.

As usual, however, the railroad made other arrangements. On 24 October 1883, only seven weeks after West End had begun, a plat was filed for the townsite of Minnewaukan, about a mile south of Heerman's town. The land, at the edge of the Fort Totten reservation, had been obtained with Sioux half-breed scrip, patented in 1882, and was platted by the owner, D. L. Wilbur, who deeded one-half of the lots to a trustee for the Northern Pacific as a donation. Minnewaukan was a railroad town, but it had no railroad until 1885. The town grew slowly in its early years when it should have boomed, falling far short of the Northern Pacific's expectations. Even the promise of a railroad was enough to lure West End's business people to Minnewaukan, however, and by the summer of 1884 West End had met the same fate as New Chicago. Heerman's daughter later said that her father lost many thousands of dollars at West End. If so, it may have consoled him that the Northern Pacific's plans to make Minnewaukan a city larger than Devils Lake also failed.[16]

It would be an exaggeration to say that all speculative townsite ventures met the same fate—instant oblivion—at the hands of railroad builders. Some of them remained for a short time as inland towns, although none achieved long-term viability. Equally erroneous would be the position that no existing towns ever were able to attract the railroad builders. To put the matter in perspective, there was one town that did develop the way people at that time evidently believed would be typical—a town that sought, and received, the iron horse at its doorstep.

Cando was platted in June 1884, following a decision by the Towner County commissioners to locate the county seat there. The town grew slowly, handicapped by being thirty-five miles from the railroad at Devils Lake, a two- or three-day trip for farmers marketing grain. Only six business houses were in operation at Cando in 1886.[17] When the St. Paul, Minneapolis & Manitoba reached Churchs Ferry that year, plans were discussed for a branch line north from there that would serve Cando. If local citizens expected the new line to come through their town, they had not been paying close attention to the fate of others with similar hopes. James J. Hill, who had put six townsites out of business just getting his railroad around Devils Lake and had managed to avoid every inland town in the Mouse River loop, surely could not have been counted on to build through Cando.

Solomon G. Comstock, whose Northwest Land Company was handling townsites for Hill on the new extension north of Churchs Ferry, was concerned that no decision had been made on a townsite in that vicinity, and he inquired in St. Paul about the railroad's plans. General Manager Allan Manvel offered the opinion that "the line ought to be run to the old town of Cando," but he noted that Mr. Hill would make the decision. Nine days later, Manvel reported that "Mr. Hill thinks we should leave the townsite of Cando to the local people and let them build up the town."[18] When the line reached Cando, the Northwest Land Company platted a small addition that joined the original townsite with the tracks, but only a few blocks separated the railroad from the county courthouse. Neither Comstock's nor Hill's correspondence indicates why Hill chose this occasion to accommodate the wishes of local citizens. Cando nonetheless remains as an example of what could have been done in many other cases where towns were platted ahead of the railroad, where existing developments could have been assisted, rather than destroyed, in the settlement process.[19]

The townsite promoter has played a colorful role in popular accounts of the American West. Perhaps best personified in the affable, born-liar Col. Beriah Sellers of Mark Twain's *The Gilded Age*, promoters have traditionally been pictured with a satchel full of other people's money, on their way to the next town to find another batch of suckers. Colonel Sellers' weakness, however, was his own inability to distinguish truth from fiction. A similar verdict must apply to the real-life Dakota townsite promoters whose deceptions and falsehoods look more like self-deception and foolish pride when placed in context.

Most speculators could be found guilty of not knowing how to make a tract of empty prairie grow into a city. No one doubted that northern Dakota would have cities, and, as homesteaders began to arrive, it was apparent that trade centers would be needed immediately. People of various means, abilities, and connections set about to create them. Two approaches were taken that, in their most unsuccessful form, could be labeled "stores without towns" and "towns without stores."

The merchant who opened a store at an isolated location, ahead of the railroad, often did not get around to legally platting a town around it, although his place had a name because it was a post office. An isolated general store and perhaps a blacksmith, but generally not more than two or three businesses within sight of one another, consituted the settlement. They were towns in name and function, but they lacked formal structure. Their sites were not surveyed and they had no streets, nor were any building lots marked off. In the East and South, such places are called hamlets or crossroads stores; especially in the South, they were an important part of the settlement fabric. In northern Dakota they were known as inland towns, and they were failures in almost every case. Their merchants lost trade to the closest railroad town, even if it were one hundred miles away. When the railroad came closer, merchants abandoned their inland towns for lots on the new railroad townsite.

Townsite speculators, at the other extreme, sometimes found they had a town without stores (or residents). Marking off streets and parcels of real estate did not make a town unless people believed that the railroad was coming. Promoters exaggerated the likelihood of acquiring a railroad in order to attract merchants. In fact, the railroad almost never chose to build its line through somebody else's townsite because they wanted to plat and control their own.

Most of the Dakota promoters had come from east of the Mississippi and were accustomed to a different sequence, in which existing towns played a more influential role. Railroads started their westward march from the eastern seaboard well after settlement was established beyond the Appalachians. When railroads came to the Ohio and Mississippi valleys, they commonly sought local assistance in the form of bond issues, free right-of-way, or other concessions in return for building to and through settlements that had been in place for some time. After the railroad and settlement frontiers got somewhat into phase west of the Mississippi River, they advanced in periodic and synchronous spurts of growth. Since large portions of the West had no sizable, existing towns to be served, railroads exercised their advantage to locate and promote towns of their own making, ignoring promoters who believed they could lure the railroad their way through the same devices that had been used in the East and Middle West a generation earlier. (fig. 8.)

The successful towns were those platted by the railroads or their designated agents. Because only the highest officers in the company knew where the tracks were going to be laid, they often were able to purchase land for right-of-way and townsites at a low price before anybody knew what was coming. Those who carefully watched the strategies of railroad construction and settlement learned the new routine so that by the 1890s there were many fewer towns like Gwynne City, West End, and Harrisburgh being entered on the plat books.

What local people did not see, however, were the enormous stacks of engineering blueprints back at railroad headquarters, showing existing lines in yellow, projected lines in red, competitors' projected lines in green, with stations and sidings—some already named—inked in white for mile after

Figure 8. Two exceptions to the rule. Lincoln Valley (*top*) was an anomaly because it survived for many years as a viable inland town. By the 1970s, however, it had become a ghost town and was used as such to illustrate "Thousands Flee the Towns of America's Lonely Plains," *New York Times*, 14 February 1971. Cando (*bottom*) was one of the few towns in the study area platted before the railroads arrived that also managed to lure the iron horse to its doorstep.

mile of road the company intended to build. The larger system mattered little to the local merchant, who was concerned with having a prosperous town and building a trade for his store, but it meant a great deal to the president of the railroad who was organizing a region thousands of square miles in extent in order to funnel traffic to his line.

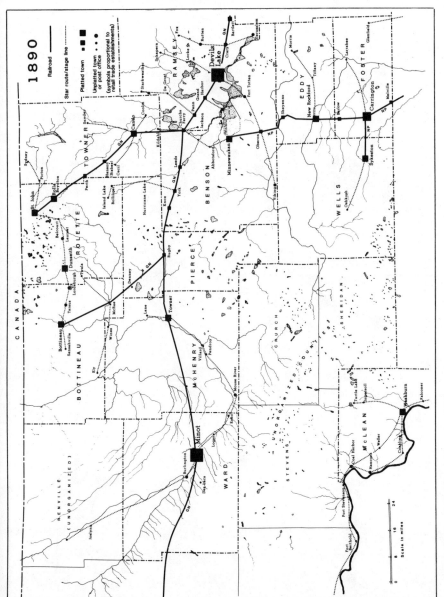

Figure 9. North Dakota study area, 1890

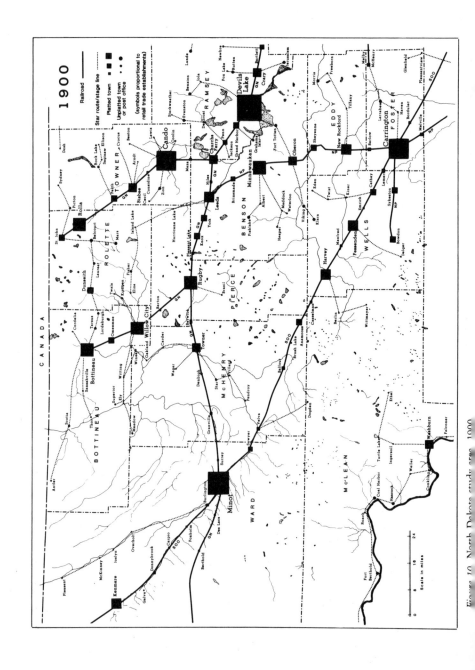

Figure 10. North Dakota study area, 1900.

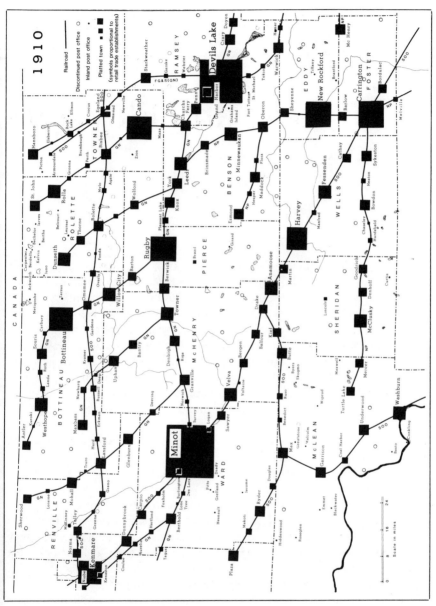

Figure 11. North Dakota study area, 1910

Chapter 5

Tracks and Elevators

Railroads entered the townsite business for two, largely independent sets of reasons. One derived from the role railroads played in colonization activities, a sideline especially important to the land-grant roads, but one shared by nearly every company that laid its tracks in the latter half of the nineteenth century. Most companies had land, colonization, or immigrant departments whose officials worked to secure the presence of an increased agricultural population in the vicinity of their lines. Townsite activity generally was placed under other departments of the road or was handled by individuals who drew no salary from the company but acted as designated agents for the towns.[1] Regardless of the business relationship that prevailed, those in charge of townsite development also shared the function of attracting people to on-line communities. Their revenue was derived from the sale of lots in the various towns they developed.

The other stimulus for townsite development came from the desirability of locating stations and sidetracks in an orderly fashion so as to achieve operating economies. Too many stations meant too little business at each one; too few resulted in loss of business to whatever competition may have been present. Revenue from the sale of town lots was a short-term prospect; more important was a series of viable, trade center towns along a railroad line that would sustain a profitable volume of business into the indefinite future. The presence or absence of competing lines is the key to understanding the level of townsite activity exhibited by a company, and traffic considerations thus take precedence over real estate sales as the reason why railroads were in this business at all.

A railroad company's first priority, however, was the long-haul traffic it could win either by generating new business or by taking it away from a competitor. If the immediate concern was construction of a transcontinental or other long-distance line, railroads understandably paid much less attention to townsites; their corporate gaze was fixed on the distant horizon, not on the little towns they could build up along the line getting there. James J. Hill's line from Devils Lake to Minot, part of a record-breaking spurt of construction that reached west to Great Falls, Mont., was one example. His immediate objective was to tap the Montana copper traffic and to establish a route that could later be extended over the Rockies to the Pacific Northwest. Only four townsites were planned on the first 120-mile segment west of Devils Lake. As North Dakota's railnet grew more weblike in later years, however, the capture of local trade became the primary objective. Most new lines constructed after 1900 were short branches, and the company's strategy was to place "all the towns on the line that the country will stand."[2]

After the first transcontinental lines had been built, the construction of new lines of road was generally prompted by traffic competition between companies, whether the business sought was long or short haul. At the local level, this competition always produced the same result—the addition of more trade center towns every time a new line was laid. Because towns were a railroad's point of access to the local agricultural economy, they multiplied in number most rapidly when two or more companies were battling to sustain or increase their share of local business. The correlation between the number of miles of track built and the number of new towns platted was, therefore, strongest in the later period, when all railroads were trying to capture as much traffic from the local hinterlands as they could (fig. 12). Corporate strategies for traffic dominance thus take precedence over all other reasons, including local demand for trade centers, that might explain the location and timing of town-founding activity.

Three railroads were responsible for most of the construction and townsite activity in the North Dakota study area. The Northern Pacific, largest but financially the weakest, entered from the southeast. The St. Paul, Minneapolis & Manitoba (known as the Great Northern after 1889), which was financially the strongest, monopolized the northern part of the study area until 1893. After that year, it faced a series of battles with the third major company, the Soo Line, for dominance in the area. All three were Minneapolis or St. Paul companies that had substantial foreign financial backing. All three hauled North Dakota wheat to the Minneapolis mills and the Duluth-Superior docks, and all either had or wanted their own lines to the Pacific coast.

The rivalries between these three corporations is a subject in its own right that is treated in detail elsewhere, but a few major points of contact should be established for what follows.[3] The Northern Pacific, which re-

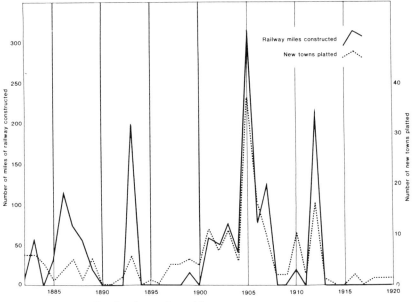

Figure 12. Railroad and townsite activity, 1882–1920

ceived the only land grant for construction across North Dakota, entered bankruptcy in 1873 (the year it reached Bismarck), was reorganized, and completed its line to Tacoma in 1883. The company went under again in 1893, the same year that the Great Northern reached Seattle. James J. Hill played a major role in the Northern Pacific's second reorganization. One of the consequences of Hill's participation was the subsequent inability of Northern Pacific to construct any new lines that might threaten the traffic coming to Hill's Great Northern. The Northern Pacific built very few miles of track in the study area after it came under Hill's influence, and its role in townsite activities virtually stopped.

Hill did not, and could not, control the Soo, however. The company was born of efforts by Minneapolis millers, first to build a line east for transporting flour destined for export to Europe, and second to build to the wheat fields of western Minnesota for purposes of securing the traffic that was bypassing Minneapolis on its way to Milwaukee or Chicago mills. Its corporate title after 1888 — the Minneapolis, St. Paul & Sault Ste. Marie — reflected the first ambition, that of a direct line to the east from Minneapolis. The Soo's first president, William D. Washburn, and most of its early directors were prominent in the Minneapolis milling industry.[4]

The Canadian Pacific acquired control of the financially troubled Soo Line in 1888, believing that Hill would turn over his eastbound traffic to the Soo-Canadian Pacific at Minneapolis for shipment via Sault Ste. Marie to Montreal or other eastern ports. Hill did not honor whatever agreement there may have been to that effect, instead routing his eastbound traffic via Chicago. The Canadian Pacific retaliated by extending the Soo Line into North Dakota, following a course just east of the Coteau du Missouri, to reach the Saskatchewan boundary and a connection with the Canadian Pacific at Portal. This line, completed in 1893, was the first in the region that could be ascribed directly to traffic competition. The Canadian Pacific's goal was a long-distance connection to avoid routing any traffic from the Northwest over Hill's Great Northern. Typical of lines constructed with this purpose in mind, the Soo's diagonal route saw little townsite activity at the time of its construction.[5] The depression of the mid-1890s further dampened efforts to build up towns along the line.

The timing of railroad construction activities was controlled, in part, by a company's ability to market the construction bonds that financed new lines of road. Most of the lines in this region were begun during upswings in the national level of business activity. The construction peaks of 1881, 1886, 1892, 1902, 1905, and 1912 all coincided with periods of economic expansion nationwide when the climate for investment was relatively favorable. The troughs between these peaks coincided with downturns in those same cycles of activity, the mid-1890s being one example. Because town platting was so closely linked with railroad construction, the graph of new town founding also corresponds closely with national business trends (fig. 12).

There were also local indicators that spurred or retarded new developments. North Dakota's pattern of precipitation had not been recorded long enough to allow settlers to know whether sequences of wet or dry years were normal or abnormal. Boomers, naturally, claimed that a sequence of wetter-than-normal years represented the true record, whereas pessimists were sure that droughts were really more frequent than the record to date had shown. Between 1889 and 1910, North Dakota experienced only five years that had precipitation totals below the long-term average that was eventually established.[6] There was a natural tendency to believe that these wetter-than-average conditions were normal, which, in turn, encouraged farmers to plant larger acreages and expect larger yields than they had in earlier years.

The same evidence encouraged an additional immigration of agricultural settlers who purchased existing farms or joined a new wave of dryland speculators who were plowing under the sod grass on the Coteau and the Missouri Slope. As the demand for North Dakota farmland increased, railroads expected to extend their lines into the newly settled lands. The actual extension of railroads into unserved areas was not an automatic consequence of the new population growth, nor did the railroads build new lines in hopes of acquiring an expanded agricultural population. In fact, railroad companies delayed these extensions as long as they could and responded only when it was advantageous for them to do so.

Wheat yields in North Dakota generally averaged between ten and twenty bushels to the acre. Taking the midpoint of that range, the output of a quarter section of land would be twenty wagon loads of grain. If the elevator were no more than eight miles away, a farmer could make one round trip in a day, including loading, hauling, waiting, unloading, and returning to his farm. Twenty days of work for marketing a quarter section of wheat at a distance of eight miles would become, roughly, forty days if the elevator were far enough away so that he could not complete a round trip in one day. Farmers were accustomed to hauling their late summer's harvest for months thereafter, well into the freezing cold and snow that began the winter season, but there was a limit to the amount of time they were willing to spend and the hardships they would endure simply transporting what they had already grown. There was other farm work to do, even in the relatively slack fall season. Hiring transportation to accomplish the farm-to-market move would take whatever profit there was from selling the crop.

Farmers who lived more than, say, eight miles from the railroad therefore invested less of their time, money, and land in cash grain farming. Most who lived beyond twenty miles sowed only a small acreage in such crops, and some omitted this activity from their operations entirely because of the time it took to haul the crop to the nearest elevator. In the transition from homesteading to commercial agriculture, time spent on the farm had become valuable, and the occasional long-distance trips to distant trade centers that had characterized the early settlement period became less common. Farmers were more likely to patronize the closest store in order to save time. The largest expenditure of time off the farm was spent hauling grain to market, and it was the need for a local grain elevator that most often prompted farmers to write letters to railroad presidents pleading their case for a new branch line or siding.

It was not an unreasonable request. A typical country elevator at that time had a storage capacity of thirty to fifty thousand bushels of grain. It could turn over this capacity two to three times for each year's crop, depending on railroad car supply and the rate at which grain was brought to the elevator. With a yield of fifteen bushels to the acre, and assuming that at least 10 percent of the land area was in wheat, a single elevator could thus be supported on the business brought from within a circle of five mile's radius, well within the distance grain farmers were willing to travel (fig. 13).[7] The restraint, of course, was that the elevator had to be served by a railroad.

Letters and petitions from farmers asking for rail service are scattered within various groups of records constituting the Great Northern and North-

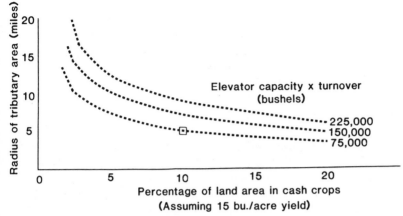

Figure 13. Area required to support a country grain elevator

ern Pacific company archives. Thirty-five such requests received by the two railroads between 1892 and 1910 represent a consensus among, perhaps, ten times that many individuals, and they reveal a consistent pattern.[8] Farmers were in no position to dictate to the company the precise route they should build, but the mileage equivalents can be roughly calculated. The average request was for extensions of approximately thirty five miles from some existing terminal. The minimum length of line requested was ten miles, which suggests that farmers were willing to undertake trips of at least that length and not feel handicapped. Invariably their pleas were accompanied by unverifiable statistics supporting their beliefs that they and their neighbors would raise more grain, thus creating more traffic for the company, if a branch were extended in their direction. Especially interesting were the letters coming to the Great Northern from farmers just south of the international boundary who claimed that grain from their area was being hauled across the border and sold at elevators on the Canadian side, a documented practice known to be winked at by local officials.[9]

Railroad response to these pleas for service was generally noncommittal. New extensions might be built, a company official would write, but there were no definite plans. When the requests were addressed to James J. Hill personally, he often used the occasion to give the entreating farmer a brief lesson in railroad finance:

> Our company has built many miles of both through and local railway in North Dakota. Some of this mileage is paying investment; but we have in your State about 300 miles which not only fails to pay its interest on a valuation of $15,000 per mile, but a large part does not pay the cost of moving the train.[10]

By 1898, his replies had become more pointed:

> We are very glad to do everything we can to aid in the best develop-
> ment of the country served by our lines . . . Notwithstanding this, we
> are at the present time defending law suits seeking to reduce our rates
> and make us lose still more money in the operation of our railway in
> North Dakota. Under these circumstances you will hardly be surprised
> if we are not willing to make further investments in a state where the
> disposition of its officers is to confiscate the investment already made.[11]

Hill's mantle of righteousness probably did not fool the farmers, who were strongly behind any efforts to reduce rates on grain shipments (even though North Dakota's railroad commissioners could not effect interstate rate reductions, the real goal). Nor did the farmers count themselves particularly fortunate to have as many miles of track as already existed. They knew, and so did Hill, that $15,000 per mile was an inflated valuation; that branch lines were cheaply constructed with iron rails ripped up when the main line was relaid with steel; that a typical station in prime wheat country shipped one hundred cars of grain every season to Duluth or Minneapolis, which Hill's road hauled every mile of the way; and, above all, that grain production would increase as soon as farmers had an elevator close enough to make large-scale production profitable. Why was the railroad so slow to respond?

Simply put, the railroad did not care how far a farmer had to travel to market his grain. Farmers near an on-line community raised large acreages, those at a distance much less, but as long as it had all the business, a railroad was willing to haul whatever came its way and avoid the expense of constructing new lines. Railroads could discriminate against the distant producer, knowing that he would produce some grain and would absorb the disadvantage by spending more time hauling the crop than he preferred, but that he would bring some traffic to the company in any case.

Wheat acreages increased slowly in the study area from 1894 to 1898 in response to a steadily advancing market price, but they fell back nearly to the 1894 level when the price began to slip after the 1898 season (fig. 14). Such a response is characteristic of marginal producers, who can operate profitably when the price goes up but are forced out when the price drops. Easier access to markets would have given those producers a more comfortable margin against price fluctuations. The nationwide economic recovery from the depression of the 1890s, which made it possible for railroads to sell their construction bonds once again, was translated into a resumption of branch line activity after 1900. From then until railroad expansion reached its final plateau in 1912, wheat acreages advanced in direct proportion to railway construction as more and more farmers found themselves within easy reach of grain elevators.

The lack of railroads in northern North Dakota had led to the formation

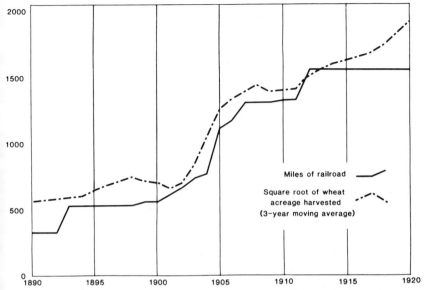

Figure 14. Railroads and wheat acreage, 1890–1920. Wheat acreages computed from *Annual Reports*, North Dakota Commissioner of Agriculture and Labor. Acreage is expressed as its square root for dimensional equivalence with railroad miles.

of several "farmers' roads," independent companies that would operate their own elevators, control their own townsites, and construct and operate their own railways. One of them, Joseph M. Kelly's Farmers Grain and Shipping Company Railroad, built a line from Devils Lake to Starkweather in 1902.[12] The Brazil Grain and Shipping Company, which held unrealistically ambitious plans for a line from Dunseith to Washburn and Bismarck, and the Leeds, Dunseith & Northern, which projected a line connecting those points, were not built, although they stimulated considerable interest and concern among the managements of the Great Northern, Soo Line, and Northern Pacific. Once again James J. Hill proved himself ablest among the men who made decisions in the railroad offices of Minneapolis and St. Paul, by gaining control of Kelly's road north from Devils Lake and scaring off the other two with news that his company was going to build the lines they had in mind as soon as "conditions of traffic" warranted.[13]

The few miles of track laid between 1901 and 1904 were minor compared with the boom that occurred in 1905 when the Soo Line invaded Northern North Dakota, constructing what became known as its "Wheat Line" from Kenmare to Thief River Falls, Minnesota. By this time, Louis W. Hill had succeeded his father at the helm of the Great Northern. He responded much as the elder Hill would have, by constructing new branches across the Wheat Line so that the Soo would have to fight for traffic practically every mile of the way.[14] His response demonstrated again that competition for traffic was what stimulated new construction, not the demands of local farmers—let alone the prospect of increasing the region's farm output by making new lines available. Townsites platted at regular intervals along these new lines grew out of the need to locate stations that each railroad hoped would draw business otherwise lost to the other.

The construction of a new branch line and all the towns that accompanied it did not always provide the service sought by local farmers. Despite large increases in railway mileage, there remained areas, especially those without competing lines, where a railroad found it unnecessary to locate the sidetracks to serve grain elevators and loading platforms. Without such access, the presence of railroad tracks meant nothing.

When faced with this problem, farmers could petition the state commissioners of railroads to require that the facilities be constructed. Official petitions were followed by an investigation by the commissioners, but the petitions were granted only if sufficient need could be demonstrated. When a group of Sheridan County farmers petitioned to force the Northern Pacific to build a sidetrack between McClusky and Mercer to serve an elevator the farmers planned to build there, the commissioners denied the request, noting that "the crops in the vicinity . . . were not sufficiently bounteous to warrant building the elevator so the sidetrack was not considered."[15]

Railroads frequently asked that farmers' petitions be denied or postponed. A petition from the Carrington area, asking the Soo Line to build a wye there to connect with the Northern Pacific (which farmers erroneously believed would lead to competition between the companies and hence to lower grain rates), brought a typical reaction. Edmund Pennington, the Soo's general manager, echoed the words of James J. Hill when he wrote the commissioners: "You will admit that we have built a long line of railway through a sparsely settled country and are entitled to all the revenue coming from the territory, providing we move the freight at as low rates as apply via other lines." The commissioners sided with Pennington.[16]

Most petitions for facilities were granted, and this led indirectly to a further proliferation of townsites. Farmers did not, nor could they, petition for a trade center town, but every new elevator created new patterns of local trips that caught the attention of railroad townsite agents or independent promoter-merchants who believed a town could be sustained at each new focus of activity. By 1916, the railroad commissioners reported that "the demand for better shipping facilities has caused numerous petitions for new railway sidings, and as a result a number of new stations dot the map."[17] Towns that came about via petition were late additions, usually with no more than one or two stores, and they were too small to attract additional population.

Grain elevators differed from most other town businesses because they were owned by outsiders and were located along the tracks rather than on the townsite itself. Elevator sites were not sold by townsite agents but rather were leased from the railroad's freight department. The "line" elevator companies conducted their operations along one or more lines of track, and they usually worked with a single railroad company. Minneapolis and Duluth companies dominated the line elevator business.

The St. Anthony & Dakota elevator concern owned 150 country elevators along the Great Northern in 1904 with a total capacity of over five million bushels. The firm's president, W. H. Dunwoody, was a Great Northern stockholder. When Dunwoody began to show interest in the Soo Line, the Great Northern's vice-president for traffic responded by denying St. Anthony & Dakota any more elevator locations. "We do not care to extend him any further favors. . . . It has always been our policy to try and confine our favors to the elevator interests that are interested only on our line." Dunwoody retreated from his attempt to colonize the Soo and was rewarded with seven new Great Northern sites the next year for his cooperation.[18]

The number of grain elevators built along each line of track corresponded closely with the level of townsite activity, which, in turn, was a function of the railroad's objectives in building the line. The study region contained only thirty-two elevators in 1888; fifteen of them were owned by the two largest line operators, St. Anthony & Dakota and Minneapolis & Northern. Later, when capture of local traffic became the railroads' principal objective, the Minneapolis line chains were best able to respond because they each could command the capital necessary for simultaneous construction of dozens of elevators. The 1905 war that ensued between the Soo and Great Northern when the Soo's Wheat Line was built resulted in about five hundred miles of new railroad, fifty new towns, and 179 elevators, all constructed in a year's time. By the end of 1905, the study area contained 475 elevators. The five largest line companies operating along each railroad had 55 percent of the Northern Pacific, 56 percent of the Soo, and 64 percent of the Great Northern elevator site leases.[19]

Although elevator construction was under control of the larger line chains, many country elevators were sold later to smaller private concerns or to local farmers. By 1918, less than half of North Dakota's elevators were owned by lines; the remainder was divided about equally between farmers and independent owners.[20] Presence of a farmers' elevator at a town often served as a check against the others. All elevators and track buyers shipped grain over the same railroads to the same markets, and the country price was not set locally; but farmers with their own elevator or warehouse could avoid paying the high storage rates often charged by lines or independents. Country elevators derived their principal income from grain storage and therefore were not as vigorous as they might have been in arranging car supply with the railroad to expedite the product to market. Dissatisfied farmers could seek redress of their grievances with an elevator company by filing a complaint with the railroad commissioners who issued (and reviewed every four years) the state licenses that allowed elevators to operate.

The many points of difference between grain growers, shippers, and haulers suggest that each group held in mind a different optimal geography of its activities. Railroads wanted to deal with just a few line elevator companies, giving each one a lease in every town. Competing with one other, they would never divert business to another railroad because their elevators were along the tracks of one company only. The elevator companies, naturally, preferred the reverse of those two conditions, and they sometimes challenged the railroads. Privately owned elevators wanted to hold the farmers' grain to earn storage fees, but farmers countered with their own competing elevators to prevent unnecessary charges. Railroads wished to limit elevator locations in all areas except where a competing line threatened their captive trade, but farmers could petition for a new site by demonstrating need. A single result generally followed from this interplay of conflicting objectives.

The most pressing need for the farmer was a conveniently located elevator. In wheat country like northern North Dakota, one elevator could be supported by grain brought from within a five-mile radius. Translated into the transportation geometry of a regular grid of section-line roads, this would have produced a lattice of diamond-shaped market areas with elevators spaced about nine miles apart, resulting in an acceptable length of haul even for the most peripheral grain grower (fig. 15-1). There were two problems with this solution, however. If the single elevator at the center of the market area chose to take advantage of its monopoly and offered a low bushel price or charged exorbitant storage rates, then producers within its trade area would have no alternative than to undertake trips of twice the distance to the next nearest point. Furthermore, railroads were not prepared to construct a network of lines anywhere near the density required to serve single elevators spaced so close together, nor could anyone, including the state railroad commissioners, require them to make such an investment. Farmers were thus forced to accept a tradeoff: more widely spaced elevator locations, which meant longer hauls for some, but with the benefit of having market areas large enough to support more than one elevator, thereby making competition possible.

Because railroads wanted to limit the number of track miles and stations in order to achieve operating economies, they preferred to locate several elevators at each station (fig. 15-2). Markets could be as large or as small as local grain production warranted, hence lines of track could be spaced far enough apart to keep the total mileage within acceptable limits. Placing towns too

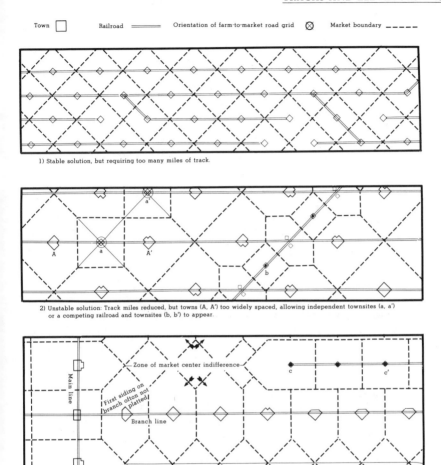

Town ☐   Railroad ═══   Orientation of farm-to-market road grid ⊗   Market boundary _ _ _ _

1) Stable solution, but requiring too many miles of track.

2) Unstable solution: Track miles reduced, but towns (A, A') too widely spaced, allowing independent townsites (a, a') or a competing railroad and townsites (b, b') to appear.

3) More stable solution: Towns closely spaced along line. Railroad line cuts short axis of oblong market area. Competing railroad and townsites (c, c') forced away from existing towns.

Figure 15. Locational strategies

far apart made it possible for independent promoters to squeeze in a trade center at the halfway point between two of the railroad's towns. If all the sites left open from such a strategy were eventually taken, it would have cut the market area of each original town in half, reducing the viability of all centers. This strategy (fig. 15-2) also encouraged competing railroads to build through existing towns—a development eagerly sought by local residents, but one the existing railroad sought to avoid if possible.

A better solution for the railroad was to segregate all farmers farthest from a railroad station into that portion of the market area also farthest from the railroad track (fig. 15-3). The market areas resulting from such a strategy were oblong. Towns, whether platted by railroad affiliates or independents, were perhaps eight miles apart along the track but three times farther apart across the back country between lines. This pattern was the common result in the Great Plains. The distribution benefited the railroads because they were able to concentrate elevators into fewer locations, construct fewer miles of track, and still haul all of the grain produced in the area. No matter what arrangement of lines and stations they made, however, every railroad was subject to invasion of its territory by a competitor. Oblong market areas forced competing railroad lines away from existing towns, making this arrangement at least marginally better than any alternative.

Whenever a company planned an extension or a new line, it commonly made some careful calculations based on local soil conditions and productivity of the farming population before estimating the amount of traffic that would be gained. The method followed was essentially that of market area analysis, whereby average conditions in the area are multiplied by the number of square miles tributary to each center. Tributary areas were calculated under the assumption that farmers would haul their grain to the closest elevator and would patronize whatever trade center was there. Railroad engineers who undertook these calculations were effectively creating their own ad hoc theory of location; their assumptions about human locational behavior were not codified as any theory, but the resulting projections did not differ significantly from what a latter-day economic geographer would have derived from the same set of "givens."

The Soo's traffic projection on their Wheat Line is one such example (fig. 16). The company estimated that there would be nearly two million acres within nine miles of the line, two-thirds of which would be closer to its tracks than to those of the Great Northern.[21] Like other roads, however, the Soo did not project that their competitor would retaliate with new lines of its own. The Great Northern countered the Soo's invasion by running new branches along the outer margins of the market areas on its existing lines. This strategy helped to preserve the traffic volume on the branches constructed earlier by serving farmers who had been at the "back end" of the market before, but the Soo was left with much less than it projected on the assumption of no retaliation.

We have no information on the actual trade areas of country elevators, although the boundaries can be derived reasonably well from the tendency to market grain at the closest point (fig. 17). Each new elevator site produced a shrinkage of the areas tributary to those surrounding. The proportion of the average trade area within eight miles of an elevator increased from 25 percent in 1888 to more than 94 percent by the end of the railroad-building era in 1912.[22] The grain production stimulated by this increased accessibility supported the new elevators, although some of them were

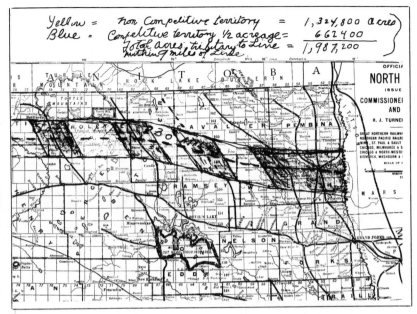

Figure 16. Locational strategies in practice. Map of northeastern North Dakota showing calculations made by Soo Line officials in their projections of traffic to be gained from building the Wheat Line, 1904–1905. From historical materials in the Soo Line Railway Collection, Minnesota Historical Society, Division of Archives and Manuscripts.

moved out of older trade centers to sites along newly constructed branches in order to keep pace with changing conditions.

As would be expected, new branch lines tended to follow the market boundaries between existing centers (fig. 17). This growth decreased the long dimension of the oblong market areas, but closer spacing along the line produced by a filling in of centers also reduced the length of the shorter axis of the trade area by a roughly equal amount. Market shapes were preserved in the transformation from a sparse to a dense network. No new lines were constructed in the study area after 1912, although railroad building went on elsewhere for another decade. The 1912 map shows why this was the final episode: no gaps large enough to support another line of road remained to be exploited. Railroad building came to a halt, and thus so did the creation of new trade centers.

In summary, this chapter establishes the priority of railroads in effecting a new settlement system. Railroad companies were interested in townsites primarily for considerations of traffic rather than real estate sales. If the motivation for constructing a line was to acquire long-distance traffic, rail-

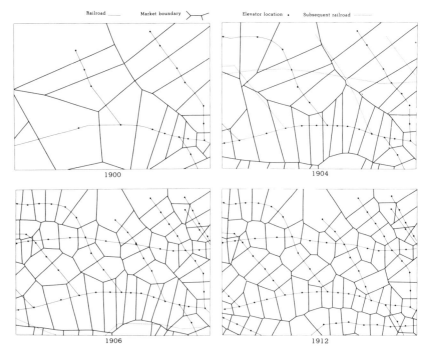

Figure 17. Growth of railnet and shrinkage of market areas, 1900–1912, in the central portion of the North Dakota study area. New lines of track tended to follow market boundaries, serving farmers most remote from existing elevator towns.

roads paid little attention (at least initially) to townsites that might be built up along the way. If the purpose was local traffic capture, however, townsites were placed as close together as possible. The construction of new lines took place during relatively favorable periods for investment, hence the platting of townsites corresponds with national business trends as well.

Railroads did not lead grain farmers into unsettled country away from their main lines; rather, they lagged behind the settlement of agricultural population and extended lines only after the demand for transportation was well established, and often then only when a competitor threatened to serve the territory. Farmers, seeking more locations for access than railroads provided, petitioned for additional elevator sites. The petitioned sites were often those where the railroad had omitted service because there were no competing lines nearby.

Towns were spaced closely on each line, and the areas tributary to each were elongated to prevent insertion of new towns or elevator sites along the line. This strategy segregated the farmers who faced the longest hauls into that portion of the market area farthest from the railroad, where they had no choice but to absorb the locational disadvantage. When new lines were built they often followed the outer market boundaries, thus attracting the trade of those who had previously been most remote.

It is thus no exaggeration to state that the *network* of towns — their location, spacing, number, and dates of founding — was largely the incidental result of decisions railroad managers made on how to best protect and extend their business. Assuming correctly that farmers would raise grain if they could, and would market it at the closest elevator when they did, railroad men plotted their lines and dotted them with towns in order to capture as much traffic as possible. No one else, regardless of their purpose in founding a town, could compete with the logic and the capital that railroads brought to the task of laying out the system they wanted.

Chapter 6

Railroad Towns

In his monumental history of the Chicago, Burlington & Quincy Railroad, Richard C. Overton argued that the relations between railroads, townsites, and the men of influence who connected one with the other produced a generally beneficial result. By following their own interests, railroad-affiliated townsite promoters created an orderly, permanent development that benefited the local citizenry as much as it did the promoters. "Whether the new towns and farming areas which these companies fostered could have been developed without speculative capital, or whether their development was premature, are moot points," Overton wrote.[1] His generally favorable evaluation balanced a popular view that railroad townsite promotion was little more than a saga of greed and corruption, but neither his analysis nor those of others are sufficient to render moot the question of corporate involvement in the town business.

The record of railroads and their townsites varies from company to company and, thereby, from region to region, but in no instance was the involvement passive. Railroad townsite strategies were most aggressive when independent parties or competing railroads threatened to usurp what was taken as a corporate prerogative—to plant towns where and when the railroad wished. If independent townsites found a permanent home somewhere along a line, it was only because the railroad allowed it; and they did so only when they judged as poor the prospects for success of a town at a given location at a given time. Whether through their own promotions or by what might have seemed benign neglect, all railroad companies watched with extreme care any attempts to promote towns on or near their lines.

The model of town settlement adopted by the railroads was one that had evolved gradually in the course of European and American urbanization. The same model had been used by the many independent townsite boomers who hoped to interest a railroad in their plans. *Structure* assumed priority over *activity* in the railroad town. A site was selected first and was then platted as a series of streets and separated blocks divided into building lots. Only after the structure was completely specified were any townlike activities allowed to locate there.[2]

It was not an ingrained belief in the virtues of urban design that led to a mapped prefiguration of a town, but rather an imperative to control development. Unlike the speculative townsite, whose promoters anticipated profit from real estate sales, the railroad town was a device for organizing the traffic that would come to the company as a result. Also unlike its other local predecessor, the inland town, railroad strategy was to make all parcels of land other than those they wished to control unfit for business activity. This was easily accomplished by the transportation cost advantage that railroad town merchants were known to enjoy over their inland counterparts.

Railroad companies engaged in townsite activity whenever and wherever they built new lines. Agreements made with townsite affiliates effectively lapsed once those lines were completed. Some companies (such as the Soo) maintained a long-term arrangement with outside parties who platted and sold their towns, but more commonly railroads reorganized their townsite affiliations when new construction was projected. The work of various townsite agents is thus demarcated more by time than by place.

The Northern Pacific's early townsite attempts (in the study area and elsewhere) were supervised by that company's Land Department, although the methods used to sell town lots differed from their other land sales efforts.[3] The company used three separate schemes to involve local capital in the townsites platted on railroad land. At Sykeston, Carrington, and Melville the railroad held an undivided one-half interest in all lots; at Minnewaukan it owned half the lots, in alternate arrangement, with a syndicate that owned the rest; and at Oberon and New Rockford the company owned land in various blocks of the townsite.

Sykeston began with a boom in 1883, with the sale of eighty-six lots at an average price of $71 in the first month after it was platted. One year later, only five more lots had been sold; by 1889, the company had collected less than a third of what it was owed on the sales to that date, a mere $2,383. Richard Sykes donated some of the unsold land for parks and a cemetery and then purchased three hundred remaining lots at $1 each in 1899.[4] The massive default on lot payments reflected an overestimation of the town's potential. Further setbacks occurred when its trade area was truncated by two new towns platted along the Soo Line in 1893 and when it lost the county seat to Fessenden in 1894. Sykeston eventually achieved stability as a trade center, although its early start was no advantage (fig. 18).

Carrington and Melville were both joint ventures between the Northern Pacific and the Carrington and Casey Land Co. Melville was a failure, bringing only $175 in its first decade of existence. A large block of lots was sold for taxes in 1898. Carrington, in contrast, was an instant success. Lots ranged from $125 to $300 each when they first went on sale in 1882, and two-thirds of the nearly $30,000 in lot sales had been paid up by 1886.[5] A county seat and minor railroad terminal, Carrington drew trade from a large area and saw many subsequent additions to the original plat. The unequal success of the two undoubtedly reflects Carrington and Casey's bold promotion of Carrington and their simultaneous neglect of Melville.

New Rockford, sixteen miles north, also became a county seat that drew considerable trade, but it was not a success in the Northern Pacific's estimation. The railroad had to sell its own lots, which were scattered about New Rockford's sixty-seven-block townsite. In 1883–84, lots sold at an average of $220 each, but sales dwindled rapidly after that time. In 1894, the railroad's land commissioner reported to the company's appointed receiver that New Rockford was thriving although lot sales were slow. The Northern Pacific reduced its average price to $58 per lot, but the $300 paid annually in taxes on the unsold lots was an expenditure the bankrupt railroad could ill afford. In 1897, they sold the nearly six hundred remaining lots to a single buyer for $434.[6]

The Northern Pacific's interest at Minnewaukan represented one-half of the lots on the townsite, which were held in trust for the company after their donation by the syndicate responsible for acquiring and platting the site. The same arrangement held at Bismarck, Mandan, Helena, Montana, North Yakima, Washington, and other "trustee towns" in which the company hoped their lots would increase in value proportional to the sales made by the syndicate. In March 1884, five months after Minnewaukan came on the market, the railroad had sold 24 lots while the syndicate had sold 160 (mainly to eastern investors), both at an average price of $215 to $230 per lot. The railroad's land commissioner blamed its poor record at Minnewaukan on the company itself for not completing the line on time, claiming that another $100,000 in town lots could be sold there in a year if the railroad arrived by June 1884. When the tracks finally were laid in 1885, Minnewaukan's growth had slowed to a crawl. By 1893, nearly ten years after the town had gone on sale, the Northern Pacific had sold only 111 lots at an average price of $60. In 1897 they cleared the books, as they had at New Rockford, with a lump-sum sale of all remaining lots for $1,000.[7]

The Northern Pacific's experimentation with town lot ventures reflected

Figure 18. Northern Pacific towns. Melville (*top*) was platted by the Carrington & Casey Land Company in 1882. The town was attractive enough to put the adjacent, independent townsite of Newport out of business, but Melville saw little subsequent growth. Sykeston (*bottom*), once the seat of Wells County, suffered a setback when it lost the county seat to Fessenden, a Soo Line town.

the confusion generally marking that company's succession of managers. The railroad itself made feeble efforts to sell town lots, apparently expecting the various partners with whom it had entered into townsite agreements to handle the promotion. This worked at Carrington, but New Rockford and Minnewaukan both fell short of expectations. Sykeston, Melville, and

Oberon, all planned as smaller trade centers, were proportionately even less successful. The Northern Pacific discontinued direct involvement in town-sites in the 1890s after it had disposed of its earlier efforts, and it left this sideline to local promoters. It was a strategy not without perils of its own, however, as the railroad was to learn.

The branch from Carrington to Sykeston was built in 1883 at the request of Richard Sykes, who had purchased the Northern Pacific's alternate sections in six townships of Wells and Foster counties. Sykes claimed that the railroad had promised him a longer extension that would better serve the area he had purchased from the company, but financial troubles on the railroad made that impossible. In 1898 he resumed his efforts to get the line extended fifteen miles west, to the edge of his land, where he planned a new townsite that he hoped would be the marketing center for a new influx of Russian-Germans (ethnic Germans who had lived in south Russia) from Eureka, South Dakota. The line was built in 1899, and Sykes's new town of Bowdon became the railhead.[8]

The extension was not merely an accommodation to good customer Richard Sykes, however. The Northern Pacific extended west from Sykeston and constructed another branch from Oberon to Esmond in 1901 to secure its territory against the inroads the Soo Line had made in the diagonal strip northwest from Carrington. The Soo was relatively popular locally and frequent rumors held that it would build new branches away from its main line to serve farmers remote from grain marketing centers. The Northern Pacific, determined to get its share of the traffic, surveyed a new line west from Bowdon in 1900 that would discourage the Soo from building its way and that would also increase the value of the agricultural land the Northern Pacific still held near the fifty-mile limit of its grant.

The Northern Pacific's land commissioner predicted that their 150,000 acres west of Bowdon would increase in value by 50 percent as a result of the new line. This softened the impact of the chief engineer's report, which projected construction costs in excess of $12,000 per mile through the hilly region at the edge of the Coteau du Missouri.[9] The line was extended twenty-six miles to Denhoff in 1902, and the survey was simultaneously run another eighty-five miles west to the Missouri River where the railroad hoped to tap the coal traffic that was developing from W. D. Washburn's mining and railroad venture, the Bismarck, Washburn & Great Falls.

The new terminal location, which became Denhoff, was known to Northern Pacific officials in 1901; but it had been literally given away by the company's chief engineer, who explained to the president:

> The only available site for a station at the end of the branch was on government land. The townsite was eagerly sought by A. A. White, R. Sykes, and others. Mr. Geo. C. Howe of Duluth owns a large amount

of land in this vicinity, and having in mind the many favors which the Railway Company has received from him without compensation, I gave him such advance information as would permit him to acquire the townsite, believing that this would meet with your approval.[10]

Denhoff may have been the only possible site for a town at the end of the branch, but it was a poor one. Farmers claimed they needed four horses on a grain wagon to get over the hills west of town, and many preferred to travel north to the Soo, twice the distance, because of the level terrain.[11] Denhoff clearly was not a place that would draw traffic from the competition.

Between 1902 and 1904, the Northern Pacific sent at least four parties into the field west of Denhoff to consider possible options. The caution and lengthy delays were caused by another shake-up in the company's management, brought about by James J. Hill and the New York bankers, who kept a watchful eye on the affairs of a company known to spend money to no avail. The Northern Pacific's subsequent engineering reports and traffic projections were thus undertaken with extreme care, but the longer company officials studied, the more assiduously they were courted by local entrepreneurs hoping to gain the townsite favor.

There were three inland towns along the surveyed route west of Denhoff. Turtle Lake, on the shores of the lake so named, and its would-be successor, Wannemacher, a few rods away, hoped to acquire the railroad. The original settlement had given birth to its nearby rival when a dispute arose with the landowner. In the summer of 1904 the "Twin Cities" had, between them, four general stores, a bank, a hotel, and two blacksmiths all eagerly awaiting the Northern Pacific.[12] The other active townsite was McClusky, twelve miles west of Denhoff, with its two general stores and blacksmith. McClusky also aspired to be the seat of a new county that was to be formed from the eastern end of McLean.

The Northern Pacific was soon embroiled in the politics of the county seat fight. One of the contenders was Lincoln Valley, an inland town consisting of a large general store owned by interests in the nearby town of Harvey, and which run by and for the Russian-Germans who were fast becoming the dominant local group. They were, observed one Northern Pacific field engineer, "a hardworking, economical people, and seem to understand the art . . . of making a dollar stick to their fingers."[13] Lincoln Valley was rumored to be a prime contender for the county seat because the Soo would extend a branch line there in the near future. The Northern Pacific considered deviating from its own survey to run a line closer to Lincoln Valley's thrifty farmers, but decided to keep to the south. Each decision took months to accomplish and was preceded by soils analyses, interviews with farmers about their trading patterns, and then new cost, revenue, and trade area projections.

The site nearest the center of what would become Sheridan County was McClusky. William McClusky, a Denhoff banker, claimed to have received promises from an earlier Northern Pacific field party that his town would receive the railroad. He continued to press his case, but the matter was soon complicated by another aspirant. In July 1904, railroad President Howard Elliott and Vice-President Jule Hannaford came to see for themselves. They were conducted about the area by a former company employee, R. H. Johnston, who was engaged in local real estate ventures that anticipated bringing in several hundred Russian-German farmers from eastern Nebraska and establishing a townsite just east of McClusky as the county seat and railroad town. Known simply as the "Section 6" town, it was favored by some Northern Pacific officials over McClusky, five miles to the west.[14]

Even though the railroad was taking no direct interest in the new townsites, its involvement was nonetheless critical because only the railroad knew where the new stations would be located. Perhaps sensing that a public relations disaster was at hand, Howard Elliott dictated a memo in November 1904, following another visit by Mr. McClusky to St. Paul, making clear the company's position:

> I told him that when we came to build a town we would locate towns where we thought best for railroad operation, and gathering the products of the country; that we were not trying to locate towns so as to make money for owners or town-sites.[15]

It was a fair statement, but as usual it stopped short of declaring what the company would do when the townsite decision was made.

The heat of local politics no doubt warmed the various townsite partisans of Sheridan County during the winter of 1904–05, but other plans were underway in St. Paul. On March 10, Elliott sent a private communication to E. J. Pearson, the company's chief engineer, instructing him to consult immediately on the location of townsites west of Denhoff. Elliott, Pearson, and land commissioner Thomas Cooper made the selection in early May. By this time, Elliott had grown weary of the continued pressure from Johnston and McClusky. He wrote to Cooper: "I think we must invent some different plan about town sites the next time we have any building to do, because the present method seems to produce friction and bad results with everybody."[16] Their solution was to adopt the same strategy the Soo and Great Northern had been using, that of giving the locations of all new stations to an independent company that would plat and sell the townsites.

The Northern Pacific chose Charles K. Wing and J. Austin Regan, businessmen of Carrington and Fessenden, respectively, to receive the honor. They formed the McLean County Townsite Company to purchase land at sites the railroad had chosen and hired a surveyor to make the plats. On July 24, they filed the plat of Mercer, at a site in McLean County that had no competitors. Four days later Wing and Regan filed plats for Turtle Lake and McClusky. The lack of official plats for the inland towns made it easy to appropriate the existing names, which was doubtless of some benefit in the county seat election. They avoided both Mr. McClusky's existing townsite and the nameless "Section 6," platting the new town of McClusky halfway between the two contenders. Wing and Regan's McClusky became the county seat. The McClusky family later platted a small addition to the town that bore their name, a minor role compared with what they had tried to accomplish.[17]

Both of the inland towns at Turtle Lake were left four miles beyond the end of track, and their inhabitants dutifully removed themselves to the railroad townsite. If Charles Wing reflected on the fate he had dealt the residents of old Turtle Lake, it may have brought a smile of recollection to his face. As an eager, young Vermonter, Wing had come to Dakota in 1882 and opened a store at the inland town of Newport in Foster County. When the Northern Pacific dealt Newport a fatal blow by platting Melville on the adjacent section, Wing moved his store to Melville, which he left two years later to commence a successful business career in Carrington.[18] Being forced to leave Newport may have been the best thing that ever happened to him. He and Regan continued their partnership in later years, platting several more towns for the Northern Pacific. Their efforts at Turtle Lake, Mercer, and McClusky gave those towns a secure beginning, and all three became viable trade centers.

The most successful of northern Dakota's townsite promoters were Solomon G. Comstock and Almond A. White of Moorhead, Minn. Incorporated as the Northwest Land Company, they platted Minot, Towner, Rugby, Bottineau, and more than two dozen lesser places along the lines of the St. Paul, Minneapolis & Manitoba (Great Northern) in the 1880s. Comstock, one of western Minnesota's wealthiest and most influential businessmen, was the dominant partner, although both held equal shares of the land company's stock. White was the field man who purchased land, arranged for surveyors, and made sure their activities were coordinated with the railroad. The Northwest Land Company was organized in 1883 around $360,000 worth of real estate that Comstock and White held in the St. Paul, Minneapolis & Manitoba townsites in the Red River Valley. By March 1886, these towns had been sold and the business was formally liquidated, only to be reorganized two months later for the purpose of platting new towns on the railroad's lines west of Devils Lake and between Moorhead and Breckinridge, Minn.[19]

Comstock and White acquired a new and most important stockholder. One-half of the reorganized company was owned by James J. Hill. It was Hill's personal investment, as risk-free as anyone could have made in this business, given that he made the final decision on townsites from information gathered by railroad engineers and then instructed the Northwest Land Company where to plat the towns. Hill continued his interest in the company until 1892, when Comstock and White bought his undivided share of the unsold lots and, the next year, liquidated their business once more.[20]

White was able to purchase most of the desired sites in scrip or cash at relatively low prices. Rugby's site cost $500, Willow City's $400, and Barton's only $100. Erik Ramstad and his brother, who squatted along the Mouse River in 1883, built a log cabin and got three crops off the land before the railroad arrived. White paid Ramstad $1,000 for the site, which became Minot. Surveyor O. W. Burnham and his assistants worked platting seven towns from June through October 1886 and were paid $938. Minor legal expenses accounted for the only other costs in establishing the sites ready for sale.[21] Given the lot prices later established, the Northwest Land Company needed to sell no more than five or ten business lots on Main Street to recover its investment in any of the towns (fig. 19).

Townsite agents sold lots to customers already interested, but sales often were preceded by correspondence with parties who sought business possibilities. Because of widespread newspaper coverage, most inquirers already possessed a fair idea of where towns had been located. It remained for them to select the right one, where, hopefully, they could get ahead of the competition. A New England doctor who had moved to a small, southern Minnesota community asked Comstock about possibilities at Bottineau and Minot:

> Minot ought to be a good point for a good Physician & Surgeon.
> When would be the best time to go there? Is there a good Hotel? Is
> Minot near a growing town? Does her future prospects look fair for
> Minot to be a large town?[22]

F. M. Winship of Grand Forks inquired, "Can you tell me of any new openings where you think a newspaper is needed?" A Minneapolis lumberman wanted "four or five places to put lumber, say 10 or 12 cars, at good places for the season's trade." An ambitious young man from St. Hilaire, Minn., wanting to start a newspaper in one of the new towns, wrote: "I intend to locate somewhere where there is likely to be a county seat"; he also wanted to be the Northwest Land Company's agent in whatever town he chose, promising to "boom it for all there is in it." A grocery clerk from Fargo inquired, "Would there be a chance for an active young man to make little [sic] money in starting a general store along the line?" Even a Roman Catholic priest, who wrote that he would leave "our poor little bereft Dunseith" with pleasure if he could go to one of the new towns and start a congregation, wanted information about where to locate.[23]

Carpenters, blacksmiths, bankers, and many others made inquiries and often followed them up with a move to one of the new towns. The role

Figure 19. General store and former bank at Barton, N. Dak. The townsite was purchased from a homesteader by Almond A. White of the Northwest Land Company for $100 in 1886, although the official plat was not filed until 1895.

townsite agents played as information brokers should not be underestimated. They had in their audience many aspiring small-town merchants, some of substantial means and others with nothing but enthusiasm: and they were able to urge various parties to one place or another where their presence would benefit the town. The agents had their own ideas about which places would be the larger trade centers and which would be smaller, and this also guided their advice. Unquestionably, the smallest of the centers were thought to be good places for business people with little capital to start a venture. To the extent that new entrants followed the townsite agents' advice, there was a presorting of businesses and their proprietors that biased the more successful of them toward places that had been marked for growth.

Answering the many inquiries obviously was aided if the towns were given names in advance so that they could be advertised. Towner was variously known as "Newport," the name of the closest inland town, and "First Crossing," referring to the bridge over the Mouse River that had to be built there. Colonel Towner, who had helped secure land for the townsite, asked White if the town could be named for him, and the request was granted.[24]

In August 1886, no name had been chosen for the second crossing of the Mouse. Allen Manvel, general manager of the St. Paul, Minneapolis & Manitoba, asked Comstock for suggestions. Manvel knew that the railroad would not touch the inland town of Burlington. "If there is anyone in that vicinity that we can 'glorify' by giving a name to a good town, please let me know." Comstock penciled on the bottom of Manvel's letter, "Preston, Colton, or Lincoln," and sent the letter back to St. Paul. It came back to Comstock with his suggestions crossed out and the name "Minot" written in place.

Henry D. Minot, second vice-president of the St. Paul, Minneapolis & Manitoba, thus received the honor of having a "good town" named after him, except that the town scarcely fit that description in 1886. It was the base camp for a gang of eight thousand construction laborers that Hill had amassed to build his road west into Montana. Prostitution, gambling, and saloons were the typical businesses. The winter of 1886–87 saw the departure of the construction force, and by February there were only half a dozen persons who remained to hold down the townsite until spring. R. H. Copeland, writing in the solitude of his all-but-abandoned inland town of Villard, extended Minot a few sour grapes: "Each vendor is compelled to drink his own whisky, the merchant to be his sole customer, and each to live through the winter by an interchange all about of what one may have and the other needs."[25]

Comstock and White filed their plat, a modest twenty-one blocks, on 9 July 1887. One year later Minot still retained many of its bawdier attractions, but it had acquired eighty-two places of business that rated mention in the R. L. Polk directory.[26] Minot was a success, even if it did have a reputation for sin that few cities in the Northwest could match. It had become, almost instantly, the kind of up-and-coming town Hill wanted to have along his tracks, and he favored the city for years thereafter. With the employment brought by the Great Northern yards, shops, and operating departments, Minot grew larger than any of its neighbors.

When the Soo built across North Dakota in 1893, it formed an agreement with the Minnesota Loan & Trust Company of Minneapolis to plat the new towns. Lemert, Cathay, Emrick, and Fessenden were platted that year, Harvey was added the next, and Velva and Kenmare joined the list in 1897. Subsequent Soo towns along the diagonal route in northern North Dakota brought the total to eleven, but ten other towns were platted along the same line by private parties.[27] The Great Northern line from Devils Lake to Minot eventually held seventeen platted towns, although Comstock and White platted only four of them and held one (Pleasant Lake) from the market until 1902. Both of these lines, built with long-distance objectives in mind, became fields for independent promoters who, in a few cases, managed to create minor successes where the railroad obviously doubted the prospects for town growth.

Anamoose and Balfour on the Soo were platted in 1899 by W. E. Cooke, a retail lumber dealer. Cooke had line yards in each town and thereby helped himself to a bit more than he was able to realize from the towns. Evidently a cautious man, his initial plats of both places covered just four city blocks. Only seven hundred feet separated "West" and "East" streets in Balfour, and the town was no larger in the other direction. Later additions to both places reflected the business growth that came from serving large rural trade areas.[28]

George Stubbins and his family came to North Dakota from northern Iowa in 1899 and soon found a niche in western McHenry County. Son Clayton laid out the town of Granville in 1900, where they based a family banking business and managed more than four thousand acres of surrounding farmland. Clayton's brother Eugene repeated the performance the next year, with a townsite and a family bank at Norwich, seven miles west of Granville. The Stubbinses were pragmatic, if somewhat unorthodox, town promoters. Granville's plat began at Main Street, but the stores on one side faced open fields on the other. Six years later, they doubled the town by platting its mirror image on the other side of Main where they built an impressive bank building that must have inspired the confidence of their depositors. As befitting their New England, Congregational heritage, the streets in both towns bore such names as Lincoln, Grant, Harrison, and Sherman (fig. 20).[29]

Other independents began to fill in the gaps along the Great Northern and Soo lines that led to Minot, especially when prosperity began to return in the late 1890s. Norwegian-born Charles T. Studness, who had come to Minnewaukan as a store clerk for T. E. Mather in 1883, established his own business at the new town of Churchs Ferry in 1886. As his business prospered, he expanded it further by acquiring interest in general mercantile stores in nearby towns, and he also began buying land. Sensing the upturn but proceeding cautiously, Studness platted the four-block townsite of York along the Great Northern tracks in 1898 and organized a general mercantile and implement business there.[30]

The Great Northern later chose York as the origin of its Dunseith branch, thereby arousing the ire of one Melvin Delamater, general merchant in and creator of Knox, six miles west of York. Delamater, who identified himself to sports-loving Louis Hill of the Great Northern as the man who "drove you out from here one time for chickens," claimed his town was a better site, and he was willing to grant right-of-way for the branch line. Hill told him that the railroad could not get an adequate water supply at Knox, to which Delamater retorted, "I see by the paper the water tank at York *exploded*, so it can't be the water plant that is to blame for the deal, eh?" Delamater predicted that the angle of the branch line north of his town would so curtail the trade area that all of Knox's businessmen would leave. Louis Hill then replied that it was an adverse grade, not the water supply, that made them choose York, and that he would "indeed be sorry to learn that the building of this line had affected the business of Knox."[31] The two towns remained roughly equal in size.

Independent townsites generally started smaller and grew more slowly than those that railroads brought into being. The difference, however, resulted mainly from the independents' later start after the excitement of new construction had passed. When a railroad town and an independent were platted simultaneously, there was little difference in their later success. Most independent towns were created at existing sidings in open country where the railroad had chosen not to commence further development. The reason for leaving such sites open was nearly always the same: if no competing lines threatened the traffic from that point, then adding another town only divided the business. A railroad could try to prevent an intruder's success if

Figure 20. Granville, N. Dak., was an independent townsite platted by the Stubbins family along the Great Northern main line east of Minot in 1900. In 1906 they doubled the town's area by platting another sixteen blocks on the other side of Main Street (*left side of photo*), where they built an imposing structure to house the family-owned bank.

it wished, by simultaneously platting an adjacent townsite, but little would be gained if all the traffic moved over their line anyway.

The threat of competition could also quickly reverse the railroad's interest in a site. In an unusual move, the Great Northern purchased land between Souris and Westhope in 1903 for townsite purposes, although no town was contemplated until the next year when company officials first learned of the Soo's plans for the Wheat Line. Landowner Guy L. Scott, who had charged the Great Northern a handsome $2,800 for the forty acres and then laid out his own town on the adjacent quarter, approached Great Northern officials in 1904 with a proposal to join forces in promoting the town (Landa). The railroad recognized Scott's serious intention of building a trade center there, one that would close a gap along their line that the Soo might capture, so they gladly resold the site to him — for $3,000.[32]

Ad hoc townsite strategies were the exception, however. When the Great Northern resumed branch line construction in 1901, it entered into an agreement to plat ten towns with Frederick H. Stoltze, a St. Paul lumber and coal dealer who operated line yards in a dozen Great Northern communities. Stoltze was to purchase townsite land at each station the Great Northern planned, but he used a novel means to acquire the sites without paying the high prices local landowners might ask.

The Northern Pacific had waited so long to select the land within its fifty-mile indemnity limits that there was an insufficient amount remaining to satisfy the original grant. Their land commissioner was allowed to select parcels well outside the original limits in lieu of the number of sections within fifty miles that were no longer available. Stoltze gave his list of tracts that had to be acquired to the Northern Pacific's land commissioner, who then requested these descriptions from the Grand Forks, Devils Lake, and Minot receivers of the U.S. Land Office. Stoltze acquired the townsites for Westhope, Glenburn, Lansford, Mohall, and parts of several others in this fashion, paying the $10 per acre price the railroad asked. Thus, some of the Great Northern's towns were platted on land purchased from the Northern Pacific.[33]

Frederick Stoltze was no public relations success, much to the Great Northern's regret. At Mohall, where he platted the townsite in opposition to an earlier plat filed by Martin O. Hall, he ran a fence around the main part of his town, gaining himself and the railroad considerable notoriety.[34] Louis Hill knew that Stoltze, despite his success in many of the towns, was not the man to entrust with future townsites — especially those fringing on territory that could be captured by the Soo Line in its aggressive entry into northern North Dakota.

The Soo placed all twenty-five townsites on the Thief River Falls-Kenmare Wheat Line in the reliable hands of the Minnesota Loan and Trust

Company, continuing an earlier and generally successful relationship. The railroad also created the position of townsite agent, whose job it was to handle lot sales and to coordinate the numerous details with Minnesota Loan and Trust. The man they hired, Cyrus A. Campbell, proved to be a good choice. He immediately began to trumpet the advantages of locating on the "New Soo Line," gaining the attention of newspaper editors across northern North Dakota whose readers were already in the grip of townsite fever.

The *Bottineau Courant* initiated a new column, "Townsite Talk," in March 1905 by reprinting a *Minneapolis Times* story on Campbell. He announced a new policy. Whereas in the past Soo towns had been platted after the railroad was built, it was to be the policy henceforth:

> to locate stations and survey and plat all townsites ahead of the line,
> thus enabling business men to get located and have their buildings up
> and stocks in readiness for the heavy fall business, when the construc-
> tion crews arrive.[35]

This meant that railroad towns would have to be built without the railroad's assistance, that all the lumber and materials for stores and residences would have to be hauled overland by wagon. What Campbell did not need to mention was that anyone locating in one of the new towns who waited for the railroad to deliver the materials was risking loss of advantage to a competitor willing to pay overland drayage costs.

The Soo platted towns ahead of construction to establish the new trading patterns in its favor. Incoming merchants were well advised to follow through according to the railroad's plan, although it meant added costs for them at a time they could scarcely afford it. Neither could the Great Northern afford to waste any time in platting towns along the new branches it had projected across the Wheat Line, and that company immediately set its own plans to establish townsites ahead of construction.

Louis Hill needed a reliable person to place in charge, a counterpart of the Soo's Campbell. He turned to a personal friend, David Newton Tallman. Born in rural New York state, Tallman had taken a civil engineering degree and, as was common at that time, moved west to seek a career in railroading. At the age of 21, Tallman landed a clerk's job with the Great Northern at Willmar, Minn., and was soon promoted. He also married the daughter of one of Willmar's wealthiest pioneer citizens. By 1905, the energetic young Tallman was in the banking business at Willmar and presided over the Minnesota Central Telephone Company. In April of that year, he organized the Willmar-based Dakota Development Company, which eventually assumed responsibility for forty-five townsites along the Great Northern.[36]

Like Stoltze and others who operated businesses amenable to line-chain branching, Tallman established small banks in many of his towns. A firm

believer in small towns and branch banking, Tallman became a natural partner in the railroad's strategy of traffic capture and remained the principal
outsider involved in Great Northern townsites for the next fifteen years. The
rise, and subsequent fall, of his own career was to parallel closely the fortunes of the small railroad towns he founded.

Chapter 7

Town Building

On a rainy evening in July 1905, Henry Stene, a banking associate of Dave Tallman's from the Willmar area, was making time across the Turtle Mountain country, determined to catch the daily train from Westhope. He had spent a week in North Dakota inspecting a dozen new townsites that his friend Tallman was launching, and he was full of enthusiasm for what he saw.

Despite the railroad's absence, the hustling businessmen at Antler and Maxbass had half a dozen store buildings in place to handle the trade that was already coming their way. Upham was also growing fast, although its trade area was foreshortened by the Soo's competing towns of Russell and Kramer. Three other towns seemed unlikely to grow because they were located on swampy sites, he thought, but all bid fair, at least, to be the sort of small trading centers their creators intended. The only serious problem was the Soo's plans for the town of Rolette, just a few hundred yards from the Great Northern's town of McCumber. Confusion reigned there that summer as merchants argued with each other over which town had the better prospect. All the new towns would be linked to the railroad in time to haul the season's harvest.

There were many Scandinavian farmers in the vicinity, which pleased Stene, but also quite a number of French-Canadians, a less welcome sight to this Minnesotan who made agricultural loans. The homestead era had passed; good farmland was bringing $15 to $20 per acre, inflated by the excitement of new town building. As Stene and his party approached Westhope they were guided by the silhouette of nine grain elevators in a row, all the evidence any investor would need of what the territory could produce. Stene told Tallman to count him in on the investments they had planned, just as he was sure that others from western Minnesota would want to participate in the townsite boom in North Dakota.[1]

Stene had witnessed an unusual event. The simultaneous creation of so many new trade center towns had never happened before, nor would it again. Bottineau County's courthouse was alive that summer, with an average of one new townsite plat coming in each week, every one of them an instrument in the battle for traffic between two railroads. Filing the plat, of course, was only a beginning.

The birth of a Great Plains railroad town was attended by a circle of admiring well-wishers. There were high hopes for individual success and, beyond that, a shared spirit of civic pride that emerged before the first balloon-frame, false-front store building was raised. Town lot buyers often were strangers to one another, but they were confronted by a common task. It remained for them to translate the surveyors plat into a living, breathing trade center town, to fulfill the predetermined design the townsite company had provided. The process that transformed one into the other was not reinvented every time a new town was born, nor even was the plat itself any more likely than a copy of the last few the surveyor had made, granting only the barest of concessions to local topography. What moved from one site to the next was a set of ideas held in the minds of designers, buyers, and sellers of space about the proper form and function of towns.

Plats had to look like credible towns. Their "common" look, while often criticized, also had a reassuring effect that grander innovations might not have provided. The late-nineteenth-century conventions of urban design that guided them held that the simple grid pattern was sufficient for smaller cities and towns, that alleys were desirable, and that the functions of various city streets should govern their width.[2] These principles were accepted by railroad town builders, although another popular idea, that city blocks should be oblong rather than square, generally was not. Square blocks, with deeper lots, allowed a clutter of small buildings to form along the back alleys, whereas longer but shallower blocks forced buildings to the front. The sparse, uneven look of residential sections that developed in many towns can be attributed to the design.

The standard railroad-town block was 300 feet square, with lots 140 feet deep and backed by a 20-foot alley. Block faces were divided into six residential lots (50 feet wide) or into twelve 25-foot business lots. The narrow lots, which sold at two or three times the price of residential lots, gave the impression of activity to a business district before there was any. Long, narrow lots on Main Street also guaranteed that the first buildings would assume a uniform size and shape, which, in turn, favored the presence of many small, independent merchants.

The width of the streets on a plat suggested where the greatest activity would congregate. If Main Street was 100 feet wide, the principal cross street was generally 80 feet and residential streets 60 feet, establishing a clear hierarchy. Few railroad town plats showed parks or other public spaces, although these amenities often were created later from unsold land, which unfortunately kept green space out of the town center and on the periphery.

The sizes of town lots, the widths of the streets, and the position of the railroad were thus the principal cues new residents had in choosing a location on the townsite. Three distinct morphologies, characterized by street patterns, placements of the business district, and railroad location, differentiate the entire history of the railroad town from the 1850s to the 1920s throughout North America (fig. 21).[3]

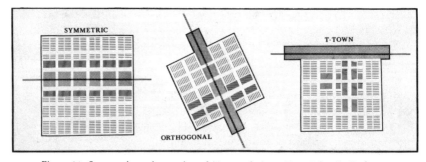

Figure 21. Symmetric, orthogonal, and T-town designs. From John C. Hudson, "Towns of the Western Railroads," *Great Plains Quarterly* 2, no. 1 (1982).

The earliest idea, and one popularized by the Illinois Central Associates, was a parallel arrangement with the railroad track as the axis of symmetry. The prototype is obscure, although possible precedents include the canal towns of western New York state where business houses were lined facing the waterway. Such an arrangement, with the railroad as centerpiece, made passage of the iron horse a daily public display of the new age of transportation.

There were two business streets in the symmetric railroad town, with buildings facing each other across a 300-foot railroad right-of-way designed for elevators, lumberyards, and other enterprises needing direct rail access. Land along the tracks was underused, and eventually some towns acquired a portion of it for parks. The two business streets rarely developed equally, especially in the smaller places. In plan, the two halves of the town were separate but equal, and in railroad towns of the southern states the design was a convenient demarcation of black and white that gave a built-in assist to segregationist practices. Outside the South, the distinction was economic. If First Avenue North was the principal business street, First Avenue South was literally "the other side of the tracks," with a row of saloons and cheap hotels.

The Northern Pacific Railway was responsible for most of the symmetric plats in the northern Great Plains, including New Rockford, Minnewaukan, and Sykeston in the study area. Only New Rockford fulfilled the original design, however. Sykeston and Minnewaukan developed along their Main Streets, perpendicular to the tracks. The adjustment in practice reflected the undesirability of having a strip of land a block wide separating the two parts of the business district. Inserting the railroad led to additional congestion where it was least desirable. Symmetric plats were used rarely after the 1890s, perhaps victim to the fading, Victorian-era fascination with steam railroads.

The orthogonal plat, placing businesses on both sides of the same street, was favored by many western railroads. The depot generally was located near the Main Street crossing, in the middle of the townsite. It was such a commonplace of town morphology that incoming merchants were confused by deviations. Railroad field engineers, however, cared little about the cues provided by such an arrangement, and preferred to locate the depot where access to the water tank used to service steam locomotives was convenient. Where townsite agents saw a thriving town, with Main Street lots commanding $200–$250 apiece, railroad men saw a servicing facility, and their different objectives sometimes conflicted.

A. A. White was astonished when he arrived at Rugby in 1886 to find the depot nearly completed at a site well west of Main Street. The same plan was already underway at Towner. He wrote Solomon Comstock an anguished letter:

> I have spent the past three days in trying to overcome the difficulty of the location. At first I thought we should have to abandon the Main St., as some parties threw up their locations on Main St., but I have succeeded in getting everything on to Main St. as intended and have not made any concessions in prices. Everything will be all right only there is not much money here, and the businessmen are rather light weight.[4]

He pleaded with Comstock to use his influence to prevent the same development at Towner, otherwise he could "not hold the business on Main St." there. It seems reasonable to conclude that White's problem was not isolated, and that there were many other towns where business people might have located on cheaper lots away from the designated Main Street had not the townsite agents urged and cajoled them to the high-priced locations.

Despite the platting of a single business street at right angles to the track, towns tended to develop more on one side of the railroad than on the other. Practice once again led planning, so that by the late 1890s most towns were not even planned to straddle the railroad. In the newer designs, Main Street began at the tracks, creating an arrangement in which the railroad formed the bar of a T-shaped configuration. This proved to be a stable solution, more acceptable both to railroads and to townspeople. The elimination of crossings in the business district was a relief to increasingly accident-cautious railroads, and the isolation of the tracks to one side of town made them less conspicuous to residents. A later Great Northern official observed that "we want to so arrange the property that we can compell all of the town developments to be on one side of the track," and he advocated the railroad's purchase of a strip along the outside of its line to prevent developments that might lead to subseqent demands for crossings.[5]

The single business street of the T-town lacked sufficient differentiation along its length to permit one intersection to stand out as more important. In 1905, the Soo Line began a variation on the T-town form by platting business lots a few blocks up the cross street away from the principal intersection; the Great Northern's towns also soon reflected the idea.[6] The "crossed-T" form was a better anchor on business locations and produced a tighter cluster nearest the center, where lots were most expensive. Banks were almost forced to locate on one of the corner lots at this intersection, following the popular idea that this is where they belonged.

Once the railroad had been moved to the side of the plat, it was possible to reintroduce a point focus, such as a center square, to replace the linear focus imposed by a bisecting railroad line. Central squares and greens were known and admired by Americans familiar with towns that predated the railroad, and thus their reintroduction in some of the later railroad towns is not surprising (figs. 22 and 23). D. N. Tallman created four North Dakota towns (Antler, Maxbass, McCumber, and Sarles) around a scaled-down, Philadelphia-style center square designed to contain his banks. The Soo Line platted Kenmare, Plaza, Columbus, Ryder, and Imperial with a somewhat similar central focus but with city parks rather than a shrine of business as the centerpiece.[7] Such devices can hardly be called innovations. They do suggest that tastes in urban design changed slowly enough to allow parks and squares to reemerge after intervening ideas, such as the symmetric railroad town, had been discarded.

The evolution of town form proceeded from the undifferentiated grids platted by early speculators to the detailed modifications of the T-town (table 2). Each shift was informed by experience. Styles changed to accommodate the railroads' wishes, to be sure, but the tendency toward plats richer in cues about town development reflected what townsite agents had learned from their pricing strategies. Simultaneously, those who platted towns were learning to estimate more accurately how much growth each might sustain, although it was not until the beginning of the twentieth cen-

Figure 22. Plaza, N. Dak., was platted by the Soo Line's Tri-State Land Company in 1906 around a two-hundred-foot-square city park. The town prospered as a major grain-shipping point.

tury that townsite agents were skilled enough to create plats of realistic size (fig. 24).

The boom of the 1880s in northern Dakota witnessed many attempts to create great cities in true speculator's fashion, that is, simply by announcing that rapid growth was soon to commence. An extensive gridiron of city blocks on the plat was a simple and inexpensive way to suggest what the future would bring. The tendency to overestimate was not confined to the wildest of speculators: railroad towns were begun with equally grandiose ambitions, following a pattern common to cities elsewhere in the Great Plains. In the 1880s, the average townsite platted in the study area contained forty city blocks, but the poor record of many railroad towns, plus the outright failure of the speculators' schemes, dampened further enthusiasm for gargantuan designs.

The depression of the 1890s was probably responsible for the reversal. Plats first recorded during this period averaged a mere seven or eight blocks each. Such modest ventures seemed unlikely candidates to stimulate the interest of others, and many did not. As confidence was restored in the early 1900s, the average size of plats inched upward once more to a size of ten or twelve blocks, realistically large enough to attract investors but small enough to prevent the tax burden of unsold lots. These numbers describe the average, around which there were some deviations, but the tendency

Figure 23. Antler, N. Dak., was platted by David N. Tallman in 1905 at the end of the branch line west from Bottineau. The eighty-foot-square central green was used, in characteristic Tallman fashion, for one of his banks. As an example of town design not commonly found in the West, Antler's central square was deemed significant enough to be designated as a historic district by the state in 1976.

Table 2. Characteristics of Town Plats in the North Dakota Study Area, 1880-1919

Characteristic	1880-1884	1885-1889	1890-1894	1895-1899	1900-1904	1905-1909	1910-1914	1915-1919
Plats and Additions								
Number of new town plats	17	15	8	15	47	72	27	3
Number of new blocks	677	241	55	110	424	820	258	22
Average size of plat (blocks)	40	16	7	7	9	11	10	7
Additional blocks platted (68 sample towns)	32	44	12	102	429	566	109	32
Location of New Plats								
Nonrailroad, total	11	2	0	0	6	3	0	0
On railroads, by persons:								
platting one or two towns	5	7	4	8	23	9	1	3
platting three or more towns	1	6	4	7	18	60	26	0
Number of Blocks in New Plats								
Nonrailroad, total;	344	33	0	0	89	19	0	0
average	31	17	—	—	15	6	—	—
On railroads, by persons:								
platting one or two towns	266	93	21	52	193	56	6	22
average	53	13	5	7	8	6	6	7
platting three or more towns	67	115	34	58	142	745	252	0
average	67	19	9	8	8	12	10	—
Number of Plats by Style								
Undifferentiated grid	12	2	0	0	5	4	0	0
Symmetric	2	2	2	1	1	0	0	1
Orthogonal	3	5	1	1	3	1	0	0
T-town	0	6	5	12	36	29	10	2
Crossed-T	0	0	0	1	0	34	17	0
Center square	0	0	0	0	2	4	0	0

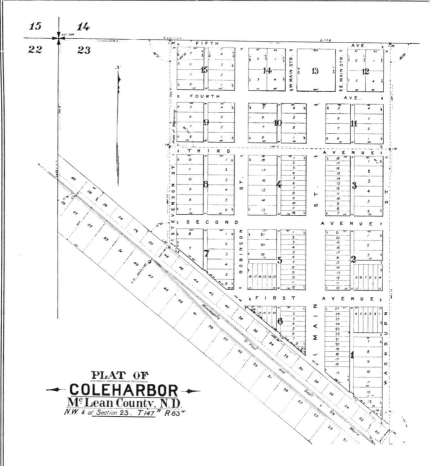

Figure 24. Plat of Coleharbor, N. Dak., prepared for advertising purposes by the Tri-State Land Company in 1906. The original plat (blocks 1–6) was filed by the Minnesota Loan and Trust Company in 1905. Courtesy John Bergene, Soo Line Railroad.

first to overestimate and then to underestimate potential town growth was shared by smaller as well as by larger townsite agencies. Those who platted only one or two towns remained cautious, however. Their plats remained smaller in size than those filed on behalf of railroad companies (table 2).

Townsite agents sought to avoid the role of leading taxpayer in the towns they founded, not only to escape payments but also because large numbers of unsold lots detracted from the image of growth they wished to project. Comstock and White delayed filing their town plats as long as they could and, in several cases, sought to reduce the valuation on their unsold lots for tax purposes. In the first year at Bottineau, for example, they paid about 30 percent of the town's real estate taxes on some four hundred lots that had not been sold. Their initial prices of $200 or more per lot were reduced to $30 the next year, roughly the value of $25 each at which the unsold parcels were carried on their own books.[8] Such a reduction did not indicate that Bottineau was a failure. This was a typical cut in price reflecting the inevitable slump in demand that followed a year or less after an opening sale.

Townsite agents seldom realized revenue equal to the value of lot sales. The terms of sale commonly were one-third down with the balance in two annual payments, but many buyers never made the payments. In the early years of western railroad townsites, most lots were sold over-the-counter at fixed prices by a resident agent of the company. If that agent were less than aggressive or honest, collections fell behind. The St. Paul, Minneapolis & Manitoba had such a man in charge of the Devils Lake townsite. Despite constant urgings from St. Paul, he did not balance the townsite company's books until April 1884 when he finally produced a statement showing collections of only $11,000 on what was reported to be more than $200,000 worth of sales.[9] The railroad kept prodding him to collect delinquent payments, but after a series of excuses that clearly did not impress St. Paul headquarters he was removed from the job.

The Budde brothers of Devils Lake, who operated general mercantile businesses there and in Bottineau, Minnewaukan, and Churchs Ferry, found themselves overextended. They were unable to make even the down payment on their Bottineau property, on which they had already placed a building and were operating in business. In August 1887 they asked Comstock for a 30-day extension:

> We have accommodated farmers to over $20,000 to be paid with the proceeds of this harvest. Also helped Bottineau people to about $2,000 which we will get soon. You can get what we owe when you say it must come, but wish you would help us a little now.[10]

The Buddes obviously were not the most prudent of managers, but neither were they of the irresponsible kind that skipped town after a few lucrative months in the trade at a boom location. Their embarrassment was common among merchants in the smaller centers, who generally began with less capital and found it even more difficult to obtain credit.

Most townsite agents realized that they had to be flexible in order to build a successful community. Few ministers of the gospel passed up the chance to ask for a free building lot for a church, and most such requests were granted routinely. These free lots were generally at the far corners of the original plat, where small-town churches remain to this day. Mrs. F. E. Champlin of Bottineau asked Comstock and White: "What are the prospects of my Baby getting a lot on the townsite, as it has been done elsewhere, and people here seem to think she ought to have one. I await most anxiously your reply." Requests to use unsold lots (free) for a pasture for the family cow, to place a temporary building (free) on a salable lot, and many others were received and frequently granted. Because townsite agents received little good publicity, they undoubtedly used such opportunities to show that they were human, too.[11]

By 1900, townsite agents had acquired new strategies for boosting initial lot sales. For one, they began with an opening-day auction. Competitive bidding pitted merchant against merchant for the putatively choicest lots on the townsite. Also common was to hold opening sales on succesive days for all the towns along a line, so that those disappointed in one town had the option of following along to the next where bidding might be less intense. The Soo Line's townsite agent, C. A. Campbell, announced that he would turn over to the local community all proceeds in excess of fixed prices brought at the lot auction, a public relations coup for the railroad that turned the occasion into something of a charity event.[12]

All towns about to be launched with an auction, no matter what their prospects for growth, were advertised widely in the press. Those that attracted few buyers could be advertised later as still holding many "opportunities" for the aggressive merchant interested in building a "good trade in a fine location." The same adjectives of boosterism were recombined endlessly to describe the prospects of any town, although sometimes it was hard to be convincing (fig. 25). An exhausted Dave Tallman once dispatched a publicity release to Great Northern headquarters after a long opening day: "The sale at Calvin was very good—sold thirty-one lots for about $18,000—and good prospects for more soon"; and then he added "have your 'fluent writer' add a little spice to the enclosed. I naturally want the newspaper article a little larger in volume of business done—anticipating to some extent the business that will soon follow." In this case, at least, the optimism was justified: Tallman platted a four-block addition to Calvin six months later.[13]

Starting with a conservative grid of ten or twelve blocks and then

BENEDICT

The Topsy Town that just grew by itself, because of the splendid surroundings. It can't help but prosper. A wide awake business place with live progressive business men. Room for more "good people" to make money in Benedict.

For information address,

C. A. CAMPBELL,

Or Local Townsite Agent,
BENEDICT, N. D.

Townsite Agent "Soo Line,"
MINNEAPOLIS, MINN.

Figure 25. Benedict, N. Dak., platted by the Tri-State Land Company in 1908, was described in glowing, if vague, terms by the railroad. Its original seventeen-block plat proved to be more than equal to the demand for town lots.

platting new additions from the balance of the purchased tract as demand warranted was the best way of avoiding taxes on unsold lots (fig. 26). In this way the plat grew apace with sales. The only element of strategy was deciding when to add more blocks to keep alive the possibilities of further growth without creating an impression that the town was a failure by having too much unsold property. Prospective buyers were discouraged easily if it appeared there was no room for growth, just as they were put off if they saw too few parcels with "Sold" written across them. Again, the plat was more than a device for locating property lines; it was also a record and projection of the town's development.

The Soo Line reorganized its town lot sales in 1906 by forming the railroad-owned Tri-State Land Company, which assumed the role Minnesota Loan and Trust had played earlier, undertaking responsibility for all new townsite activity.[14] Early in 1908, the Soo issued a remarkable pamphlet entitled "Dozens of New Towns" that showed the real estate available in towns

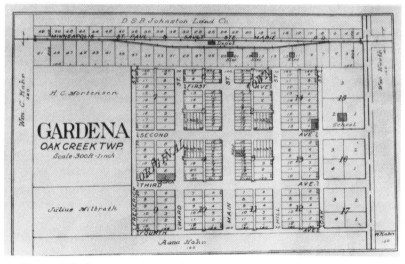

Figure 26. Gardena, N. Dak., platted by the Soo Line during the 1905 "war" with the Great Northern, saw enough growth in its first year to warrant a six-block addition to the original eight-block plat, although the intersection of Main Street and First Avenue stands vacant today. Map from *Standard Atlas of Bottineau County* (Chicago: George Ogle & Co., 1929).

along their lines where there was "a chance for every man to carve out a fortune."[15]

According to maps shown in the pamphlet, the land company had sold 41 percent of the business lots and 55 percent of the residential lots of the initial plats for those towns in the North Dakota study area platted between 1902 and 1907, including fourteen on the Wheat Line, all eight on the line west of Drake to Plaza and Coleharbor, and two (Logan and Bergen) on the main line. At Drake (platted in 1902) and Rolette (1905), they had sold 90 percent of the business lots and had added more, although no new 25-foot parcels had been added in the other towns. About 30 percent of the lots in residential additions had also been sold at that time. The sales were substantially in excess of the number of lots eventually deeded to the purchasers because of default on payments, but the sales record was good in view of the fact that the Great Northern simultaneously was promoting and selling as many new towns in the same area.

Soo/Tri-State platted additional blocks in all towns where more than 30 percent of the Main Street business lots were sold within one year, suggesting the margin by which they desired to have plats lead actual sales. Comparable figures are not available for the Great Northern towns, although scattered evidence suggests that this same figure represented enough success to warrant plat additions in its towns as well. Some of the towns with no plat additions later became viable trade centers simply because their initial designs proved equal to eventual demand. Many other places sustaining no subsequent additions were those that stimulated little interest in the initial lot sale.

Of all towns in the study area, the tendency was for those with the largest initial plats to receive subsequent additions, although the reason for this was complicated by timing (table 3). Many of the plats larger than twelve blocks were the early ones, and they often grew larger because of their earlier start in a period when trade areas were much larger. On the other hand, original plats of no more than twelve city blocks were about evenly divided in the proportion that received subsequent additions. The size of the original plat thus is only weakly related to the subsequent addition of new blocks.

The timing of new additions also depended strongly on the overall level of business activity. The 1905 peak in town platting was accompanied by additions of new blocks to existing towns (see table 2). New towns did not necessarily inhibit the growth prospects of existing communities. As one newspaper editor suggested:

> The building of railroad lines instead of scaring the citizens of Cando
> or making them feel the business of this place will be lessened thereby,
> seems rather to have strengthened their confidence in our little city, for

Table 3. Town Plats, Additions, and Population Growth in the North Dakota Study Area

	Size of Initial Plat	
Characteristic	1-12 blocks	More than 12 blocks
Additions		
Number of towns with:		
No subsequent plat additions	65	27
At least one plat addition	67	40
1920 Populations		
Towns platted 1881-1889		
1920 population less than 100	5	9
100 or more	2	15
Towns platted 1890-1899		
1920 population less than 100	5	0
100 or more	15	2
Towns platted 1900-1909		
1920 population less than 100	58	12
100 or more	25	26
Towns platted 1910-1919		
1920 population less than 100	25	4
100 or more	3	1

we note with pleasure that within a few more days, more good business
and residence properties will be in the course of construction than has
ever been built here in one season.[16]

Even though new towns often drew their merchants—and sometimes even
their business buildings—from nearby, existing centers, the effect was not
to make the longer-established towns shrink in population. Those leaving
were replaced by new in-migrants. Growth could be sustained, at least in
the short run, because of the close relationship between railroad construction and expansion of the cash-grain economy. As railroads were built,
wheat acreages increased; and the proportional relationship created a new
economic base for trade centers. Whether the increased trading volume supported the new towns or was diverted to existing trade centers had to be settled competitively between towns.

All townsite agents held their own ideas as to which places would grow
largest. They concentrated their major sales efforts on a relatively few sites,
especially those they projected as future county seats. Towns with obviously
limited trade areas, squeezed in along the line at the railroad's insistence for
purposes of traffic capture, were not promoted with the same vigor. D. N.
Tallman's "recipe" for a successful town was three to five lumberyards, one
or two banks, two to three general stores, one or two hardware stores and
farm machinery dealers, plus as many more individual tradespeople as could

be attracted — usually a single drugstore, hotel, newspaper, butcher, restaurant, and livery stable.[17] He scaled this recipe up or down, depending on his projections for the town's future growth. Naturally, the size of town he platted bore a close relationship to the amount of anticipated business. There was, in the plans of Tallman and other's, a certain self-fulfilling aspect: towns designed to be small were likely to remain small.

Excluding the 1890–99 period, when nearly all town plats recorded were conservative, there is a clear relationship between size of the initial plat and later population growth: towns with small plats, which reflected their creators' notions of how successful they would become, had fewer people and were less likely to be incorporated by 1920 than were places with larger initial plats (table 3). One cannot conclude, however, that design rather than economics was responsible for the difference. The notions that guided townsite agencies in choosing the size of the plat and that affected their efforts to attract tradespeople to one place rather than another were based clearly on projections of economic viability. The relationship suggests, instead, that town growth should not be viewed simply as the aggregate result of many independent business successes or failures; the designers also played a significant role by matching their promotional efforts to what they regarded as the prospects for growth.

Some townsites, whether because of undesirable locations, lack of promotion, or both, failed to attract more than a few lot buyers. Failure in towns platted along railroad lines generally can be attributed to their late entry when there was little trade to be captured at the market boundaries between existing towns already spaced as closely together as population density could sustain. Townsite companies wished to avoid taxes on their unsold lots and sometimes moved swiftly to vacate plats where it was apparent no growth would follow, thus cutting short the losses already evident.

Approximately 18 percent of the plats filed in the North Dakota study area were later vacated partially (at least 50 percent of the blocks removed from the plat) or in total. The legal procedure of vacation removed the property from the category of town real estate, and most such parcels were resold to neighboring farmers for croplands or pasture. This 18 percent does not include an even larger component of town real estate, the thousands of lots sold at bargain prices to local realtors who were then faced with the problem of disposing of the land before taxes consumed whatever profit might be realized.

The Soo's incorporation of the Tri-State Land Company in 1906 was soon followed by creation of the Dakota & Great Northern Townsite Company, which the Great Northern designed to handle all subsequent townsite activities.[18] Both railroads were dissatisfied with the results of their efforts to create towns at the other's expense in the 1905 war over the Wheat Line.

Consolidation of townsite activities directly under company control was intended to produce better coordination, and hence more successful results, although both the Great Northern and the Soo would learn that townsite agents were not to be blamed for the failure of miniscule trade center towns too weak to grow.

Records of the Dakota & Great Northern Townsite Company show that even towns marginal as trade centers did not necessarily lose money for the company. In 1906 the Great Northern extended a branch northwest from Berthold into territory it considered too profitable for the Soo alone to control. The result was the usual chain of new towns, three of which — Aurelia, Kenaston, and Niobe — were in Ward County. The townsite company paid more than $24,000 for the three sites in the boom year of 1906, a far larger sum than had been the custom, illustrating another reason why later townsites were less profitable. They sold less than one-third of the lots platted in the three towns but collected more than $30,000 from the sales.[19]

When the railroad undertook a general accounting of the sites in the 1930s it decided to dispose of the unsold lands as quickly as possible. Sales at Kenaston and Niobe produced a small profit, whereas Aurelia was a net loss. The Great Northern resolved to pay no more taxes at Aurelia by selling the remaining lots at whatever price could be had; the buyer would pay the back taxes. Aurelia's 195 unsold lots remained on the books at a value of $2,834, the "effective loss for income tax purposes" if no buyer was found. The company managed to find buyers at all three sites, however, and emerged with black ink on the ledger. It was not until 1952 and 1966, respectively, that Aurelia's and Kenaston's unsold blocks were finally vacated by their purchasers after decades of population loss.[20]

When the Great Northern was engaged in legal procedures to divest itself of unprofitable townsites in the 1930s, the company's assistant right-of-way, land and tax commissioner, W. N. S. Ivins, gave a deposition that amounted to a postmortem on the townsite business. He stated that the company was:

> conservative in the area of land platted as a townsite, being careful to plat no more than it might reasonably expect to sell, with a small margin of loss for normal growth; that its whole object and motive in platting townsites is to develop communities along the lines of the railway and has not at any time engaged in the business on a speculative basis. . . . There is no means whereby it can be definitely predicted that any particular townsite will be a success, that being dependent wholly upon the development of the back-country tributary to the townsite. . . . It is the practice in platting townsites to provide a plat of sufficient size to accommodate such population as may be reasonably expected to locate there; and that if that population does not develop quickly, the town becomes dormant and unsold, platted property of little value, and difficult to dispose of at any price.[21]

Ivins neglected to mention why his company had platted so many towns, especially on the evidence of poor performance of some earlier ventures. Nor did he give any indication of their method for calculating the population "reasonably expected to locate" in any town. Such information would have revealed a good deal more about the townsite strategies of the Great Northern, as well as other railroads. The primary objective, however, was always the same — to capture traffic.

The success or failure of a townsite company was measured not in terms of the success or failure of merchants who located in a town, but rather in terms of the number of lots sold. The railroad company, in turn, measured town success in terms of whatever traffic it did not lose to a competitor as a result of the town's presence.

The speculative capital that railroad townsite companies invested at various locations could equally well have been invested by others. In many cases outsiders did desire a role, but they were rebuffed by railroad companies that wanted to control the business for their own purposes. A railroad allowed independent townsites only when there was no competition from another railroad. They created too many towns in the vicinity of their competitors' lines, too few elsewhere.

That the railroads were able to launch so many new towns scarcely was testimony to their wisdom in doing so, although the record speaks well of townsite agents as salesmen. Town plats eventually were scaled in proportion to the sales each site might generate, which, in turn, was evidently a function of the size and productivity of the trade area. Competition for trade, which commenced as soon as a new town was platted near an existing center, worked against the new-town merchant, especially if his town's trading area was insufficiently large. The decline of many small centers, so often linked with the advent of automobile ownership, thus began well before the shift from rail to road networks.

A definitive statement on the success of railroad towns as a type thus can be given only in terms of the criteria held by the various interests involved. If lot sales are taken as the measure, then the rate of failure was comparatively low. Townsite agencies were able to recover their investment with the sale of a fraction of the platted lots and dump the rest to avoid taxes. The most generous definition of success was that held by railroad companies, whose needs were met if the site had no more than a single grain elevator in operation to serve the purpose of traffic capture. Population growth and economic stability were the merchants' concerns, and neither followed just because people purchased town lots and commenced business activity at a site. A successful town, by these criteria, required the emergence of coherent economic and social relationships within the community. The business and social lives of town inhabitants are the subjects of the next two chapters.

Chapter 8

Merchants and Trade Centers

Northern Dakota's first merchants came from the Northeast and the upper Middle West. They were part of a westward migration that included American-born farmers and laborers as well as thousands of the foreign-born, all of whom anticipated a good life in a new land. Anyone planning to enter into trade at one of the prairie towns generally had a specific destination in mind that was familiar from railroad advertising or from others who promoted immigration. In later years, after the region had produced its own population, migrants to the new towns were of more local origin; but those who began in the 1880s were likely to have come some distance.[1]

William and Sarah Plummer, with sons Clarence and Bertrand, arrived at Minnewaukan from their native Waterford, Maine, in June 1884. The stage ride up from the end of track at New Rockford included a fording of the Sheyenne, an event as memorable for them as the New England baked-bean dinner Mrs. Plummer's sister prepared for their arrival. Like many in the Maine-New Hampshire border country, William was a lumberman. Now, however, he would have to shift from manufacturer to seller. He purchased his first stock from a West End merchant who was quitting that town (soon to be bypassed by the railroad) and established a yard at Minnewaukan. Clarence, a graduate of Bridgton Academy, founded Minnewaukan's first school.[2]

Until 1886 or 1887 there were only inland merchants west of Minnewaukan, and they offered little competition for early merchants like William Plummer and Thomas Mather (chap. 3). The town's trading area included more than one thousand square miles then being opened to settlement. Plummer supplied building materials to ranchers in the Mouse River loop and to scattered homesteaders, most of whom preferred to construct their first dwellings of sawed lumber (which they knew how to work) rather than of sod or that scarce commodity, timber. In 1891 Plummer added farm machinery and hardware lines to his business by purchasing the stock of a local firm that had been dissolved. Dry goods, boots, shoes, groceries, and other general mercantile items were added in 1893, by which time his trade amounted to $75,000 annually. Profits were invested in improved farmlands, which led the Plummer family into the grain business—a sideline that eventually caused them to construct their own elevator.[3] William Plummer's background in no way specifically prepared him for what he was to undertake in Dakota, but he proceeded methodically, applying the business principles he did know to a new set of opportunities. In less than a decade William Plummer was pillar of a new community, just as he had been in the Maine village he left behind.

Plummer's role as a leading citizen of Minnewaukan made him a source of advice, especially for young people, concerning business possibilities in his town and general area. Some sought clerical or apprenticeship positions, others were searching for sites where their line of trade was not already served. Minnewaukan residents may not have been aware of Plummer's role as an information broker on the town's business status, but interested outsiders were. He also frequently passed along information learned from traveling salesmen and manufacturers' agents concerning the prospects for business growth in other towns. The information network that Plummer and his circle of drummer acquaintances maintained was casual, fed by desultory conversations; yet it was of great value in a region of hundreds of small towns, none of them well known beyond the few miles of its trading reach.

Cora Shannon of Sanborn, N. Dak., wrote to Plummer:

> I was told that there was only one milliner in your town and that other
> seasons she has not carried a very large stock. I am going to a number
> of towns on your branch line and would like to stop at your town for a
> few days with my millinery goods. I was told by the salesman of the
> wholesale house that your town was a very good town for millinery.[4]

Plummer's "gatekeeper" function was honorary and voluntary. The recruitment of business people was a function that townsite agencies were expected to perform, however. Unlike the earlier townsite speculators, who were interested only in selling lots (it did not matter to whom), railroad-affiliated agents attempted to create a viable mix of businesses that would get each town off to a good start. The matching of people and their trades with the various towns was made easier by the flexibility of business conditions in small centers and by the eagerness with which recruits began ventures for which they lacked experience.

Townsite agents were information brokers, but their income was derived from real estate sales. They often sold more lots to more people than was warranted by the trading volume the town could capture. The supernumerary merchant population eventually had to adjust to the real level of trade through a competitive cycle in which new merchants vied for a stable niche. A somewhat similar view was expressed by Thorstein Veblen who saw all towns as little more than real estate speculations.[5] Inflated land values attracted and were sustained by additional in-migration, which left too little business for each firm. Retailers compensated by pushing up prices, and the farmers suffered. Veblen's view was correct as far as it went; what he neglected was the elimination of the less successful through the inevitable competition that began as soon as a town was born.

For every William Plummer there were perhaps two hundred others of lesser means and abilities. It is risky to generalize about so large and diverse a group, but three major entrepreneurial categories were represented in the ranks of early business people in Dakota towns. Most numerous were the young men and women who had been engaged as clerks or apprentices in business houses of longer-established communities and who sought an opportunity to start their own shops. Railroad townsites were virtually tailor-made for the purpose: capital requirements were small, and experimentation was encouraged by the lack of existing competitors. If they failed at one line, there remained the possibility of switching to another that would afford a better prospect for success.

Two other types of initial entrepreneurs were common. One was a permanent class of movers who shifted locations in phase with the peak of activity as it moved from one new town to the next. Because the volume of trade characteristically declined once the initial construction phase had passed, the movers sold out or carried their stocks to a new boom location to exploit the same niche there. The third group consisted of established merchants, usually from nearby trade centers, who moved a small stock of goods to a new townsite and opened a branch business. Some later sold the branches to local merchants or, if trade prospects were especially good, relocated their headquarters to the new town.

Those starting businesses with the intention of remaining shared one other trait in common. Most were deeply in debt, short of working capital, and unable to do much about their plight until local farmers had been paid for the next harvest. One means of increasing capital was to acquire a new business partner, and this was done so frequently that it is difficult to trace business ownership from most available records. Anderson & Berg's general store might become Berg & Smith six months later, then Berg, Smith & Jensen, Smith & Jensen, and, perhaps after two years, Jensen's General Store. Ownership changed constantly through the dissolving and reforming of partnerships, yet at no point in the sequence did it change totally.

Just as common was the addition and deletion of various lines of goods each time a new partner, with new ideas, was acquired. If Anderson began a general mercantile business, and if Berg was a hardware dealer, Smith a farm machinery man, and Jensen a grocer, the business of the firm becomes difficult to describe. Changes in ownership often were accompanied by a change in buildings either by moving to a new structure elsewhere on the townsite or by moving a larger building onto the existing site. (Those who have traveled the Great Plains know that the moving of buildings remains a regional habit to this day.)

The acquisition of new partners could become a business in itself. Fessenden had a man practiced in the art:

> "Uncle" Shadley was very hard of hearing, but was a great friend of the little boys who liked to hang around the mill and listen to his stories. [He] always sold half interest in his business to some men who had a few hundred dollars to invest, but since his business consisted chiefly of grinding a little feed, which would, just about, bring him enough to keep him in groceries (he batched in the mill) his Partners usually left him as soon as they found out that they had bought a gold-brick. There was Henry Speiser, a Frenchman by the name of Boleau, a German-Russian, John Swanson, and John Pudville, all had, in turn, bought half interest in the mill from "Uncle" Shadley.[6]

The memory of "Uncle" Shadley may have grown richer in the intervening years before this account was written, but his method of acquiring new life for a small business was not an isolated case.

The matching of people, structures, and activities was a continuing process in the new towns. New possibilities opened each time one venture was abandoned for another. Those interested in expanding often did so by purchasing unrelated businesses and operating them simultaneously, staying with each until one proved stable. Occupational mobility within the merchant class was fed by new additions from among the ranks of homesteader-farmers who desired an easier life in town, but the size of the business class was maintained by a corresponding exodus of tradespeople leaving to seek opportunities elsewhere.[7]

The exceptional degree of mobility can be attributed to the manner in which trade centers were founded. Adjustments that might have taken years in towns that grew in piecemeal fashion (that is, where *activity* assumed priority over *structure*) were compressed into a matter of months. Railroad towns were born full-grown, with as many—and often more—business houses in operation in their early months as some would ever see again. The appearance of a fully formed town, however, did not signal economic maturity. Filling in the plat with buildings was another step in making the place look like a town, but the method of instant growth was no substitute for the relations of business activity that made the town function, nor even did this mode of settlement creation short-circuit any of the adjustments that were inevitable; it simply compressed them into a shorter span of time. Fires, sometimes tragic, added another dimension to the cycle. Whether acts of God or, more usually, of mortals, fires would jump from one frame structure to another and destroy an entire town in a matter of hours. Towns so new they lacked any form of local government, let alone fire-fighting equipment, were helpless in the face of such disasters. Some tragedies inspired collective action that brought about a quick rebuilding, although an early fire marked the end for other towns, especially those already experiencing financial troubles. News of a town fire spread almost as quickly as the flames. Minnewaukan experienced a disastrous conflagration in 1895, soon after which Plummer began receiving letters from lumber suppliers hoping for a share of the inevitable boom in sales that would accompany rebuilding.

A definition of business turnover is elusive in a context where fluidity was the norm and persistence the exception, but a general understanding of the nature of change is important because it bears on many other aspects of town life, including economic stability and social cohesiveness. If a business is defined as having a change in ownership (or disappearing) whenever all partners of an existing firm have departed, then the ownership changes due strictly to acquiring new partners are eliminated. Detailed but unverifiable business histories of Towner (Great Northern, started in 1886), Esmond (Northern Pacific, 1901), and Glenburn (Great Northern, 1903), provide enough information to compute typical life spans of firms in those towns during their early years.[8] The median duration was five years at Towner, six at Esmond, and three at Glenburn. In all three cases, a few of the firms dating from the origin of the town remained fifteen years thereafter. Median values clearly overestimate the true record, however, because many ephemeral businesses did not survive long enough to make an impression on anyone.

A tradesperson remaining in a single business for several years might represent anything from startling success to near failure. Persistence cannot be equated with success any more than turnover can with failure; business mobility could be positive, in response to new opportunities; or negative, forced by economic circumstances.

Persistence rates (number of businesses remaining after x years with at least one of the initial partners present) were calculated from Polk directory listings for all towns in the study area for a series of sample periods (table 4). Two-year persistence rates averaged about 50 percent; that is, half the businesses remained two years after the count. For longer periods, naturally, the rates are lower, but there is a marked difference between rates of equal duration at various times.

The ten-year persistence rate from 1890 to 1900 was 32 percent, but

Table 4. Business Persistence Rates in the North Dakota Study Area, 1886-1910

Period	Total	Number of Businesses at Beginning of Period			
		Fewer Than 10		10 or More	
		1-4	5-9	10-29	>29
1886-1888	.53	.69	.39	.41	
1888-1890	.48	.48	.63	.29	
1886-1890	.28	.33	.25	.24	
1890-1900	.32	.34	.28	.35	
1900-1902	.53	.53	.51	.51	.60
1902-1904	.54	.55	.38	.59	.60
1900-1904	.28	.18	.37	.31	.43
1904-1910					
(towns existing in 1900)	.32	.40	.27	.26	.35
1904-1910					
(towns created 1900-1904)	.20	.17	.29	.26	
1900-1910	.11	.05	.17	.13	.22
Conditional Probabilities					
1888-1890/1886-1888	.53	.48	.64	.59	
	(.48)	(.48)	(.63)	(.29)	
1902-1904/1900-1902	.53	.34	.73	.61	.72
	(.54)	(.55)	(.33)	(.59)	(.60)
1904-1910/1900-1904	.39	.28	.46	.42	.51
	(.32)	(.40)	(.27)	(.26)	(.35)

only 11 percent from 1900 to 1910. The greater stability in the earlier period reflects another well-known tendency, that people tend to remain where they are when the economy is sluggish, clinging to whatever they have rather than attempting a new start elsewhere. The upswing of 1900–1910 created many new opportunities; characteristically, there was a sharply reduced tendency to remain in one's old location, doing business as usual. The other component of this high turnover rate in the first decade of the twentieth century is made up of the inland businesses that were abandoned when railroad townsites were platted nearby. This, too, reflects opportunity rather than a lack thereof.

The relationship between business persistence and size of place is not a simple one. Inland towns had the highest rate of turnover because of their own limited life spans, and this accounts for lower rates in the smallest places during some periods. There also was a tendency toward persistence over longer time periods in the largest trade centers. The differential might be explained by several factors, including the likelihood that merchants in larger towns were better managers and had more capital at their disposal so that they were better able to withstand fluctuations in business activity. Larger towns also commanded a larger volume of trade, which also may have led to a greater satisfaction for merchants there, decreasing their likelihood of moving or starting a new venture.

A common pattern can be observed in most human mobility data. Known as the "inertia" effect, it is an explanation given for the increased tendency to remain in a place the longer one has been there.[9] Similarly with small businesses: the longer the history, the better should be the prospects for survival. Business people who survived the first few years at a location would be expected to have a greater chance of remaining, say, another two years, than would those just starting who had yet to experience the early causes of failure that evidently plagued so many. The absence of an inertia effect, on the other hand, indicates that experience and stability are of no value in predicting future persistence. In such circumstances, personal factors are less likely explanations for mobility; instability of the trade center itself is a more likely cause. Many merchants who later proved themselves by establishing successful businesses elsewhere were forced out of inland towns when those places were bypassed by railroads.

Inertia values can be computed directly from the persistence rates by defining conditional probabilities of survival.[10] For example, the likelihood of remaining from 1888 to 1890, given persistence from 1886 to 1888, is $p = .53$, slightly higher than the $p = .48$ "straight" probability of survival from 1888 to 1890. There was an evident inertia effect in the larger trade centers that was reflected in consistently higher conditional survival probabilities for the sample periods. The reverse holds true of the smallest centers. In some cases, longevity diminished the likelihood of remaining; this was especially true of inland towns, where longevity indicated simply that the area was well settled and ripe for development by the railroad, which, in turn, meant abandonment of the old trade locations in favor of the new townsites along the tracks.

Turnover was more likely in newly created towns than it was in more established centers, at least for an active townsite period such as 1904–1910. Many of the smallest centers at this time were inland towns founded after 1900 but abandoned before 1910. Again, however, size-of-place clearly affects the rate of persistence.

Although turnover is open to conflicting interpretations, the greater persistence found in larger centers remains clear. Why this should be so is largely a function of two distinct causes. Townsite agents directed business people with a history of success to the centers they expected would grow largest, and they remained satisfied with whatever interest they might stimulate in the smaller places. The bias of preselection was compounded by the difficulty many smaller towns experienced in building a stable trade among farmers already used to patronizing the larger, existing centers. Had small-town instability not been so pervasive, there might have developed a less significant divergence among what seemed to be at the beginning a series of uniformly good locations at which to commence a business venture.

The store William Plummer built after the 1895 fire housed an ever-expanding line of goods (fig. 27). He and his sons (who were formally incorporated into the business in 1901) constantly sought new lines to offer, tested salability, and followed through to obtain more reliable and cheaper suppliers. They asked wholesalers and manufacturers for quotations on horse collars, wallpaper, cookies, gloves, grease, tents, potatoes, pulleys, and hundreds of other items. Most groceries came via wholesalers in the Twin Cities, Fargo, or Jamestown, but the Plummers dealt directly with many others. They bought buggy whips from a venerable Massachusetts manufacturer, hat pins from Marshall Field in Chicago, eggs from local farmers, cedar shingles from Grays Harbor, Wash., rice from a growers co-op in Houston, and steel ranges direct from a South Bend factory. The attention to detail required of such a far-flung network of transactions was accomplished with Yankee forthrightness. When the Plummers discovered that the Adamant Wall Plaster Company of Minneapolis sent them an inferior product, they returned what remained and gave the company a lecture on the subject.[11]

Figure 27. Main store building of the William Plummer Company, ca. 1900, as it appeared on the firm's letterhead.

By the end of the nineteenth century, small-town merchants could not survive by selling only a few staple commodities. Brand names and styles were becoming a factor in retail trade, and this stimulated a new competition. Clarence Plummer addressed Wyman, Partridge & Company, wholesale dry-goods jobbers of Minneapolis, on a local problem:

> Your Great Northern traveler got in the way of selling to Craigue & Gibbs in this town because he also sold to Craigue's brother-in-law, T. E. Mather, of Leeds. Now that Mather is discontinuing his Leeds store it occurs to us that perhaps you could see your way clear to discontinue selling to the successors of Craigue & Gibbs, who recently dissolved. As you may readily see, in a town of this size—less than 500 people "counting the babies" or about 75 families—it leads to petty annoyances to have the same goods on our shelves that our competitor has on his.[12]

Because the Plummers were valued customers, their request was honored; presumably, those who appeared in public with a Plummer-supplied suit or dress were again secure in their status. The letter incidentally reveals another aspect of business life: Mather had left Minnewaukan because of the competition brought by the Plummer firm and his brother-in-law had failed there for the same reason. Rivalries within the town were a counterpart of the trade competition between separate communities.

Whether the economics of location was already understood or learned in the process matters little, but those who survived did learn. William Plummer's successful business at Minnewaukan can be attributed to his own skill and hard work, but it was also partly the result of Minnewaukan's early start as a trade center, its county-seat status, and the lack of any new railroad construction west of the town for fifteen years thereafter. These conditions did not hold for most towns, and those operating businesses in them had to seek other ways of expanding their trade.

One of the severest handicaps of the smaller trade centers was their small market areas. If those who entered into business at a new townsite held the ideals appropriate to their calling, they would not forever be content to serve a small, local trade. Opportunities for growth were limited, however, by the proximity of competing centers. The more towns there were, the less possibility there was for extending one's market area. Price competition invited retaliation, while expanding the offering of goods and services required capital in excess of the trading volume small towns would likely realize. Acquiring new partners was not a long-term solution, nor was the simultaneous operation of several, unrelated businesses. The most obvious strategy was branching—in effect, to offer the same line at a series of locations that could, in aggregate, amount to a large-volume business. (fig. 28).

Towns themselves were branch outlets (of the railroads), and most grain elevators and lumberyards were owned by outside line chains. General mercantile businesses, banks, and other providers of goods or services were more likely to be owned within the region, but some commercial functions were amenable to extension via branching. Most railway lines offered daily-except-Sunday service because of the mail contracts they held, and this facilitated communication with towns up and down the line. Outlets of a parent firm commonly were located along a single line of track or otherwise were arranged so that frequent, direct contact was possible, thus allowing the owner to maintain a smaller inventory at the branch. The Plummers carefully managed their own inventory and evidently were even more cautious with the store they briefly operated at Brinsmade, from whose manager they

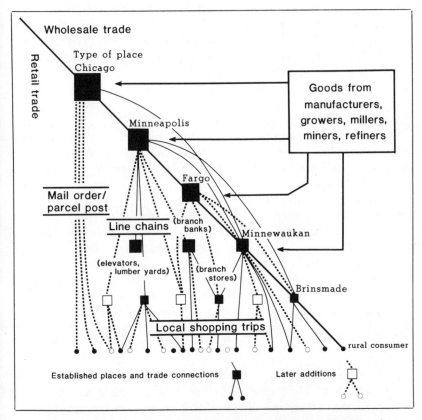

Figure 28. Hierarchy of towns and economic linkages. Wholesale and retail trade took place within, and helped to shape, the hierarchy of places. Chains of banks, grain elevators, lumber yards, and general stores evolved to exploit the commercial opportunities present in the hierarchy. The mail-order house with parcel-post delivery was the ultimate line chain, creating retail outlets dispersed to the level of individual consumers.

once received this poignant request: "Dear Sirs: Brinsmade is out of flour, please ship me up a sack on the freight tonight."[13]

Branch banks did not require frequent contact with headquarters, and their ownership pattern was correspondingly more dispersed. North Dakota law required a capital investment of only $10,000 of anyone aspiring to be a banker. Entry was encouraged by the leniency, but failure was all the more likely. Frequent turnovers in small-town bank ownership invited established bankers to expand their spheres of operation. Thomas L. Beiseker, of Indiana German background, grew up in Austin, Minn., and moved to Sykeston in 1893 where he organized Wells County's first bank. His aggressive attempts to relieve the Northern Pacific of its Wells County land at below-market prices put him in disfavor with that company, but he soon found success in banking. He moved his bank to Fessenden when the county seat went there in 1894, and he controlled banks in New Rockford, Harvey, and Cathay as well before he reached the age of forty. By 1910, Beiseker's empire had grown to include nineteen North Dakota banks and loan companies plus several in Minnesota and Montana (fig. 29). His headquarters at Fessenden virtually controlled the agricultural loan business of Wells and Sheridan counties.[14]

David N. Tallman, the Willmar banker and Great Northern townsite promoter, probably held the record in branch banking. His own controlling interest in each bank was supplemented with the investment of friends from the Willmar area, some of whom became cashiers in the new branches. Sigurdt B. Qvale, the mayor of Willmar, was Tallman's chief partner in the ventures. Qvale personally saw to the opening of forty-two banks in North Dakota and Montana towns of the Great Northern.[15] Some of Tallman's banks were clearly acts of faith in townsites that others thought had few prospects. He placed a branch at his town of Nanson, N. Dak., a townsite so swampy that the grain elevator contractors scheduled to build there pronounced it unfit for occupancy. Three weeks after Newburg was platted, Tallman received a petition from local farmers to create an alternative site because of the same problem of low, wet ground, but he placed a branch bank at Newburg nonetheless.[16] Wolford, Calvin, Antler, Maxbass, McCumber, Sarles, Bantry, and Barton also received Tallman banks.

At least a dozen other men owned or held controlling interest in chains of northern North Dakota banks. By effectively expanding the area within which they could make agricultural loans, branch bankers reaped the benefits during good times but were correspondingly more vulnerable when grain prices dropped or crops failed. The liabilities of line-chaining matched its advantages: as a method of reaching rural consumers, the strategy worked in direct proportion to the general health of the agricultural sector.

The economics of trade area formation derives from differences in prices

Figure 29. The former State Bank at Chaseley, one among dozens of branch banks that appeared in North Dakota. This one was part of T. L. Beiseker's chain.

charged for goods in various centers and also from the responses consumers exhibit toward fluctuations in those prices. There is a well-known relationship between the elasticity of consumer demand and the consumer's location within the market area. Individuals living farther from the trade center increase their purchases in response to falling prices, and decrease them as prices rise, more sharply than do those living nearer the point of supply because the greater transportation costs are absorbed by distant consumers.[17] The smaller the market area, the smaller also is the proportion of consumers who must absorb the cost disadvantage of distant location. It thus follows that price cutting works more to the advantage of the larger trade center (with a larger market area) and least to the advantage of the small center whose customers are local. As a corollary, the smaller the average size of the market area in a region, the less likely it will be that the average consumer will purchase goods at prices set competitively between centers. Higher prices accompany the subdivision of a region into smaller market areas.

Although small-town businesses were in no position to initiate price competition, those same businesses could be made more profitable at fixed prices if they enjoyed the benefits of volume buying from wholesalers. Line-chaining can be seen as an attempt to overcome the competitive disadvantage in smaller centers, although the profits accruing to the strategy were accumulated by a parent firm that was generally located in one of the larger, nearby towns.

That this variety of tentacular outreach in marketing strategies appeared when it did can be ascribed directly to growth of the regional railnet, which made it possible for entrepreneurs in larger centers to reach into the new towns along the tracks to expand their own sphere of operations. The increasing reluctance of farmers to undertake long trips to reach lower prices in the larger towns demanded a response: if rural consumers were not met at least half way, the business would be lost to local centers. A branching strategy not only accomplished this end but also allowed city merchants to sell at higher prices in their distant outlets (with small trading areas) than they did at the home store. Reorganization of consumer travel patterns into smaller market areas reduced price competition between towns, which further reinforced the advantages of branching. Veblen's conclusion is again demonstrated, although with different reasoning.

The terms "small" and "large" are relative ones as applied to trade centers. All merchants tried to minimize costs after the fashion of centers relatively larger in size, no matter what the absolute size of their trade happened to be. The success of the William Plummer Company derived in part from its domination of a large market in comparison with those of nearby general stores, but the firm was hampered by its distance from wholesale suppliers. They sought to mitigate the disadvantage through cooperation with their own competitors. Whenever Plummer ordered goods of less-than-carload quantity from, say, a Twin Cities jobber, he tried to coordinate his purchase with others in the vicinity so that all would reap the benefits of lower, carload rates. The rate difference sometimes amounted to half his usual markup on commodities like potatoes, canned goods, or smaller farm implements.[18]

The counterpart of local strategies to deal in volume and extend retail trade were efforts by urban wholesalers to extend their own sales to smaller towns in much the same fashion. The John V. Farwell Company, a Chicago jobber of dry goods, carpets, and yard goods, maintained such a business with Plummer. The disastrous crop year of 1910, which left Minnewaukan's largest firm unable to settle its account, brought dunning letters. Clarence Plummer wrote to them that "Chicago is too far distant a market for North Dakota dealers to buy in," implying that Farwell did not understand why he was short. The Chicago firm disagreed: "We think Chicago is the market for North Dakota dealers, as we are able to carry those that need extra time as well as any of the Twin City jobbers and we feel we can offer other inducements in the way of prices."[19]

Any wholesaler or retailer who wished to serve North Dakota, or any other grain-producing region with a small population dispersed over a large area, immediately confronted the problem of transport costs. Farmers who wrote letters to railroad presidents seeking new branch lines had urban counterparts—men who sought to extend their trading network into areas without rail service. Great Northern, Northern Pacific, and Soo Line corporate records contain a number of such letters, fewer in proportion than those addressed by farmers but written with the same objective of extending new lines of track. Merchants in Minot, Grand Forks, Jamestown, and Fargo saw benefits to themselves in such extensions.[20]

City "commercial clubs," seeking to attract new railroads to their communities, petitioned freight-rate reductions on goods they might ship to or receive from customers in their hinterlands. Those in a single industry also organized for the purpose of petitioning lower rates. City laundries, for example, tried to extend their reach to remote trade centers via railway shipments. One Grand Forks laundry arranged with Great Northern station agents to ship a weekly basket to the city, and others soon created similar outposts. The level of business evidently was good because the North Dakota Launderers Association sought a reduction in freight rates, claiming that "many thousands of baskets of laundered and soiled articles are shipped back and forth between local points." Tailors, similarly uncommon in smaller trade centers, attempted the same sort of outreach via railway service; but they complained that laundries avoided paying the higher rate on tailored garments sent for dry cleaning by packing all items in the same basket.[21]

Such disputes were settled before the state's commissioners of railroads. Small transactions of a frequent nature to dozens of scattered outlets naturally focused attention on rates for small shipments. Because these shipments were unprofitable, railroads tried to eliminate them by setting a one-hundred-pound minimum rate. In 1910 the commissioners upheld the minimum charge of 25 cents, which effectively made a flat gradient of railroad transport costs within a distance of 30 to 40 miles of a city; for 50 cents the same goods could be shipped 125 miles.[22] Urban merchants were thus able to extend the *range* of goods and services they provided to smaller centers whose own market areas were too small to support such offerings as laundries, tailors, floral shops, and other specialty lines.[23]

Small towns also faced a critical commercial threshold in terms of the volume of business transacted with the rest of the system. In 1901, the state of North Dakota enacted legislation requiring railroads to maintain station agencies at all points originating at least $25,000 annually in freight shipments. The result was an immediate closure of agencies where the traffic volume fell below this minimum. J. Austin Regan, the Fessenden merchant and sometime promoter of Northern Pacific townsites, was also a North Dakota state senator; in 1903, he successfully introduced legislation to decrease the threshold to $15,000.[24] Railroad companies continued to test the limits of the law.

A town lacking its own railway agent was not merely at a disadvantage in terms of service. Any place without an open agency assumed freight charges of the nearest point taking a higher rate. The market areas of towns without an agent thus were reduced, a discouraging factor especially for farmers marketing their grain at stations that, through no fault of their own, handled too little business to require an agent.

The tribute exacted by small towns from railroad companies who may have forgotten who created them in the first place also extended to passenger service. Also in 1901, North Dakota's legislators responded to railroad indifference toward local centers by requiring all passenger trains (later amended to "all but one") to "stop upon their arrival . . . at each county seat." In 1907 the state enacted daily passenger or mixed passenger-freight service requirements on all lines. The support for this legislation came from those directly affected—the residents of small towns and, equally important, the urban-based merchants whose business depended on regular service to the branch outlets they wished to develop. The Northern Pacific sought the good offices of Alexander McKenzie, the self-styled political boss of North Dakota who had done the company many favors, to get the train service laws repealed; but their efforts produced little relief.[25] Not until the 1960s did the state of North Dakota joining the rest of the nation in repealing all branch line passenger service requirements.

Urban and small-town merchants operated as a coalition in their attempt to link outlying centers with their suppliers. The railroads' reluctance to provide convenient service to their own towns suggests, on the other hand, a quite realistic assessment of the marginal character of many towns, just as it shows the railroads' true role in the townsite business—to capture whatever traffic might be lost to a competitor as a result of not creating the town. If their own level of service went unchallenged, railroads found little incentive in providing anything beyond the minimum.

The mail-order house provided trade centers, large and small, with a new and unexpected source of competition in the early twentieth century. The impact was felt in two stages, the first being introduction of rural free delivery (RFD) by the post office. In 1901 the North Dakota study area had only one RFD route (operating from Bottineau); by 1912 the number had grown to 199. The introduction of RFD service was accompanied by the closure of small, rural post offices in many parts of the nation, but in North Dakota fourth-class operations (gross receipts of less than $1,900 per year) were the norm. Some fourth-class offices in the state supported as many as four RFD routes, all serving a thinly scattered population.[26]

RFD service also eliminated many inland post offices, thereby reducing further the number of inland stores and the frequency of farmers' trips to town. Small-town merchants were the most powerful opponents of this new service, which made rural customers less dependent on their local trade center. They soon realized, however, that there were benefits as well. Perhaps in the belief that people would trade in the town where their mail was received, many merchants later sought to increase the number of RFD routes for the local post office, creating a wider service area and hence drawing upon more potential customers.[27]

On 1 January 1913, the post office inaugurated parcel post delivery, a development that substantially increased the value of RFD delivery to the farmer. Those who wished to avoid the higher prices and, perhaps, the inferior goods of their local trade center, could simply order what they wanted from a mail-order catalog and have the postal carrier deliver the order to the farm; the only additional cost was the rather low parcel post charges on the shipment. Opposition to parcel post came from small-town merchants and from urban wholesalers who correctly anticipated the impact the new service would have.[28]

Mail-order houses offered all the goods carried in a well-stocked general store, including groceries. One year after parcel post began, C. J. Kelly, a Devils Lake merchant, advertised as follows:

> $100,000 is annually sent to mail order houses from Devils Lake for merchandise. Now I think I know the reason and I am going to divert a big percentage of this amount into the local banks and incidentally into my own pocket.[29]

He compared prices on $15.10 worth of Sears Roebuck groceries, versus $15.58 for roughly the same items from his store. The parcel post charges from Chicago were $1.60, which boosted the mail-order price slightly higher than his. This small margin in favor of the local merchant suggests the potency of competition brought by the new service, notwithstanding the convenience of home delivery, which more than erased the difference for some customers. Selling at "Devils Lake prices," once a boast of inland merchants who wished they could afford to, soon became an irrelevant claim. By 1914, merchants in Devils Lake or any other town who could not compete with catalog prices were in danger. Were it not for the social advantages of a trip to town (as opposed to a trip to the mailbox), even more trade might have been diverted through the mail service.

The mail-order house was the ultimate line chain, effectively creating retail outlets dispersed to the level of individual consumers (fig. 28). Its appearance at the end of the formative period for plains country towns was partially in response to changing business relationships outside the region, but its impact capped an adjustment process within the Great Plains that was begun by railroads and their townsite strategies. Prospects for urban growth within the region were limited. No great industrial cities employing thousands of workers were to grow there, yet there existed a potential for further commercial growth inherent in the network of transportation routes and towns already in place.

Small-town merchants moved to extend their influence to still smaller centers via branching. Businessmen in larger cities broadened their market areas through agencies that communicated with them by rail service. Wholesaling developed similarly by the first decade of the twentieth century, moving into North Dakota's half-dozen largest cities instead of remaining a function only of the Twin Cities or Chicago. Business activity ultimately came into configuration with the transport system that served it, and the benefits of centrality moved up through the hierarchy to create an urban system that changed very little in its gross structure thereafter.

In this sense, railroads were as effective in limiting small-town growth as they were in making growth possible. Jeffrey Williamson has shown, in his analysis of late-nineteenth-century American economic growth, that railroads retarded urbanization in the Middle West because of the relative ease with which agricultural staples could be exported in exchange for manufactured goods from the urbanized Northeast.[30] One need not revert to explanations that evoke an anti-urban bias in the northern plains to explain the lack of large cities. The advantage that Minnewaukan held over Brinsmade was the same as the one that Fargo held over Minnewaukan and, in turn, that Minneapolis could command over Fargo. Once the tracks were laid, trains could run in either direction.

Chapter 9

Social Relations

Some observers of rural America have seen towns as a major force in forming the values of an entire nation. In Thorstein Veblen's estimation, the country town was perhaps the greatest American institution, "shaping public sentiment and giving character to American culture." Years later, historian John D. Hicks introduced his autobiographical essay on small-town life with a tongue-in-cheek description of "The Significance of the Town in American History," a la Frederick Jackson Turner; but Hicks nonetheless described town and country of the old, agricultural America as "a viable civilization . . . fairly well equipped to meet the needs of the people it served," and added that urban America of later years could scarcely claim as much. Veblen, writing in the 1920s, excoriated the country town for its crass materialism; Hicks, writing in the context of urban unrest of the late 1960s, looked back with nostalgia.[1]

The significance accorded small towns derives in part from a widely held belief that they once were bastions of *community*, a quality of the human condition held in high esteem by all generations but that has managed nonetheless to elude a lasting definition. Part of the difficulty lies in the difference between the singular and plural—*communities* need not be more than social groupings in a definable territory. Plains country towns are more easily recognized as communities than as localities bound together through common emotions, beliefs, and experiences; they were, from the beginning, *Gesellschaft* rather than *Gemeinschaft*. Places settled almost instantaneously by people uprooted from hundreds of diverse origins could hardly have been otherwise. If community ever had been part of the American frontier, it was effectively lost west of the Appalachians in the coming of westward migration streams.[2]

Nor did a sense of community grow in place once the new plains dwellers got acquainted with one another. Social customs carried into the region were soon expressed in familiar forms, a process described by James Malin in his account of Kansas in the 1870s:

> Settlers were scattered, acquaintances were wide, often as extensive as a conventional county, and there had not yet emerged any fixed centers of organization. Individual settlers felt free to meet at different places and to participate in activities that might bring them together. Later this larger area became more differentiated, centering around a local trading center for some activities, or a schoolhouse or other convenient place. With the settling-in of numbers, the major religious denominations set up separate services, school district lines were drawn, and families became identified specifically with particular social interests and groups. With the establishment of a village, the differentiation between town and country began.[3]

Malin's description of town and country social separation omits a step in the process. Pioneer social life, although undeniably more extensive and encompassing in scope and territorial reach than the social system of later years, did not disintegrate with the creation of towns. Small trade centers, especially the unplatted, inland towns, also became social centers for the entire local area. The openness of these small places contrasted sharply with the larger, platted towns, whose inhabitants self-consciously worked to create an internal, more or less closed, set of relationships befitting their "urban" status.

The bases for the congregational aspects of early social relations lay both in the diversity and homogeneity of the settlers themselves. About half of the Dakota frontier households of the 1880s were made up of single males, one-third were nuclear families with or without children present, and most of the remainder were multiple-person households of various composition. These proportions varied little between the livestock-general farming economy of the Missouri and Mouse river districts and the grain-producing counties farther east.[4]

Most of the new arrivals were young and male. The median age of Towner County's population in 1885 was 23, in Wells County, 25; Ward and Renville (unorganized) had a median of 24 years of age. In that year, 40 percent of the new settlers in the Mouse River loop were foreign-born, as were about one-third in Towner County and slightly more than one-quarter in Wells County. Canadian, English, Scots, German, and Scandinavian ancestry were most common.[5]

If married, the settlers had most likely just begun families. Courting rituals of the unmarried provided a ready-made basis for social gatherings, which were undertaken all the more earnestly because single men outnumbered women of marrying age by a ratio of three or four to one. Endogamy was the rule among Russian-Germans and Norwegians, both present in numbers large enough to enable young people to find mates within their own group. Those from other European countries or born in the United States showed much less tendency to select marriage partners in common with their own ethnic or regional heritage.[6] Ethnically homogeneous communities were also bound together through their religious preferences, offering yet another basis for social cohesiveness. In later years it was the most endogamous communities that were likely to retain children born to those marriages.[7]

Commonality in age, family status, and occupation helped form the bonds for areal groupings where clear religious or ethnic identity were lacking. Where people of diverse backgrounds settled side by side, dissimilarity of origins was overshadowed by the conventions of neighborliness. Regardless of who lived on the adjoining homesteads, they were equally engaged in a common enterprise hundreds or even thousands of miles from the places they had left. It was under these circumstances that people undertook weeklong shopping trips to distant trade centers, bringing back goods for themselves and their neighbors.

The most common basis for the early social gatherings was simply visiting—getting acquainted, sharing ideas, and generally having a good time. Ole Hanson, a Norwegian immigrant who settled north of Devils Lake in 1884, later recalled the ecumenical nature of these gatherings. Norwegians, Irish, Bohemians, and Russian Jews (who had been settled there by a New York immigration agency) participated equally in the local social life.[8] Differences were forgotten in their mutual curiosity about one another and in their eagerness to understand the strange, new land they inhabited.

If there were a local focus of activity around which such gatherings could be formed, the most likely candidate was the nearest inland store and post office. The inland merchant may have been more useful socially than economically, given the information transacted incidentally through conversations at his store. The smallest of the railroad-platted towns also became social centers for the surrounding community. Truro's lone store in 1905 saw a regular, daily ritual. The men of the neighborhood gathered there each evening to wait for the mail train, Truro's only contact with the world outside. It was all the better when the train was late because more time was spent around the stove telling stories, smoking, and playing cards, activities that helped break the long winter desolation.[9]

The best evidence that inland town dwellers saw themselves as one with the neighboring farm population comes from the inflated population estimates that were made. Few inland towns had more than a half-dozen inhabitants, but many towns were reported in business directories as having populations of fifty, one hundred, or more. Those who belonged to the town thus were defined as those who used it in one way or another, not merely those who lived there. Descriptions of inland towns published in the Polk business directories included such occupations as brick-maker, coal miner, jeweler, and physician, activities so grossly incommensurate with the town's tiny size as to be identifiable as hobbies, sidelines, or just plain fantasies of nearby rancher-farmers.

The lack of a formal plat and the scattered nature of the businesses encouraged an outward-looking, embracing definition of town population. There was no demarcation of the inland town's margins because no limits were recognized there. The outer trade boundary of the store and post office was the only functional definition that mattered. The introduction of town-like functions, which provided nodal points in local networks of communication, was thus not enough to produce the social differentiation of town and country. As long as the towns were small and informal, they played a congregative rather than segregative social role. In this respect inland towns of the Great Plains reflected their direct antecedents, the crossroads stores and hamlets of the Northeast, Upland South, and Middle West, long established as foci of rural neighborhoods.

To reduce the point to a critical distinction, we can identify the relative priority of *structure* versus *activity* as making the difference between socially inclusive or exclusive towns. When *activity* was the organizing principle, towns were seen less as entities in themselves than as fixed points of contact that oriented daily life for everyone. This priority was reversed by specifying the *structure* first. Platting a town reserved that site for a certain mix of human endeavors, just as it proscribed others. Laying out streets, putting up buildings, and affixing labels demanded activities that would pump life into the structural forms thereby created. The larger and more complex the plans laid for the town, the greater was the effort required to make it work. Town residents had to have some means of harnessing a bright future to a design that required it. "Boosting" is thus a most appropriate name for their efforts.

The urge to formally organize things—anything—was part of the merchant's ethos. Baseball teams are a good example. Although some of the better recruits were local farm boys, the team itself was identified with a town and especially with the merchants who sponsored it. Baseball rivalries seem to have emerged as soon as a group of neighboring towns could field separate teams, and summer Sundays were spent urging the "local nine" to victory over the upstarts from down the track who dared to challenge them. The sporting drama clearly reflected an underlying need to prove one's own town superior in all things, whether in trade activity or other forms of competition. Semiprofessional baseball teams became a vehicle for boosting towns throughout the spring wheat region of North Dakota and Montana, and Americans who settled Alberta took the custom there as well.[10]

Dances, card parties, and picnics were to rural folk what brass bands, lodge meetings, and literary clubs were to town dwellers.[11] Probably there was no difference in their fondness for social gatherings, but there was a characteristic difference in approach. Most often the town-based events were larger and were organized for a specific purpose, such as raising money for yet another amenity that added further evidence of civic pride. Rural socializing, on the other hand, most often was an end in itself, a means for breaking down the isolation. Agricultural fairs, although they celebrated the bounteous nature of the surrounding countryside, were nonetheless town based and supported by merchants — not only for the business they drew but also for the recognition gained.

The predilection that townspeople had for lodges and secret societies was a direct import from their northeastern or middle western, small-town origins. Rare was the town that could not boast of a Modern Woodmen or Odd Fellows organization within two years after the first buildings appeared on the townsite, and most fraternal organizations had their women's counterparts that were no less active.[12] These were the social gathering points for town dwellers. Among the officers of the lodges, poetry clubs, church groups, and various auxiliaries were the names of all leading merchants and their spouses. Successful farmers, especially in later years, joined these groups but rarely participated to the same degree that townfolk did.

Three factors — distance, ethnic differences, and cultural background — reinforced the social segregation of town and country. The distances that rural people traveled to socialize were shorter than the shopping or marketing trips they undertook. Social neighborhoods (areas within which people have a significant proportion of their contacts with one another) were consistently smaller than trade areas throughout the United States, and they remain so today.[13] Schools and churches, which could be supported by fewer families than it took to keep a store in business, consequently had tributary areas smaller in size. They became the institutions around which rural neighborhoods were organized.

The first churches built in newly settled areas were located with respect to their congregations, with no distinction between town and country. Some of the early church buildings in North Dakota towns were moved in from the country for purposes of a central location, and some rural churches were small, town buildings that belonged originally to congregations that had outgrown them. The reorganization of churches along town/country lines depended on the size of the denomination and its local concentration of membership. Lutherans, largest in numbers and with a tradition of churches located for their own sake rather than oriented to townsites, were split into rural and village parishes more often than the other denominations.[14]

There was also an ethnic distinction between farmers and merchants. Those in the trade were most often American-born with native-born parents, whereas the foreign-born — especially those from non-English-speaking Europe — were more likely to begin as farmers. The difference was magnified by railroad efforts to attract population. Immigration agents fought one another to attract the hard-working Russian-German wheat farmers to lands along their own line, but they would not have tried to entice them or others they perceived as peasants to begin a store on a railroad townsite. The image of town life that fed this distinction in the minds of railroad-affiliated agents was based clearly upon the middle western trade center, with its Yankee-dominated class of small entrepreneurs. Many European immigrants succeeded in establishing themselves at railroad townsites, but custom did not dictate strong efforts to attract them there.

The significance of cultural background cannot be underestimated in the differentiation of town and country — as well as town and town — that emerged. Harriet Manly Wing, of the same New England heritage as her husband Charles, the successful Carrington merchant, was possessed of a normal-school education and began a kindergarten in that city. A highlight of her memories of Dakota pioneer life was the Grand Ball held to inaugurate the new Foster County courthouse in 1888, an event at which "all dressed in formal clothes." (When the next Foster County courthouse was completed, in 1910, formal dress was omitted and so was the inaugural ball.)[15]

Minnie Davenport Craig left Boston in 1907 and came to Esmond, North Dakota, as the bride of E. O. Craig, president of Esmond's First International Bank. She returned to Massachusetts for one year to complete her studies at the New England Conservatory of Music, after which she almost single-handedly began to organize Esmond's society along lines familiar to her. She inspired several local youngsters to musical careers that brought a degree of recognition to the town, and she extended her influence to others through a thirteen-year tenure on the school board. Such activities, plus leadership in the local Congregational church, Womens Christian Temperance Union, and local Womens Study Club, were overshadowed later by her election (six times) to the North Dakota House of Representatives and her election as Speaker of that body in 1933.[16]

The infusion of a more eastern, urban "high" culture into northern North Dakota's towns and cities flowed from the very presence of people like Wing and Craig, and so did a sense of social responsibility. Sarah Horr Plummer, the wife of William, taught school in Maine before the family moved to Minnewaukan. William served as a volunteer under General

Sheridan at Winchester, following the lead of his father and brother who had gone to Kansas to fight for the free-state forces. Sarah's sentiments were no less strong, for it was at her insistence that their Maine farm employ two freedmen who had come north in search of work.[17]

Sarah Plummer's dedication to the abolitionist cause was matched by her support of temperance work and the Presbyterian church in the early days of Minnewaukan. With apparent indifference toward their surroundings, she and her temperance group held their early meetings in a room adjoining the bar at the large Arlington Hotel that graced that city. She also organized, financed, and maintained a free reading room at the Arlington until its proprietor, Ransom R. Wise, a Jamestown businessman who had been one of Minnewaukan's early boomers, dismantled the building and moved it to Brainerd, Minnesota, in 1888. When Sarah Plummer's son Clarence organized Minnewaukan's first school, she provided space for it in her own home.

Devils Lake was one of more than one hundred American cities that had acquired its own chautauqua organization by the 1890s. The grounds were connected with the city via a small railroad line, and (also like the parent institution in western New York) Devils Lake's chautauqua had its own boat dock. The wooded grounds on the north shore of Devils Lake were beautiful to Sarah Plummer, and she lived there in an open tent during the summer of 1899 seeking to regain her health. She died before the end of that year— in Pomona, California, where she had joined other health-seekers.[18]

The mantle fell upon a new Mrs. Plummer. Clarence was married in 1903 to Laura Nelson, who had left the sod house of her Swedish-Norwegian parents at age 16 to take a position as salesclerk at the Plummer store. The Plummer family's influence on her was evident, beginning with an education that they financed. The young woman attended the Normal Department at the University of North Dakota and taught one year before her marriage. Laura Nelson Plummer became an active member of the Presbyterian church, Ladies Aid Society, Missionary Society, W.C.T.U., Timely Topics Club, and Order of Eastern Star. The poetry she was encouraged to write was published in various state and local magazines.[19]

It was the larger towns that benefited from the literary and musical prowess of a few such residents, but town size was not the governing factor. Larger towns were those founded earliest, which meant that their first residents came from outside the region and more likely had been drawn from diverse backgrounds that included exposure to a wide range of interests. Towns founded later, while they remained smaller in size, also were more homogeneous because their initial populations came from more local origins. Without a Sarah Plummer or Minnie Craig to plant the seeds, there was little likelihood that these more exotic traditions would flower.

Social organizations brought to the new towns by women differed in their objectives from those founded by men, although they shared in common a possibly more important characteristic—that of civic betterment through personal improvement. Urban and small-town North Dakota has remained fertile "club" territory ever since. Whether the group's reason for being was baseball, poetry, or life insurance, the very act of belonging was important because of the positive attitude it suggested. This outlook, etched with acid on the pages of Sinclair Lewis's novels, became a national stereotype of small-town life, just as the political prairie fires set by angry farmers organizing for higher prices have had a generally sympathetic portrayal. The contrast is one between comfortably affluent townspeople, celebrating their status via self-congratulation, and hard-bitten dirt farmers trying to achieve what would have been theirs had not the weather, the bankers, and the railroads cheated them out of it.

Like most such stereotypes, the distinction lingered beyond the times that gave it rise. The rapid appearance of social clubs and organizations in the towns was soon followed by a much longer period of decline. Population loss was partly responsible, but so also was a less tangible decay in community spirit that eventually sank to match the bleak economic prospects many towns really had. The local newspaper editor's shift from unrestrained boosterism to a more cautious approach lagged well behind the rate at which businesses failed. There was one case (McCumber) in which a town literally disappeared without any admission of it in the local newspaper, although the overwhelming evidence of failure eventually moved most editors to at least make excuses.

By the 1920s, especially with improved roads and automobile access, farmers were traveling farther to socialize just as their shopping trips were more often directed to county-seat towns. A declining farm population led to the closure of some rural schools and churches: as that happened, the tributary areas of those remaining increased in size, sometimes encompassing the towns as well. Organization of exclusively town-based high school districts mandated another, large-scale form of spatial organization. The smaller trade centers, meanwhile, were adjusting to the reduced populations that accompanied decline in their commercial spheres and were eliminating some of the earlier, more complex social rituals. Even the standards of neighborliness declined: as one homesteader in northwestern North Dakota later recalled, after the automobile "neighbors were forgotten and were just as far away as the owner had gas to drive."[20]

Town and country tended to mingle more than before until the smallest centers were reduced to the role that inland towns had played a generation earlier—that of neighborhood meeting places whose economic function was largely incidental. U.S. Department of Agriculture social scientists who surveyed Wells County in 1947 found two significant trends: small villages were becoming stable centers of simple business enterprises to meet primary needs of rural people; and open-country institutions and social activities showed a tendency to shift to town or village centers.[21] Similar conclusions were reached in case studies done elsewhere in the nation. The agrarian "community" long sought by the USDA still was not to be found; in Wells County, at least, it had never existed.

The erosion of boundaries did not totally erase old differences, however. The USDA team in Wells County noted that "in some localities [lodges] serve to strengthen town-country relations, but fraternalism is not strong among farmers." In 1926 there had been thirty-four active lodges of fraternal organizations in Wells County, but only sixteen could be found in 1947. Farmers might have been welcomed by organizations withering from lack of interest, but they did not join. The thirty-one Homemakers Clubs once active in the county had declined to fifteen, but the Agricultural Extension Service was still pursuing this form of organization for farm women: "These groups in many cases have broadened their activities so they resemble women's clubs in town. Most of them have made donations to some organized charity." Despite the imitation, Wells County's five town-based "affiliated" women's clubs did not extend their membership beyond the city limits, nor could the Homemakers Clubs count more than a few town residents among their numbers.[22]

The significance of this social cleavage is more difficult to assess than are the factors that brought it about. Paul Voisey's study of southern Alberta presents convincing evidence that boosterism blunted rather than sharpened differences between farmers and merchants.[23] Both groups participated in these activities, and as a result there was much less friction in town-country relations than some other studies have suggested. His point applies equally well to North Dakota. Social separation did not necessarily imply antagonism. There were mutual interests, economic as well as social, and the smaller the town the more likely farmers and townspeople were to find points of contact. Such a conclusion is entirely in keeping with the observation that social neighborhoods are smaller than trading areas. Social separation based on distance alone could be continued only as long as population was large enough to support neighborhood-scale institutions.

Social differentiation was also carried into the region in the minds of the town's first inhabitants, whose ideas about the social life of commerce had been formed in prior communities of residence. Added to this was an ethnic and sometimes religious split between Anglo-Americans in town versus German and Scandinavian farmers. Social mobility later erased many of the differences, but the bases for the distinction remained. In Wells County and others, there was no evident demand that the more typically town-based or farm-based organizations encompass one another's members.

Social networks originally embracing the entire, local population were not torn apart in the process of town building and boosting. Rather, the cross-linkages became increasingly weak, while networks within towns or among farmers grew in strength as the two groups organized for their own purposes. Townspeople moved to create an internal social life that sought economic as well as cultural ends. The substance of these activities mattered little. Lodge meetings, poetry readings, and gatherings that heard testimonials on the town's promise were easy to ridicule, but it was the act of engaging in them that was important. They supplied a necessary step in making a town's physical existence believable in terms of human activity. Only later, when the realities of economic life were clear and depopulation was well underway, did the emphasis shift back to embrace town and country in a single social community.

The platting of railroad towns effectively blotted out the possibilities for trading points in all but the designated sites along the tracks where railroads desired to concentrate such activities. Social relationships among tradespeople were effectively segregated into those same locations as a result. If a trade center was so small that merchants and their families could not develop a viable, internal structure, then the center functioned as a meeting point for an open, inclusive community, fulfilling the same role as the inland town. If a railroad town developed as intended, however, its size was sufficient to demarcate the boundaries of a group preoccupied with socializing its economic role.

Chapter 10

Passing the Limits

The affair began with a sumptuous dinner laid before the distinguished functionaries of railroading, flour milling, and banking, the core of Minneapolis-St. Paul's commercial elite. After tables had been cleared there were toasts and testimonials, until finally, late in the evening, it was the guest of honor's turn. Edmund Pennington, who was completing thirty years with the Soo Line, rose to the occasion:

> It has been our good fortune to have had among us, from the earliest days, broad-brained and broad-shouldered men; men of breadth of outlook; men endowed with vision who foresee great things; men with unquestioned confidence in the possibilities of this Northwestern Empire. For its development they planned and worked, in season and out of season; in storm and sunshine, amid discouragements and the scorn and ridicule of the faithless; misunderstood, unappreciated, but never waivering, and were rewarded by the dawn of the realization of that for which they had toiled.
>
> The millions of acres that are producing the golden grain; the lowing in innumerable herds of cattle, grazing in the lowlands and valleys; the comfortable homes occupied by the tillers of the soil; the thrifty towns and villages dotting the landscape; and these magnificent commercial centers, are evidence of the faith and effort of men, such as those of whom I have been speaking and to whom we owe a debt of grateful appreciation.[1]

When the bloviations finally ceased on that cold Minneapolis night in January 1917, there could have been no doubt of the consensus. What the railroads and the Twin Cities investors had wrought was nothing short of a miracle. Nor could there be any doubt that Edmund Pennington counted himself among those men of vision whom he described in terms usually

131

reserved for the Founding Fathers. A pragmatic man whose accomplishments were little known outside the circles of railroading, he deserved his hour of recognition even if he had to provide the most glowing tribute to himself.

Ever a booster, Pennington closed the evening by reminding his friends that millions of unused acres along the Soo Line still awaited their investment, but the retrospective mood of the hour was unmistakable. James J. Hill had passed away eight months before. The colonization era on the northern plains had ended, railways had built their last new lines, and the business of town-founding had ground to a halt, never again to be resumed under their umbrella of corporate control. Had anyone been so unkind as to seize the occasion for a more factual accounting of those "thrifty towns" Pennington described, there might have been some embarrassment, especially so if the focus were leveled upon the company's efforts in northern North Dakota.

The Soo had some successes, but the overall record was not impressive. Under the auspices of either the Minnesota Loan and Trust Company (1893–1905) or the Soo-owned Tri-State Land Company (1906 and thereafter), Pennington's railroad had platted fifty-five towns in the North Dakota study area. Eleven of these were such dismal failures that the company did not even list them in their 1918 directory of on-line businesses and opportunities.[2] Another twenty-seven (50 percent) had fewer than a dozen businesses in operation (exclusive of line elevators and lumberyards) in 1918 and had populations averaging about one-hundred persons in 1920. Of the fifty-five, only two — Harvey and Kenmare — had 1920 populations of more than one thousand. Another twenty-one towns platted by others along their lines in the fourteen-county study area averaged a better record largely because of their earlier start. (The Soo arrived in Minot seven years after the town was platted; in Devils Lake, thirty years after.)

This accounting is put in better perspective by comparable figures for Great Northern towns. Comstock and White platted ten towns in the same area; eight of them were ventures of their Northwest Land Company and two (Pleasant Lake and Bisbee) were later platted by White after the partnership was dissolved. Minot's 1920 population of nearly 10,500 established that city far ahead of any others. The other nine averaged populations of 622 for the same census year, clearly a better record than the Soo, but again one that reflects the advantage of priority.

The Northwest Land Company's record was blemished on only one occasion, in a rather unusual lawsuit brought by some residents of St. John who claimed that Comstock and White had deliberately blighted their community by platting the town of Rolla only nine miles down the track. St. John's mixed French-Indian-Anglo population had settled there before the railroad arrived in 1888. A. A. White arranged for purchase of the old town-site, filed a new plat, and deeded lots to the landowners in payment for the site, which became the terminus of the Churchs Ferry branch. The usual practice of building a major trading point at the end of the line obviously was not followed by Comstock and White, who concentrated their promo-tion efforts at Rolla. The Northwest Land Company's town became the county seat and, by 1890, had so outstripped St. John as a trade center that residents of the old community declared war on the Northwest Land Com-pany, claiming they had been promised that no other town would be platted within twelve miles of theirs. Comstock and White denied the misrepresen-tation, but the court ruled against them and ordered that the parcel of land (only a small part of the St. John townsite) be deeded back to the plaintiffs.[3] The Northwest Land Company left the townsite business in the early 1890s with as good a record as any, St. John notwithstanding.

Next in the Great Northern townsite chronology was Frederick H. Stoltze, the bone trader turned lumber dealer who platted ten towns be-tween 1902 and 1904. Only one of them had fewer than 200 people in 1920, and their average population was 323. Stoltze assessed the growth prospects for his towns realistically, unlike some of his counterparts, and he managed to make all of them essentially what they were intended to be—small but viable trade centers. His success with such places, aimed at the lower limits of what would sustain a town, was also partly a function of timing. Stoltze's towns were begun in the early upswing of what North Dakota historians call that state's "Second Boom," the 1900—10 decade of relatively rapid eco-nomic growth, which saw new towns and railroad extensions into areas where farmers were ready to increase their grain acreages substantially.

Success stories in the townsite business were the exception after 1905, however. By any reasonable criterion that might be set, the least successful settlements were those established by David N. Tallman, the Willmar banker who plunged into a total of forty townsites included in the study area. Of these, twenty-one were created by his Dakota Development Com-pany during the 1905 Wheat Line war with the Soo, six were platted by his Northern Town & Land Company after that date, and the remaining thir-teen were joint ventures with a variety of other entrepreneurs during 1910–12 when the Great Northern built the "Surrey cutoff" from Fargo to Minot.[4] Although Tallman's towns were founded later, this does not account for all of their poor performance. In 1920, none of his forty towns had yet attained a population of three hundred. Census figures or accurate estimates are impossible for many of them because so few were incorporated, but at least half the towns he founded contained no more than a half-dozen locally owned business houses or more than one hundred inhabitants by 1920.

The first evidence of town saturation came in the aftermath of the 1905 debacle. The Soo's twenty-five new towns between Kenmare and Thief River Falls were matched by twenty-six platted along branches that the Great Northern hoped would foil the Soo's plans to colonize the spring wheat region. Four Great Northern towns (Olmstead, Rock Lake, Crocus, and Newville) were platted by Joseph M. Kelly's Farmers Grain & Shipping Company Railroad before that small line was absorbed. Kelly's town of Olmstead was barely five hundred yards east of the Soo's Egeland, but Louis Hill counseled him to stand by the site. "If you start your town in time," Hill wrote, "you will have all the business at the crossing, providing you have three or four good elevator interests buying grain."[5]

The editor of the *Cando Herald* visited Olmstead and Egeland and was impressed with the sound of hammers ringing long into the night as carpenters scurried to put up each town's buildings, but he puzzled over the wisdom of it all: "It is difficult for the casual observer to figure out where the patronage necessary for the support of so many general stores is to come from," he wrote, "since the most that can be expected is a radius of five miles on three sides with a town 80 rods away on the fourth."[6] Egeland became a qualified success, but Olmstead's population peaked well under one hundred inhabitants.

Field agents for R. G. Dun & Company operating in North Dakota during the summer of 1905 discovered that fifty-eight new towns were under construction in the state. More than one hundred new banks had been started, and nearly five hundred names of new business people appeared on their credit records as a result.[7] Thirty years earlier, the Dun agent had found only a few scattered stores in the hinterlands, and most of those were connected with military posts. Saturation was being approached at an alarming rate, yet this fact was evidently not comprehended by those who went ahead with more towns. The object was to build up your own business and your own town and hope that the competition failed.

Dave Tallman had high hopes for many of his towns in 1905, but no one of them pleased him more than McCumber. Platted around a center square that contained one of his banks, the site attracted a great deal of interest that summer and was advertised as the likely seat of Rolette County. The Soo countered with its own town of Rolette, within sight of McCumber on the south, and local sentiment favored the Soo as soon as its town was announced (fig. 30). Farmers there believed, probably correctly, that the Great Northern would not have been building their way had it not been for the competition.[8] Although Tallman's town was first by a few months, Rolette was promoted so vigorously that it soon overshadowed McCumber. The opening-day lot sale was held at Rolette on 10 August 1905. Some of the first buyers were McCumber businessmen, and soon they were joined by

WAIT!

FOR THE SALE OF LOTS

NEW SOO TOWN

ROLETTE

Center of Rolette County where the

Soo and Great Northern Cross

Bound to be the

COUNTY SEAT

Lots will be ready in a few days.

Don't Be Fooled.

Any town near this new Soo Town will not be worth your attention, as the Soo people are going to use their best efforts to make Rolette one of the best towns in the state. The Soo owns and controls all their towns. Not how much can they get for each lot but how many people can they get to locate and build up the town. Therefore the prices will be reasonable. This point was formerly known as Eliza.

Charles F. Craig,
Rolette, N. D.

A. M. Iverson,
Leeds, N. D.

Figure 30. Advertisement for the Soo Line's town of Rolette, which was platted within sight of D. N. Tallman's Great Northern town, McCumber. From a clipping in Great Northern Railway Collections, President's Subject Files.

others from the nearby rival. Two years later only seven businesses remained at McCumber, Rolette had won the joint school election amid charges of "Tammany politics" from McCumber, and the fate of Tallman's town was sealed.[9]

Louis Hill, who was then running the Great Northern under his father's watchful eye, somewhat meekly approached Edmund Pennington to secure a truce between McCumber and Rolette in August 1907.[10] The two roads effectively swapped their failures. The Soo gave up their town of Imperial for the Great Northern's Columbus—both on branches built as a result of a similar skirmish in the northwestern corner of the state—in exchange for the Great Northern's abandonment of McCumber for Rolette. Unfortunately, they did not extend the olive branch to one another in the cases of a dozen other towns platted so close to one another that none could achieve sufficient trading areas. Merchants in these centers might have joined forces on a single site, perhaps one of their own choosing, but that was impossible because the railroad dictated the locations of business activity. Abandoning a townsite was tantamount to giving away traffic to the competitor. Tallman and his counterparts with the Soo stayed by their towns until the last hopes for survival had been exhausted.

The problem of the size of the tributary area was the key to determining success or failure, a point well illustrated by simultaneous developments in Ward and McLean counties. The Soo purchased the Bismarck, Washburn & Great Falls Railway in 1904.[11] Its connection with this coal-traffic line at Bismarck suggested a new Soo expansion into the Missouri River country. The Soo extended the road north from Underwood to Garrison in 1905, on to Max in 1906, and then built a new line west from Drake through Max to terminate at Plaza. These lines served portions of the Coteau du Missouri suited more to stock raising than wheat culture but within which there were sections capable of producing large grain crops. In 1916, the Soo built another twenty-four miles west of Plaza into the portion of the Fort Berthold reservation opened to white settlement, terminating at Sanish on the Missouri River. This also became prime wheat country.

The ten towns built west of Drake in 1905–1906 averaged nearly four hundred inhabitants each by 1920, making them the most successful line of Soo trade centers in the region. Prosperity came to the towns because they had no close competition in a large, productive area. The Northern Pacific, sometimes allowed by the Hills to covet this territory for its own, was astonished at the traffic the Soo gained there. In 1922 the sixty-four-mile Max-Sanish portion produced nearly 3,000 cars of grain, an average of 320 cars per station, substantially in excess of what the Northern Pacific received at any but a handful of places on its entire system.[12] Despite urgings from Roseglen's merchants that continued well into the mid-1920s, the Northern

Pacific never built west of Turtle Lake, south of the Soo, as it had so often planned (fig. 31). The nexus that emerged after the 1905 war in the northern portion of the state had so locked the three major railroads into competition that every move made by one was the object of instant threats of retaliation by the others. In this context, there began one final episode of new construction and town-founding activity.

The era of railway building in the United States lingered into the automobile age of the early twentieth century, financed by investors who responded to new schemes of an old industry rather than risk their capital in newer industries not yet proven. Although the national railnet was already dense for a country of this size and there remained few inhabited areas without rail service, the major systems found that they did not have the direct lines of contact they wished. Most large companies had been formed by absorbing a series of smaller ones, built with relatively short-distance objectives. Direct routes between major cities were lacking. The Santa Fe, Rock Island, Chicago & Northwestern, Great Northern, and others undertook various "cutoff" lines after 1900 that would enable them to connect their largest cities via less circuitous routings. Hill had built the Great Northern by adding an east-west transcontinental line that connected with his earlier north-south link between the Red River Valley and Minneapolis. Traffic from west of Minot to the Twin Cities had to move through Larimore or Grand Forks, a detour from the straight-line path that increased operating costs.

With uncharacteristic indecision, the Great Northern pondered a variety of options in 1906, a "good year" of the sort that encouraged railroaders to think expansively of the future. The new Great Northern route from Aneta to Devils Lake via Warwick offered one possibility (fig. 31). A projection of that line west to Oberon, purchase of the Northern Pacific's Oberon-Esmond line, and another extension west of there toward Minot was contemplated, but the country offered little prospect for local traffic.[13] The Oberon-Esmond line, typical of many branches, was in poor condition. Its profile hugged the stagnant-ice moraine for twenty-eight undulating miles with little benefit of cut or fill, clearly not the sort of route over which the Hills wanted to direct their fast mail trains from the coast. One farmer west of Esmond pleading his case for a new route wrote to James J. Hill that his was a country inhabited by "old German bonafida settlers, the backbone of any farming community," but whatever attraction that may have held was not enough to balance the disadvantages.[14]

As part of his strategy to discourage independent railroads, James J. Hill had surveyors locate another line through the center of North Dakota in 1905. Known as the Rugby-Fort Stevenson extension, its plan was brandished several times thereafter when rumors surfaced concerning new lines

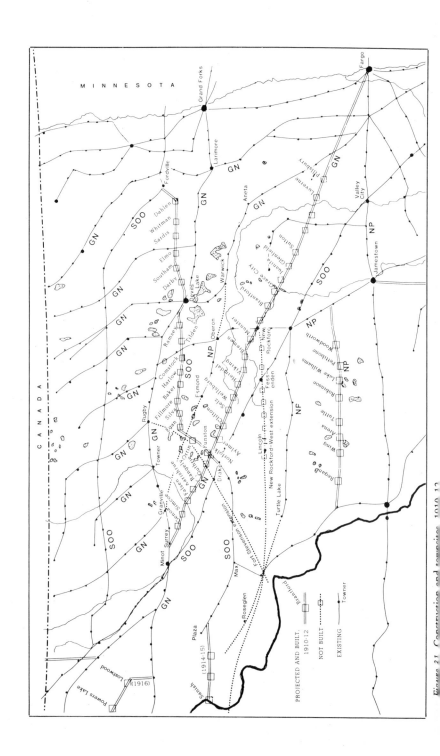

Figure 21. Construction and townsites, 1910-12

south of the Great Northern. It would have been a pointless extension for the company, given its pattern of traffic, but the mere plan was enough to prevent the Northern Pacific from extending another fifteen miles from Esmond to the inland town of Brazil.[15] Louis Hill favored building the line, but his father knew better, and the blueprints were eventually shelved permanently.

The Panic of 1907, construction of a new line along the Columbia River from Pasco to Vancouver, Washington, and the state of Minnesota's injunction against a Great Northern stock issue combined to prevent further consideration of a cutoff via Oberon. Furthermore, it was not a straight-line route from Fargo to Minot. The Great Northern's locating engineers, as sharp as any in the business, soon found a better alternative. A natural corridor stretched diagonally across the state from the Red River Valley to Minot, broken by hills and low ground in a few spots but affording a level-profile route within the morainic belts between Devils Lake and the Coteau du Missouri. When the economy recovered in 1909, James J. Hill decided the cutoff would be built. Beginning at Surrey, east of Minot, it followed an almost ruler-straight 225 mile route, terminating just west of the depot in Fargo. The saving in distance over the best existing alternative was only twenty-eight miles, but construction to high standards would allow faster trains.

There was also the matter of a grudge to be settled. James J. Hill had never forgiven the Soo for building a line to "his" town of Minot, and one that was more direct than the Great Northern's at that. When the Soo's intentions to build its Wheat Line became known to the Great Northern in 1904, Louis Hill, on his father's orders, confronted the Soo-Canadian Pacific directly in an attempt to bluff the intruder out of territory the Hills considered theirs. Since Edmund Pennington would not abandon his plans, Louis told him that the Great Northern would have to make up for its losses by taking traffic from the Soo elsewhere.[16] In 1910, he made good on the threat. Pennington learned of the Surrey cutoff route in early February, and it did not please him. For 182 miles from Valley City to Minot, the new Great Northern was staked out never more than 20 miles and often within 10 miles of the parallel Soo Line.[17]

Louis Hill confirmed the route in a letter to Pennington, and the Soo's president tried again to reason with the youngster he had watched rise to the Great Northern's presidency. "My dear Louie," he wrote, "going back to the early history of this Company, in looking over the construction of the lines, I think we have fully as much to complain of as your Company has." He recounted the Great Northern's history of building lines parallel to the Soo and suggested the company follow its earlier plan for a route via Oberon. "It would not hurt the country and towns already established and not leave yourself open for another line between your Main Line and the one you propose to construct."[18]

Had the Great Northern been interested in the cutoff only as a route for high-speed traffic it would have forgone the usual custom of platting towns. In fact, plans for townsites had been laid the day after Louis Hill announced the decision to build. By June 1910, the company's right-of-way commissioner had secured or taken options on land for thirty-three townsites along the cutoff; all but nine of them were on the portion paralleling the Soo.[19] If any lessons had been learned in the 1905 confrontation, they were forgotten, for no sooner were the Great Northern's intentions known than Edmund Pennington made good on his counterthreat to Louis Hill. In May 1910, the Soo filed papers in Bismarck for construction of a 132-mile line from Fordville (Medford) to Drake that would bisect the territory between the new and old Great Northern main lines. There would thus be 357 new miles of railroad that would require support from whatever traffic might be generated.

The Soo's Tri-State Land Company projected sixteen new towns, all of them located strategically to draw trade from the GN; they brought to four dozen the total of additional communities squeezed into the little polygonal pockets of territory that remained away from existing centers. As before, they would be boomed as offering "numerous unsurpassed business opportunities," with "every indication of becoming thriving commercial centers." The emptiness of those phrases was to be demonstrated even more forcefully than before, although no one acknowledged the inevitable in 1910.

The residents of western Benson and southern Pierce counties were dazzled by the prospects. They had waited years for a railroad, and now they would have two. "Every farmer west of Trappers coulee has visions of town sites and union depots," said the *Esmond Bee*. On 7 May, a crew of Great Northern engineers made their camp just west of the town and local residents believed, naturally, that the Oberon-Esmond line was being chosen for the cutoff. They were fooled, but that was not the object.[20] The Great Northern had surveyed west from Esmond to Towner only to keep the Northern Pacific from doing likewise, and, given the leverage that prevailed, it was enough to hold the Northern Pacific on the sidelines watching its options disappear.

The Great Northern's difficulties began in June 1910. A dry spring was followed by an even drier summer, with prospects for the poorest harvest in years. What was worse, railroad engineers discovered that their level-profile route belied a swell-and-swale topography through unsorted glacial materials that would demand heavy grading and filling, far in excess of projections. The company's chief engineer informed Louis Hill that the line would not be completed in 1910 and would require an uncommon effort to reach completion even the next year. As prospects for the harvest withered in the summer drought, Hill ordered construction to a halt in August and did not resume work until the next July.[21]

The Soo, no doubt relieved to see its rival backing away, rested plans for the Fordville-Drake extension and its towns; but the Great Northern was caught, having placed a dozen towns on sale by the end of June 1910. Although lot auctions were conducted by the railroad's townsite agent, the sites were owned by a series of small companies controlled by officers of the Tallman Investment Company. The multitiered hierarchy of ownership included Tallman, his father-in-law, officers of several Tallman banks, and Willmar businessmen, arranged this way no doubt for the purpose of spreading risk in what had become an obviously risky business. Grace City, Juanita, Brantford, and Glenfield were owned by the Foster County Realty Company, whose president, H. C. Sexton, was also cashier of Tallman's New Rockford bank that included Sigurdt Qvale of Willmar and Louis Hill among its stockholders. J. N. Kuhl, cashier of Tallman's North Dakota "headquarters" bank, the First National of Towner, presided over the McHenry County Realty Company, owner of Karlsruhe, Guthrie, and Simcoe. The Bremen-Heimdal Town and Land Company owned those two towns plus Viking (Hamberg) and Wellsburg; its president, Albert J. Clure, ran the Tallman bank at Bremen (fig. 32).[22]

The intricately dispersed obligations of this latest Tallman venture reveal that at least he understood the risk involved. Even so, he probably did not anticipate the extent to which the new towns would not succeed. Albert Clure, a sometime banker, professional baseball player, and traveling salesman, was hired by Tallman to take charge of bank organization in the new towns along the Surrey cutoff. Clure and his family were among Bremen's first inhabitants in 1910, and they remained there in select company until 1912 when the railroad finally was completed and settlers began to trickle in.[23] J. J. Arvestad bought a town lot at the opening-day auction at Grace City in June 1910, but by October of that year his hardware and implement business was on the brink of failure. Nearby farmers believed that the Great Northern had permanently abandoned the line and had no interest in switching their trading allegiances until construction resumed. The same cloud of despair hung over Guthrie's few businessmen; even the cashier of Tallman's bank there did not believe the line would ever be completed.[24] The *Esmond Bee* reported that one particularly disgruntled merchant who had established a business at Selz traveled to St. Paul to confront Great Northern officials and had returned unsatisfied. A nervous Dale Tallman sought assurances from his friend Louis Hill, but the record of correspondence indicates clearly that faith in the Great Northern had reached a low point.[25]

Figure 32. Hamberg, N. Dak., (originally named Viking) was platted by the Tallman-controlled Bremen-Heimdal Town and Land Company on the Surrey cutoff west of New Rockford in 1910. The railroad did not arrive until two years later.

Resumption of Great Northern construction in 1911 convinced the Soo that it would have to build the Fordville-Drake "counter" line, and it lost little time in acquiring right-of-way. Both companies finished construction late in the summer of 1912, by which time all of the planned townsites were on sale and attention had shifted to completing elevators to store that year's bountiful harvest. The Great Northern loaded 6.5 million bushels of grain on the new line after the 1912 season, about one-third of it "on track" at stations where elevators were not yet available. Perhaps as much as one-half of the carloadings were the result of taking business away from the parallel Soo main line. The cutoff had cost the Great Northern nearly $9 million.[26] Construction to high standards, although expensive, had given the company a valuable assist in its continuing drive to expedite freight and passenger traffic between Puget Sound and the Middle West. The cutoff was a clear success by the criterion of traffic, but the towns were quite another story.

Nine platted towns between New Rockford and Surrey had only seventeen business buildings among them by the end of 1912, excluding elevators.[27] Having lost their early opportunity for rapid growth, most of the towns struggled unsuccessfully thereafter to gain a niche in territory already well served by existing trade centers. Land for townsites had been expensive along the line, averaging nearly $7,500 for each site, but sales did not cover costs in many of them.[28] Tallman and his network of lieutenants stood by their line of miniscule trade centers nonetheless.

The Soo/Tri-State Land Company towns on the Fordville to Drake line were announced for sale on 6 July 1912.[29] The company's townsite agent held sixteen town lot auctions in ten days, moving east along the line about a week behind the company surveyors who were filing the plats at courthouses along the way.[30] The townsite agent did his best, but in the face of a resounding lack of interest. Three years later Tri-State Land Company officials would make another pilgrimage to the same courthouses to vacate seven of their sixteen plats, all of them locations that had attracted little or no attention.[31] A few towns, including Baker, Silva, Fillmore, and Harlow, managed to hold a dozen or more businesses on their two-block-long Main Streets, although none would ever reach long-term stability as trade centers. Their grain elevators collected the local harvests, and some of the abandoned townsites stand yet today in the shadow of active elevators; but those who believed that the possibilities for trading success were "sure and wide," as the Soo claimed, were sadly mistaken. Continuing the pattern established in 1905, what was successful for the railroad was a marginal failure for townsite interests and a disaster for most who tried to live there.

The Soo Line, long frustrated in its dream of achieving trans-continental status, gave the Great Northern cause to survey yet another line in 1912. The semiarid rangelands and benchlands of eastern Montana had become the new wheat bonanza, with acreages expanding at 40 to 50 percent each year, and where publicity photos showed that a man could stand neck-deep in the golden grain. Railroad men in the Twin Cities began to project new extensions across the miles dotted with homesteaders' shacks, hoping to secure traffic for themselves before competitors got the same idea. Newspaper accounts varied, but the Soo was rumored to be building a new line west from the end of one or another of its North Dakota branches, passing through either Lewistown, Mont., or Lewiston, Idaho, and somehow reaching the Pacific coast or else making a connection with the Canadian Pacific in the Rockies.[32] As can now be readily anticipated, the Great Northern immediately launched plans for its own new line across North Dakota to terminate at Lewistown, Mont. Known as the "New Rockford West extension," it was to begin at that North Dakota city and follow closely the stakes driven by Soo surveyors across the valleys of the Yellowstone and Musselshell to reach Lewistown at the edge of Montana's fertile Judith Basin, where the Great Northern's presence was already established.[33]

David Tallman appeared at railroad headquarters in St. Paul early in

1913 to offer his services as agent in charge of townsites projected along the line. His relations with the company had been strained, especially after the Great Northern commenced its own townsite company in 1906; but he had proven himself subsequently by purchasing the Great Northern's interest in townsites along the Fargo-Surrey cutoff and in several others elsewhere. Tallman learned that the railroad had located nine stations between New Rockford and Lincoln Valley, eight of them projected to be Great Northern townsites.[34] The ninth, Fessenden, was an established community; but banker T. L. Beiseker and members of the Commercial Club there were so eager to acquire another railroad that they offered to let the Great Northern build its depot in the town's main business street, where it would command due attention. Lincoln Valley, once the object of the Northern Pacific's affections, had survived the intervening decade as an inland town, its cooperative store thriving from the trade brought by the Russian-German farmers who owned it. The Great Northern purchased townsite land about one mile southwest of the farmers' store, with the apparent intention of forcing the town to move over to the railroad. Lincoln Valley, however, was destined to remain in its unique role as a successful inland town. In 1913, the Great Northern decided not to build the line.[35]

Had it not been for the war in Europe, this would have been the end of the New Rockford West extension; but constriction of European wheat supplies pushed the bushel price to $1 in 1915, the year of the "billion bushel harvest," and there was no end in sight. The new extension was planned to serve a dry-farmed wheat country that stood to earn millions from the favorable wartime conditions, and the plans were revived briefly in 1916. Tallman, who had waited patiently for three years while the company played with the New Rockford extension idea, made a final plea to Louis Hill that year, asking that he be included in whatever townsite plans were laid.

It was the loan business, Tallman wrote, that showed his efforts to the best advantage. The railroad was not able to get banks established in these little towns, but he could. In fact, he already had parties waiting to begin them in the projected towns west of New Rockford. Without banks and someone there to make loans and handle lot sales, little would come of the towns. Louis Hill "has been the best friend I have ever had," Tallman told another Great Northern official as he broadened his plea for inclusion in the company's townsite plans, but the end of their cooperative partnership was at hand.[36] Inland towns along the projected line in North Dakota and Montana continued to plead with railroad officials for another decade and more, but to no avail. The New Rockford West extension was never built.

Tallman left the scene by reaping what he had sown. His net worth, estimated at just under $1 million in 1909, reflected the real estate he had sold, not what he had been paid. Rare was the town after 1905, whether platted by Tallman or anyone else, in which lot buyers paid more than half the value of sales. Taxes on unsold property consumed most of the profits realized by holding on in the hope that buyers would make final payments. A collapse of the wartime boom was followed by agricultural depression in the 1920s. By the middle of that decade, David Tallman's banking empire was in the hands of receivers. As his biographer has noted, by the mid-1930s "David Tallman was back where he had been upon his arrival in Willmar 40 years earlier—flat broke."[37] His failure was preceded by hundreds of other bankruptcies, those of business people he had enticed to locate in trade centers that never saw success. The majority of Tallman's towns hung as loose encrustations, as freely shed by the railway that demanded them as they had been easy to attach in the first place.

Railroad companies who claimed they "opened" the plains to settlement were guilty of some exaggeration, but had they claimed they also closed it, they would have been speaking the truth as never before. Strategies for traffic capture caused railroad officials to project new lines of trade centers well after the period when town founding was an economically prudent activity for anyone to undertake. These plans continued for more than a decade after the lower limit of viable market areas became clear. Railroad companies either did not understand the limits of the system or else they proceeded cynically, hoping to attract whatever short-term business they might while knowing that the towns would not support most of the people who settled in them. Our conclusion must rest on an overall evaluation of what was known, what was projected, and what experience had taught was the rule.

It took a fair amount of ineptitude to lose money in a railroad townsite up through the 1880s. Land for those early sites, deriving either from land grants or scripted at $1.25 to $2.50 per acre, cost no more than $900 to $1,200 per town. Adding fixed costs of platting and selling to the total still demanded sales of no more than six to ten Main Street business lots to recover costs. Some of these early towns made little money for their creators; some platted with overly optimistic ideas about future growth later saw most of their lots sold for taxes, but none of them became financial drains on the local economies they were designed to serve and promote.

These conditions changed, especially after recovery from the 1890s depression. The cost of townsite land rose proportionately with the value of improved farmland, out of which most later sites had to be created. By 1910, townsite agents were paying $50 per acre for a quarter-section townsite plat. Maximum fixed prices after 1905 ranged between $750 and $950 per lot, but the higher those prices were bid up at auction, the less likely it was that their purchasers would ever complete payment. It was not uncommon for a town to bring $20,000 to $30,000 at the first sale, but after subtracting land costs and writing off the unpaid balance it was just as common for these latter-day townsites never to turn a profit, especially after taxes on unsold lots had accumulated. The problem was that each site cost roughly the same amount to bring onto the market, but the substantial profits from a few were offset by small losses from a much larger number. The occasions on which opening-day auctions brought a large volume of business decreased in frequency over time, and eventually losses became the rule rather than the exception.

Losses on later townsites might have been more staggering had it not been for the continued willingness of buyers to invest in them. Every time a new townsite was announced for sale, local newspaper editors obligingly passed judgement that the new town "bid fair to become a sizable trading point." Given the predilection editors had for booming their own town, some must have presumed that the trade supporting new centers would be self-generated. The *New Rockford Transcript* announced the birth of nearby Brantford in May 1910: "The townsite located on the J. M. Walker farm out southeast was platted last Friday and town lots will soon be on sale. The town will be named Bantford [sic] and is bound to be a good business point."[38] Had Brantford's business been good, it would have been partly at the expense of New Rockford's. The *Esmond Bee* took a somewhat more realistic view of the new Soo Line towns platted only a few miles from Esmond in 1912: "[Esmond's] merchants have become reconciled to the conditions as to decreased territory, as they will have more and better territory than the new towns and when the railroads now being constructed are completed [Esmond's] trade will not be cut into again."[39]

Towns once situated at the end of a railroad line commonly experienced decreased trade after the line was extended beyond to a new railhead. The effects of this were learned early. Extension of the St. Paul, Minneapolis & Manitoba west of Devils Lake in 1886 was accurately seen to have negative consequence for that city: "The trade of Devils Lake, which has heretofore been so brisk, will follow the order of things elsewhere, no doubt, and dissolve itself in the newly created towns further west. The stopping off place again will be a good town."[40]

The Great Northern extension from Bottineau to Souris in 1901 created a boom at the new railhead, but a short-lived one that collapsed when the line was extended to Westhope in 1903. The Souris correspondent for the *Bottineau Courant* wrote that her town was the:

> largest primary wheat market in the whole northwest. Drawing our trade as we do from a great distance, all through the fall hundreds of teams could be seen coming from the west and far into the night the process of unloading would continue. Even the banks remained open until after midnight. With the passing of the road this will come to an end, and yet we will still have a large tributary area.[41]

Despite insights such as these, there remained a widespread willingness to believe that circumstances could be overcome and that mercantile prosperity would follow if only it were sought after. The editor of the *Towner Tribune* sermonized:

> The history of one town is practically the history of another. If it is so fortunate as to have a majority of hustling, wide-awake business men it grows and goes ahead. . . . It is not a matter of soil or climate, it is simply a matter of brains and ambition whether we grow better or worse.[42]

Towner's trade center status was secure, enhanced by its early start and county-seat function, but such exhortations had no basis in fact for merchants in later communities who had to earn a living by taking trade away from the established centers.

If these comments can be taken as representative of what was believed at the local level, then it must be concluded that there was a fair knowledge of the consequences of adding towns to the settlement network, just as there was an overly optimistic assessment of what the new towns might become if only their boosters would accept the challenge. Railroad men who dictated new town locations did not reason this way, however. They made no projections of a trade center's gross income when they contemplated its location. A booming town was certainly better than a dead one, but even the most dormant trade center was enough for the railroad's purpose if it had an operating grain elevator. The cost of building the line and its projected revenue were the only variables of interest.

The calculation began with a bushel of wheat, which the railroad charged between 10 and 15 cents to haul from North Dakota to Minneapolis or Duluth. The cost of transportation represented about one-third of the railroad's price, yielding an operating profit of between 7 and 10 cents on a bushel. One boxcar could carry six hundred to nine hundred bushels, leaving a net operating income per car (assuming 7 cents per bushel profit) of approximately $50. Stations were spaced roughly eight miles apart; those in the best wheat country loaded more than four hundred cars per season, those in rolling country with poor soils only seventy-five, for a range of between nine and fifty carloads per mile per year or a net annual operating revenue ranging between $450 and $2,500 per mile. Branch-line construction costs varied between $5,000 and $10,000 per mile. Interest at 5 percent on the construction bonds required earnings between $250 and $500 per mile per year to service the debt. Other costs and revenues (such as maintenance of way costs; passenger, mail, and livestock revenues) were important on some lines, but the volume of grain handled generally determined the level of profit.

These are average figures, drawn from various sources.[43] Their range suggests why railroads were careful in calculating costs and revenues before constructing a line: a costly route through poor wheat country would produce a net loss, whereas one through flat terrain that produced large grain yields might produce an annual profit of more than $2,000 per mile. The average does not reflect annual fluctuations in grain yields, which could substantially alter these margins.

Wheat prices in the 1900–1910 period ranged between 65 and 99 cents per bushel. The railroad's 10 or 15 cents for hauling the bushel to market was subtracted — in good crop years and bad — before the remainder entered the local economy to pay off loans, purchase goods, pay taxes, and the like. A town that handled 150,000 bushels of wheat thus would have averaged receipts of perhaps $125,000 per year plus the value of other farm products sold there. An economic base of less than $200,000 per year was sufficient to support a small trade center, but it is not the nature of an urban system for all towns to approximate the average size. If one town attracts five times the average trade, the entire support for four others is removed. But those were not problems railroad men contemplated.

By 1984, more than half the townsites that railroads platted in the North Dakota study area were little more than neighborhood gathering points for local farmers, with perhaps a gasoline station, a store and post office, a tavern or two, plus one or more grain elevators. Most merchants in the towns disappeared so long ago that younger residents never knew their local trade centers as anything but a collection of decaying buildings. But the railroad network remains today much as it did sixty-five years ago — only 3 percent of the track-miles in the study area have been abandoned. Railroad profit and losses never were tied closely to the economic fortunes of the towns they served, even less so in later years when everything except grain moved on the highway.

Platting townsites in advance of settlement is a long-established custom that did not die with the failures that western railroads encountered in the early twentieth century. The idea that *structure* can precede *activity* has remained an article of faith of town promoters, even through the era of New Towns in the United States during the 1970s. Today, no less than before, however, it remains to be demonstrated that this inversion of human priorities can give rise to viable communities. Plans that assume the instant reproduction of settlement history still generate disappointing results.

Figure 33. Soo Line depot, Rolette, N. Dak.

Notes

Notes

Chapter 1. Introduction

1. Burnham to Comstock, 12 October 1886, Solomon Gilman Comstock Papers (hereafter cited as CP), box 57, folder 6; J. Ohmer to Comstock, 20 September 1886, ibid.; Rolette County, Register of Deeds, plat book; L. B. Lien, "Bottineau-Whitterton Twp.," MS in Bottineau County, Historical Data Project files (hereafter cited as HDP), p. 1.

    2. Burnham to Comstock, 12 October 1886, CP, box 57, folder 6; J. Ohmer to J. J. Hill, 10 October 1886, ibid.; Northwest Land Company ledger, box 72, vol. 33, CP.

    3. Bottineau County, Register of Deeds, plat book; L. B. Lien, "Bottineau-Plat 1890," MS in Bottineau County, HDP, pp. 2–3; Manvel to Comstock, 13 April 1887, CP, box 58, folder 4.

    4. A brief interpretation of the railroad town landscape is given by J. B. Jackson in *American Space: The Centennial Years 1865–1876* (New York: W. W. Norton & Co.; 1972), 67–69.

    5. Some authors have argued that environmental limitations, an agrarian society, and radical politics retarded urbanization; see Lawrence H. Larsen and Roger T. Johnson, "A Story That Never Was: North Dakota's Urban Development," *North Dakota History* 47 (Fall 1980): 4–10. For the plains region as a whole, however, James C. Malin's observation probably is accurate: "The cities took over, almost bodily, the forest man's concepts. Only in isolated instances did urbanization make adjustments which harmonized with grassland-desert regionalism" (*The Grassland of North America* [Lawrence, Kans.: privately printed, 1947], 321).

    6. See, for example, three articles by Donovan L. Hofsommer: "Town Building on a Texas Short Line: The Quanah, Acme and Pacific Railway, 1909–1929," *Arizona and the West* 21 (1979): 335–68; "Townsite Development along Oklahoma's Beaver, Meade and Englewood Railroad," *Southwest Heritage* 4 (Fall 1974): 27–32; and "Townsite Development on the Wichita Falls and Northwestern Railway," *Great Plains Journal* 16 (1977): 107–22. Also see H. Roger Grant, "Iowa's New Communities: Townsite Promotion along the Chicago Great Western Railway's Omaha Extension" and F. Stuart Mitchell, "Railroad Townsite Promotion in a Capitalistic Setting: Herbert Sydney Duncombe and the Midland Continental Railroad, 1906–1914," papers presented at Northern Great Plains History Conference, Sioux Falls, S. Dak.,

October 1981. Townsite promotions on the Kansas City Southern and Kansas City, Mexico and Orient are included in Keith L. Bryant, Jr., *Arthur E. Stilwell: Promoter with a Hunch* (Nashville: Vanderbilt University Press, 1971). Atchison, Topeka & Santa Fe towns in Kansas are given some treatment in L. L. Waters, *Steel Trails to Santa Fe* (Lawrence: University of Kansas Press, 1950), chap. 7; Atlantic & Pacific (later, Santa Fe) towns in Arizona and New Mexico are described in William S. Greever, *Arid Domain: The Santa Fe Railway and Its Western Land Grant* (Stanford, California: Stanford University Press, 1954), chap. 5. Nearly all railroad corporate histories contain some mention of this aspect of the business; for example, information on townsites in Missouri, Texas, and Kansas is scattered throughout V. V. Masterson, *The Katy Railroad and the Last Frontier* (Norman: University of Oklahoma Press, 1952).

7. John W. Reps, *The Making of Urban America: A History of City Planning in the United States* (Princeton, N. J.: Princeton University Press, 1965), 12–15, 161–63. Much of the evidence for direct borrowing of city planning ideas is circumstantial, although the degree of correspondence between many European city plans and those later drawn in North America offers a very good case for diffusion.

8. James E. Vance, Jr., *This Scene of Man: The Role and Structure of the City in the Geography of Western Civilization* (New York: Harper's College Press, 1977), 259.

9. Ray A. Billington, "The Origin of the Land Speculator as a Frontier Type," *Agricultural History* 19 (1945): 204–12; quotation on 210–11. Recent scholarship on the New England village suggests that a sense of community prevailed regardless of the settlement pattern actually followed; see Joseph S. Wood, "Village and Community in Early Colonial New England," *Journal of Historical Geography* 8 (1982): 333–46. The best geographical description of the New England settlement type is Glenn T. Trewartha, "Types of Rural Settlement in Colonial America," *Geographical Review* 36 (1946): 568–96.

10. Turpin C. Bannister, "Early Town Planning in New York State," *Journal of the Society of Architectural Historians* 3 (1943): 36–42; quotation on 39.

11. "Recorded Town Plats," *Engineering News* 5 (1878): 361.

12. Glenn T. Trewartha, "The Unincorporated Hamlet: One Element of the American Settlement Fabric," *Annals,* Association of American Geographers, 33 (1943): 32–81; Edward T. Price, "The Central Courthouse Square in the American County Seat," *Geographical Review* 58 (1968): 29–60; and Milton B. Newton, Jr., "Cultural Preadaptation and the Upland South," *Geoscience and Man* 5 (1974): 143–54.

13. Contemporary (and, typically, critical) accounts include: W. E. Webb, "Air Towns and Their Inhabitants," *Harper's Magazine* 51 (1875): 828–35; "The Shaping of Towns," *American Architect and Building News* 2 (1877): 195–96; and "Professor T. Hayter Lewis on the Laying Out of Town Areas," ibid., 22 (1887): 180–82. The extent of railroad influence in town platting is shown in James F. Hamburg, "Railroads and the Settlement of South Dakota during the Great Dakota Boom, 1878–1887," *South Dakota History:* 5 (1975): 165–78. Also, see David A. Montgomery, "The Development of Street-Pattern Orientation Systems: A Case Study in the Platte Valley of Nebraska" (Master's thesis, University of Nebraska-Lincoln, 1972). An interpretation of the railroad's significance in the new settlement system is given in John C. Hudson, "The Plains Country Town," in *The Great Plains: Environment and Culture,* ed. Brian W. Blouet and Frederick C. Luebke (Lincoln: University of Nebraska Press, 1979), 99–117.

14. Reps, *Urban America,* chap. 14; Paul W. Gates, *The Illinois Central Railroad and Its Colonization Work* (Cambridge, Mass.: Harvard University Press, 1934), chap. 7.

15. Richard C. Overton, *Burlington West* (Cambridge, Mass.: Harvard University Press, 1941), 286. Also see Ronald Rees, "The Small Town of Saskatchewan," *Landscape* 18, no. 3 (1969): 29–33.

16. Grenville M. Dodge, *How We Built the Union Pacific Railway* (Council Bluffs, Iowa: Monarch Printing Co., n.d.), 118. Railroad and townsite construction before, during, and after the Civil War is described in H. Craig Miner, *The St. Louis-San Francisco Transcontinental Railroad* (Lawrence: University Press of Kansas, 1972), 56–73, 78–81, 145, 156.

17. Stanley P. Hirshson, *Grenville M. Dodge: Soldier, Politician, Railroad Pioneer* (Bloomington: Indiana University Press, 1967), 173.

18. John W. Reps, *Cities of the American West: A History of Frontier Urban Planning* (Princeton, N. J.: Princeton University Press, 1979), 595, 598; and Richard C. Overton, *Gulf to Rockies, the Heritage of the Fort Worth and Denver-Colorado and Southern Railways, 1861–1898* (Austin: University of Texas Press, 1953), chap. 4 and pp. 99–101. Montgomery was also involved with townsites for the Missouri-Kansas-Texas Railroad; with Dodge' assistance, he attempted to manipulate the location of U. S. military installations in west Texas to enhance the value of lands they held there; "Texas and Colorado Railway Improvement Company," in Grenville M. Dodge Papers (hereafter cited as DP), box 218. Wallace D. Farnham, "Grenville Dodge and the Union Pacific: A Study of Historical Legend," *Journal of American History* 51 (1965): 632–50.

19. Jas. A. Evans to Dodge, 13 February 1867, W. B. Bent to J. E. House, 15 February, 1868, Dodge to Edwin M. Stanton, 16 February 1868, and Dodge to Stanton, 24 February 1868, DP, box 153; minutes, Union Pacific directors meeting, 23 May 1867, DP, box 170.

20. "Plan for the Organization of the U.P.R.R. Town Lot Department," MS in DP, box 170.

21. Ibid., p. 6.

22. Oliver Knight hypothesized that a city's zone of influence is an additive function of its location, the leadership of its entrepreneurs, the effects of local physical environment, and its role in government and banking; "Toward an Understanding of the Western Town," *Western Historical Quarterly* 4 (1973): 27–42.

23. The role of individuals is made explicit in Alan F. J. Artibise, "Boosterism and the Development of Prairie Cities, 1871-1913," in *Town and City, Aspects of Western Canadian Urban Development*, Canadian Plains Studies, no. 10, ed. Alan F. J. Artibise (Regina: Canadian Plains Research Center, 1981), 209–35. Artibise writes (230): "This overview of the early history of prairie urban development does not support the idea that local leaders through their actions created their cities, or were alone responsible for their patterns of growth and development . . . but rather that the element of urban leadership must be an integral part of any explanation of urban growth."

24. Brian J. L. Berry, who first successfully merged the ideas of central place theory with those of marketing geography, wrote: "The Hierarchy is a Spatial System. The levels of centers define a central place hierarchy in which there are distinct steps of centers providing distinct groups of goods and services to distinct market areas. The interdependent spatial patterns of centers of different levels, and the interlocking market areas of goods and services of related orders, weld the hierarchy into a central place system"; Berry, *Geography of Market Centers and Retail Distribution* (Englewood Cliffs, N. J.: Prentice-Hall, 1967), 20.

25. Walter Christaller, *Central Places in Southern Germany*, trans. Carlisle W. Baskin (Englewood Cliffs, N. J.: Prentice-Hall, 1966) and August Lösch, *The Economics of Location*, trans. William H. Woglom with the assistance of Wolfgang F. Stolper (New Haven: Yale University Press, 1954). Readers unfamiliar with the theory are advised to begin with Berry's summary (*Geography of Market Centers*, n. 25) rather than the originals.

26. James E. Vance, Jr., *The Merchant's World: The Georgraphy of Wholesaling* (Englewood Cliffs, N. J.: Prentice-Hall, 1970). Michael Conzen states that Vance's model "is fast gaining the character of a new orthodoxy," replacing central place theory; see Michael P. Conzen,

"The American Urban System in the Nineteenth Century," in *Geography and the Urban Environment: Progress in Research and Applications*, vol. 4, ed. D. T. Herbert and R. J. Johnston (London: John Wiley, 1981), chap. 9; quotation on p. 311.

27. The location principles used were based on solid calculations and should not be confused with earlier geopolitical and generally fanciful arguments such as William Gilpin's "theory," which predicted that a great urban center necessarily would develop near Kansas City; see Charles N. Glaab, "Visions of Metropolis: William Gilpin and Theories of City Growth in the American West," *Wisconsin Magazine of History* 45 (Autumn 1961): 21–31.

Chapter 2. Frontier Beginnings

1. Elwyn B. Robinson, *History of North Dakota* (Lincoln: University of Nebraska Press, 1966), 40.

2. Martin Ira Glassner, "The Mandan Migrations, PreContact to 1876," *Journal of the West* 13, no. 1 (1974): 25–46.

3. *Army Life in Dakota: Selections from the Journal of Philippe Regis Denis de Keredern de Trobriand*, trans. George F. Will (Chicago: Lakeside Press, 1941), 281.

4. Ibid., 54–57.

5. Ibid., 117; Charles De Noyer, "History of Fort Totten," *Collections*, State Historical Society of North Dakota, vol. 3 (1910), 178–237.

6. De Noyer, "Fort Totten," 213.

7. Ibid., 211–13.

8. Ray H. Mattison, "Old Fort Stevenson," *North Dakota History* 18 (1951): 74–75.

9. Manuscript credit ledgers, Western Territorial Series, vols. 2 and 3, 1876, Dun & Bradstreet Manuscripts (hereafter cited as DBM).

10. Mattison, "Fort Stevenson," 75.

11. Credit Ledger, vol. 3, 1876, DBM.

12. Lewis Atherton, *The Frontier Merchant in Mid-America* (Columbia: University of Missouri Press, 1971).

13. De Noyer, "Fort Totten," 178–98; Robinson, *North Dakota*, chap. 5.

14. Palmer to St. Paul, Minneapolis & Manitoba agent, Devils Lake, 13 March 1884, scrapbook of Devils Lake agent, vol. 5, St. Paul, Minneapolis & Manitoba Letters, Great Northern Railway Collection (hereafter cited as GNC).

15. Railroads played an active role in military logistics of the late territorial period in Dakota; see Kenneth C. Hammer, "Railroads and the Frontier Garrisons of Dakota Territory," *North Dakota History* 46 (Summer 1979): 24–34.

16. Credit ledger, vol. 3, 1876, p. 328, DBM; Neree Ethier, Pembina County questionnaires, HDP; Robinson, *North Dakota*, 65–66. New York-born Nathan Myrick was the first merchant and also the first permanent settler at La Crosse, Wis., where he located in 1841 after a brief stay at Prairie du Chien. He moved to St. Paul in 1843 and soon established himself in business there. Nathan Myrick and his brother Andrew were active in trade with the Sioux in the Minnesota River country, at one time controlling as many as seven stores in the vicinity of Big Stone and Lake Traverse. Andrew lost his life in a skirmish with Indians at Fort Ridgeley in 1862. Nathan remained in St. Paul, where he grew wealthy from real estate investments, but he continued an active involvement in the frontier trade through ownership of stores such as the one at Pembina. Morrison McMillan, "Early Settlement of LaCrosse and Monroe Counties," *Report and Collections*, State Historical Society of Wisconsin, vol 4 (1859), 383–84; Minnesota Historical Society, *Collections*, vol. 2 (1967), 180, vol. 9 (1901), 166, 444, and vol. 14 (1912), 536; George E. Warner, *History of Ramsey County, Minnesota* (Minneapolis: North Star Publishing Co., 1881), 577.

Chapter 3. Inland Towns

1. Clarence Chapman, "Sherwood, General History," MS in Renville County, HDP; "Story of Sherwood," *Sherwood Tribune*, March 1936, clipping in Renville County, HDP.

2. Terry G. Jordan, *Trails to Texas, Southern Roots of Western Cattle Ranching* (Lincoln: University of Nebraska Press, 1918); idem, "Early Northeast Texas and the Evolution of Western Ranching," *Annals,* Association of American Geographers, 67 (1977): map on p. 68; Hazel A. Pulling, "History of the Range Cattle Industry of Dakota," *South Dakota Historical Collections* 20 (1940): 486.

3. M. D. Clark and J. D. Quam, "A Brief History of Towner," MS in McHenry County, HDP; and R. L. Polk & Company, *North Dakota, South Dakota, Montana Gazetteer and Business Directory* (hereafter cited as PD), vol. 5 (1886–87).

4. *Villard Leader*, 6 March 1886; PD, vol. 5.

5. Lösch, *Economics of Location*, 106; Bonnie Barton, "The Creation of Centrality," *Annals,* Association of American Geographers, 68 (1978): 34–44.

6. Perry Johnson, Ward County questionnaires, HDP; Joseph Busch, MS in Ward County, HDP.

7. Ole Forde, Nelson County questionnaires, HDP.

8. Seasonal labor migration took homesteaders west to work on wheat bonanzas and railroad construction in the summer, east to lumber camps and sawmills in winter; John C. Hudson, "Migration to an American Frontier," *Annals,* Association of American Geographers, 66 (1976): 260.

9. Computed from bills to J. G. Lamoreaux (Jerusalem, Dakota Territory) and Coutts Marjoribanks (Newport, Dakota Territory) in scrapbook of Devils Lake agent, vol. 5, St. Paul, Minneapolis & Manitoba Letters, GNC.

10. *Villard Leader*, 10 and 17 May 1886; PD, vol. 5.

11. St. Paul, Minneapolis & Manitoba tariff posted 4 September 1885, copy in scrapbook of Devils Lake agent, vol. 5, St. Paul, Minneapolis & Manitoba Letters, GNC; *Villard Leader*, 6 March and 17 July 1886; LeRoy Barnett, "The Buffalo Bone Commerce on the Northern Plains," *North Dakota History* 39 (1972): 23–42.

12. *Villard Leader*, 17 July, 28 August, 11 September, 20 and 27 November 1886; 5 February, 12 March, 23 April, 8 June, and 3 September 1887; 13 March 1888; 22 March 1889; PD, vol. 5 (1886–87) and vol. 6 (1888–89).

13. The equivalent of cash in the money-short frontier economy of the Devils Lake region was a form of scrip. Buffalo bones were sold at stores in exchange for groceries. Whatever balance was due the bone picker was given as a receipt that could be used at other stores in the area. Usher L. Burdick, "Recollections and Reminiscences of Grahams Island," *North Dakota History* 16 (1949): 40.

14. Lösch based his derivation of the demand cone and range of a good on such small-scale manufacturing, although others in later years have tended to regard these kinds of enterprises as somehow contrary to the predictions of central place theory; see, for example, F. A. Dahms, "The Evolution of Settlement Systems: A Canadian Example, 1851–1970," *Journal of Urban History* 7 (1981): 169–204.

15. Marshall Cushing, *The Story of Our Post Office* (Boston: A. M. Thayer & Company, 1893); Wayne E. Fuller, *RFD: The Changing Face of Rural America* (Bloomington: Indiana University Press, 1964).

16. B. F. Gue, *History of Iowa*, vol. 4 (New York: Century History Company, 1903), 37–38; "Offers . . . " and "Contracts for Carrying the Mails," House Executive Documents, Congressional Serial Numbers 2111 (1882–83), 2307 (1884–85), 2474 (1886–87), 2551 (1887–88); Annual Report of the U.S. Post Office Department, 1904, p. 558.

17. Average and minimum passenger stage fares in the study region were computed from

forty-two individual rates between towns listed in various Polk directories, 1886–1900 (PD vols. 5 through 12).

18. Berry, *Geography of Market Centers*, 6, summarizes the same pattern for southwestern Iowa.

19. *LaFollette Forum*, 22 and 27 March 1906, 28 June 1906.

20. Ibid., 6 and 12 July 1906; *Plaza Pioneer*, 19 and 26 July, 16 August 1906.

Chapter 4. Townsite Speculators

1. Reps, *Cities of the American West*, 400–47 passim; Hamburg's map of South Dakota paper towns shows only thirty-five in the entire state, undoubtedly a conservative estimate; James F. Hamburg, "Paper Towns in South Dakota," *Journal of the West* 16, no. 1 (1977): 41.

2. 13 U.S. Statutes at Large (2 July 1864), pp. 379–80; 16 U.S. Stat. L. (31 May 1870), p. 378.

3. Walter Spokesfield, *History of Wells County, North Dakota, and Its Pioneers* (by author, 1929), 45–46, 60–61; E. S. Killie, "The Richard Sykes Ranch and Land Sales Helped Open Wells County to Settlement," *Wells County History*, vol. 5 (6 April 1874), 1–7. Sykes' holdings were in the odd-numbered sections of township 145 N, range 67 W in Foster County and in 145–68, 146–71, 146–70, 146–69, and 146–68 of Wells County; E. H. McHenry to C. S. Mellen, 16 January 1900, Northern Pacific Railway, President's Subject Files (hereafter cited as NPS), box 69, folder 164A.

4. Spokesfield, *Wells County*, 63.

5. Wells County, Register of Deeds, plat book; Killie, "Richard Sykes Ranch," 4.

6. Foster County, Register of Deeds, plat book; Northern Pacific Land Department (hereafter cited as NPL), Commissioner's Letterpress Books, vol. 9, 282.

7. Thomas Donaldson, *The Public Domain* (Washington, D.C.: U.S. Government Printing Office, 1884), 289, 950; A. A. White to S. G. Comstock, 24 June 1886, CP, box 57.

8. Griggs to Hill, 14 March 1882, James J. Hill papers, box 14, GNC; Robinson, *North Dakota*, 130.

9. H. V. Arnold, *The Early History of the Devils Lake Country* (Larimore, N.D.: by author, 1920), endpiece; *Larimore Pioneer*, 23 March and 15 June 1882.

10. *Larimore Pioneer*, 17 July 1882; Arnold, *Devils Lake Country*, 74.

11. Griggs to Hill, 11 August 1882, James J. Hill papers, box 14, GNC; Arnold, *Devils Lake Country*, 70–75.

12. *Larimore Pioneer*, 11 November 1882 and 12 January 1883.

13. Arnold, *Devils Lake Country*, 75; *Larimore Pioneer*, 17 August 1882; De Noyer, "Fort Totten," map facing p. 208, p. 235; Ramsey County, Register of Deeds, plat book.

14. Ramsey County, Register of Deeds, plat book; Adolphus A. Bode files, folder H, St. Paul, Minneapolis & Manitoba letters, GNC. James J. Hill to F. P. Hannafin, 21 March, 5 April, 7 April 1898, Great Northern President's Letterbooks, vol. 36, GNC.

15. "Minnewaukan, Dakota—1883," MS in Benson County, HDP; Benson County, Register of Deeds, plat book; "Pioneer Business Men in Minnewaukan," MS in Benson County, HDP.

16. Statement of Minnie Heerman Naugle, "West End," MS in Benson County, HDP; Northern Pacific Land Commissioner, Town Property Book, Minnewaukan, vol. 39, NPL; Thomas C. Cochran, *Railroad Leaders, 1845–1890* (New York: Russell and Russell, 1953), 236.

17. Newspaper clipping, undated (probably July 1886), in James J. Hill papers, box 14, GNC; PD, vol. 5 (1886–87); Roy Thompson, "The Naming of Cando," *Collections*, State Historical Society of North Dakota, vol. 3 (1910), 321–23.

18. Manvel to Comstock, 24 June, 3 July 1886, CP, box 57, folder 6.

19. Dunseith, in Rolette County, also technically qualifies as a town begun ahead of the railroad. It managed to survive the railroad's coming even though the Great Northern tried to create an alternative site, Thorne, eight miles to the south, and delayed laying tracks into Dunseith until it became clear that Thorne would not draw away Dunseith's trade. See Hudson, "North Dakota's Railway War of 1905," 13, for details.

Chapter 5. Tracks and Elevators

1. The Northern Pacific was an exception to this; the company's land department was directly involved in townsites through the middle 1890s. James B. Hedges, "The Colonization Work of the Northern Pacific Railroad," *Mississippi Valley Historical Review* 13 (1926): 311–42; and John L. Harnsberger, "Land Speculation, Promotion, and Failure, The Northern Pacific Railroad, 1870–1873," *Journal of the West* 9, no. 1 (1970): 33–45. The Atchison, Topeka & Santa Fe Railroad was more typical in its separation of agricultural and town promotion under separate departments; see Waters, *Steel Trails*; Greever, *Arid Domain*; C. L. Seagraves, "Colonization as a Factor in Traffic Development," *Santa Fe Magazine* 21 (August 1927): 19–20; and Carl B. Schmidt, "Reminiscences of Foreign Immigration Work for Kansas," *Transactions*, Kansas State Historical Society 9 (1906): 485-97.

2. L. W. Hill to W. W. Broughton, 6 January 1905, Great Northern Railway, President's Subject Files (hereafter cited as GNS), no. 3950. Townsites originally planned west of Devils Lake were Pleasant Lake (originally named Broken Bone), Rugby, Towner, and Minot. On the construction west to Great Falls and James J. Hill's dealings with Paris Gibson, who promoted the city, see Albro S. Martin, *James J. Hill and the Opening of the Northwest* (New York: Oxford University Press, 1976), and Reps, *Cities of the American West*, 571–73.

3. Martin's *James J. Hill* is strongly biased in favor of his subject. No history of the Northern Pacific's North Dakota operations exists, although details of the railroad's land grant here are described in U.S. Congress, Joint House-Senate Committee on the Investigation of the Northern Pacific Railroad Land Grant, *Hearings*, 16 parts, March 1925 to June 1928. Robinson, *North Dakota*, chap. 6, gives a general background. A detailed study of later railroad rivalry in the northern portion of the state is John C. Hudson, "North Dakota's Railway War of 1905," *North Dakota History* 48, no. 1 (1981): 4–19. Also see William J. Wilgus, *The Railway Interrelations of the Untied States and Canada* (New Haven: Yale University Press, 1937).

4. MS, "History of the Soo Line," in Lydon files, historical, Soo Line Railway Company Records (hereafter cited as SRR), 14 pp. Also see John Gjevre, *Saga of the Soo, West from Shoreham.* (LaCrosse, Wis.: Privately printed, 1973).

5. "To the Wheat Fields in 1886 and On to Canada in 1891," undated MS in Historical Materials, folder 1, SRR. A letter from Edmund Pennington of the Soo to the Canadian Pacific's Sir Thomas G. Shaughnessy, 29 January 1903, shows that the freight business on this sparsely settled line decreased by more than 60 percent per mile north and west of Harvey toward Portal where only a few towns had been platted; Lydon files, box 3, SRR.

6. Computed from *Maps of Seasonal Precipitation Percentages of Normal by States, 1886–1938*, U.S. Department of Commerce, Weather Bureau (Washington, D.C., 1942).

7. If A is the elevator's trade area then $A = tC/640 kp$, where t = turnover rate, C = elevator capacity (bushels), k = wheat yield (bushels/acre), and p = proportion of land area in wheat. Fig. 13 is calibrated using yield data in C. M. Hennis and Rex E. Willard, "Farm Practices in Grain Farming in North Dakota," U.S. Department of Agriculture Bulletin, no. 757 (Washington, D.C., 1919).

8. The principal sources of these letters and petitions were GNS-2978, GNS-3147, GNS-3263, GNS-3585, GNS-3982, and NPS-164B.

9. A. W. Clark to J. J. Hill, 18 June 1897, GNS-3227.

10. Hill to R. S. Tyler, 27 August 1897, GNS–3263.

11. Hill to Robert Wright, 19 February 1898, GNS–3263.

12. H. Roger Grant, " 'Captive Corporation': The Farmers' Grain and Shipping Company, 1896–1945," *North Dakota History* 49, no. 1 (1982): 4–10; W. B.. Hennessey, *History of North Dakota* (Bismarck, N. Dak.: Bismarck Tribune, 1910), 428; *Poor's Manual of Railroads, 1903,* 689; *Poor's,* 1910, 1218.

13. J. Blabon to L. W. Hill, 5 May 1904, A. B. Fox to J. J. Hill, 15 June, 3 August 1904, J. J. Hill to Fox, 25 June, 5 August 1904, GNS–4100; H. T. Willey to J. J. Hill, 28 December 1903, Hill to Willey, 6 January 1904, GNS–4100.

14. Hudson, "Railway War," 6.

15. North Dakota, *Report of the Commissioners of Railroads to the Governor of North Dakota* (hereafter cited as NDR), 1912, 20.

16. NDR, 1899, 20.

17. NDR, 1916, 9.

18. L. W. Hill to D. Miller, 27 August 1904, President's Letterbooks, GNC; W. W. Broughton to F. E. Ward, 22 May 1905, GNS-3982.

19. Fourth Annual Report of the Railroad Commissioners of the Dakota Territory (Bismark, 1888); NDR, 1905; Hudson, "Railway War," 16.

20. North Dakota Public Service Commission, Biennial Report of Chief Elevator Accountant, 1918. Of 1,923 elevators in the state, 917 were owned by lines, 476 were independent, and the rest were owned by farmers; NDR, 1918, 9.

21. MS map in Lydon files, box 3, SRR.

22. Tributary areas for each elevator station were constructed (fig. 17) as Theissen polygons (all points within the boundary of a convex polygon being closer to its defining center than they are to any other center). The average proportion of each polygon's area within eight miles of its defining center increased over time as follows: 1888, 25 percent; 1900, 37 percent; 1904, 57 percent; 1906, 88 percent; final (1920), 94 percent.

Chapter 6. Railroad Towns

1. Overton, *Burlington West*, 182.

2. Reps, *Cities of the American West*, x.

3. The Northern Pacific's first townsites were located along its line from Superior to Fargo in the 1870s. Difficulties encountered at Brainerd, Glyndon, and Detroit Lakes foreshadowed later problesm, owing mainly to a lack of coordination in promotion efforts in northern Dakota. Harnsberger, "Land Speculation, Promotion, and Failure," 36–40. For railroad towns in the Red River valley of Minnesota, see Thomas W. Harvey, "The Making of Railroad Towns in Minnesota's Red River Valley" (Masters thesis, Pennsylvania State University, 1982).

4. NPL, ledger, box 69, vol. 11.

5. NPL, ledger, box 69, vol. 25; Foster County, Register of Deeds, plat book.

6. NPL, ledger, box 69, vol. 25; Eddy County, Register of Deeds, plat book; W. F. Phipps to T. F. Oakes, 15 September 1894, NPS, vol. 11, folder 30.

7. NPL, ledger, box 69, vol. 25; NPL, Minnewaukan, Town Property Book. W. B. Phipps to M. P. Martin, 28 August 1894, and C. Lamborn to T. F. Oakes, 27 March 1884, NPL, Land Commissioner's Letterpress Books; Benson County, Register of Deeds, plat book.

8. E. H. McHenry to J. W. Kendrick, 26 October 1897, Sykes to C. S. Mellen, 9, 13, and 21 July 1898, McHenry to Mellen, 21 May 1898 and 16 January 1900, NPS, box 69, file 164; Wells County, Register of Deeds, plat book; *Wells County History*, vol. 5, no. 4, 1974.

9. McHenry to Mellen, 16 January 1900, and Phipps to Mellen, 8 June 1900, NPS, box 69, folder 164.

10. McHenry to Mellen, 15 July 1901, NPS, box 69, folder 164.

11. W. J. Smith to E. J. Pearson, 6 August 1904, p. 7, NPS, box 70, folder 132.

12. Pearson to Smith, NPS, box 70, folder 132; G. S. Kyle to Pearson, 4 October 1904, and G. B. Walker to T. Cooper, 9 June 1904, NPS, box 69, folder 164-B; "Turtle Lake Township," MS in McLean County, HDP; PD, vol. 14.

13. Kyle to Pearson, 4 October 1904, NPS, box 69, folder 164-B.

14. J. Steinbrecker to H. Elliot, 31 May 1904, R. H. Johnston to J. M. Hannaford, 27 June 1904, Johnston to Elliott, 12 July 1904, Hannaford to Elliott, August 2 1904, NPS, box 69, folder 164-B.

15. Memorandum by Elliott, 10 November 1904, NPS, box 69, folder 164-B.

16. Elliott to Pearson, 10 March 1905, Elliott to Cooper, 14 May and 29 May 1905, NPS, box 69, folder 164-B.

17. McLean and Sheridan counties, Register of Deeds, plat books.

18. Charles K Wing, Foster County questionnaires, HDP; "City of Fessenden," MS in Wells County, HDP; Spokesfield, *Wells County History*, 457; Hennessy, *History of North Dakota*, 525, 627.

19. Northwest Land Company, articles of incorporation; CP, box 72, vol. 33. Gregory C. Harness, "Solomon Gilman Comstock: Prairie Laywer, Legislator and Businessman" (Masters thesis, Moorhead State College, 1976); chap. 9 describes Comstock's role in townsite matters.

20. Northwest Land Company papers, CP, box 57, folder 6.

21. Northwest Land Company, land contracts for Minot, CP, box 50; contracts for Rugby, CP, box 52; contracts for Barton and Willow City, CP, box 53; O. W. Bunham, financial statement, CP, box 57; account of Erik Ramstad, MS in Ward County, HDP.

22. L. J. Demming to Comstock, 17 November 1886, CP, box 58, folder 2.

23. Letters to Comstock from Fr. L. Reishaus, 12 September 1886, T. D. Rice, 3 June 1886, K. Stenerson, 26 May 1886, J. S. Arnold, 29 April 1887, CP, box 57.

24. A. A. White to Comstock, 25 June 1886, CP, box 57.

25. *Villard Leader*, 5 February 1887; A. Manvel to Comstock, 25 August 1886, CP, box 52.

26. Ward County, Register of Deeds, plat book; PD, vol. 6.

27. The Minnesota Loan and Trust Company was organized in March 1883 with $200,000 capital stock owned mainly by Minneapolis businessmen (Minnesota, Secretary of State, Articles of Incorporation, Book H, p. 430). This company platted the Soo's North Dakota towns until the railroad organized the Tri-State Land Company in 1906. The Minnesota Loan and Trust towns in the study area were Cathay, Coleharbor, Drake, Eckman, Egeland, Emrick, Fessenden, Gardena, Garrison, Grano, Harvey, Hurd, Kenmare, Kramer, Mylo, Overly, Rolette, Russell, Sawyer, Tolley, and Velva.

28. McHenry County, Register of Deeds, plat book.

29. Ibid.; Hennessy, *History of North Dakota*, 550.

30. C. T. Studness, Benson County questionnaires, HDP; Benson County, Register of Deeds, plat book; PD, vol. 14.

31. Delamater to Hill, 13 February 1905, Hill to Delamater, 14 February 1905, Delamater to Hill, 13 March 1905, GNS-3892.

32. Bottineau County, Register of Deeds, plat book; G. L. Scott to L. W. Hill, 17 August 1904, Hill to C. Hayden, 24 September 1904, Hayden to Hill, 10 October 1904, Hill to Hayden, 12 October 1904, GNS-3950, folder 5.

33. W. B. Phipps to F. M. Stoltze, 15 and 22 December 1902, 10, 12 and 31 January 1903; NPL, Land Commissioner's Letterpress Books. vol. 103.

34. *Fargo Forum*, 15 June 1904.

35. *Bottineau Courant*, 31 March 1905.

36. Minnesota Historical Society, *Collections*, vol. 14 (1912), 766; Frank E. Vyzralek,

"David Newton Tallman and the Development of Townsites Along the Great Northern Railway, 1905–1920," paper presented at Northern Plains History Conference, Sioux Falls, October 1981.

Chapter 7. Town Building

1. Stene to Tallman, 24 July 1905, GNS–3950.

2. W. H. Dorsey, "The Laying Out of Towns," *Engineering News* 26 (1891): 192–93, and J. J. Donovan, "The Laying Out of Cities and Additions Thereto," *Engineering News* 26 (1891): 605, summarize late nineteenth-century planning ideas in the practical terms of the engineer.

3. Hudson, "Towns of the Western Railroads," 47–48. The three types had many variations, depending especially on the angle formed between the railroad line and the township-and-range survey grid. There are also many examples of "proposed designs" for railroad towns found in the literature, but the more intricate the design, the less likely it was to be used. See, for example, the proposal of Sanford Fleming (1877) shown in J. Edward Martin, *Railway Stations of Western Canada* (White Rock, British Columbia: Studio E, 1980), 4–5.

4. White to Comstock, 31 August 1886, CP, box 57, folder 5.

5. C. R. Gray to J. T. Maher, 11 April 1913, GNS–5188; M. C. Byers, "Standard Station Grounds for Use in Prairie Country," MS in GNS–5865; R. Budd to Byers, 2 July 1913, GNS–5856.

6. The "crossed-T" form, distinguished by incorporation of a business cross street, first appeared in the study area in the plat of Kramer, surveyed in early June 1905 by C. F. Bode for Minnesota Loan and Trust (Soo Line) and in the plats of the nearby towns of Deep and Newburg, surveyed the same week by T. M. Fowble for the Dakota Development Company (Great Northern); Bottineau County, Register of Deeds, plat book. The same idea was used in every subsequent town platted by the two railroads in 1905.

7. Price, "The Central Courthouse Square," 29–60. Tallman's central squares followed the Philadelphia style identified by Price, although they were only eighty feet square in size. Kenmare's square was a standard city block (block 2 of the original townsite) with business lots arranged facing it on three sides. Ryder and Plaza had central city parks, two-hundred feet square, with business lots facing on two sides only. Bottineau, Ward, and Mountrail counties, Register of Deeds, plat books.

8. L. B. Lien, "Bottineau Plat–1890," MS in Bottineau County, HDP; Northwest Land Company, balance sheet, 1 September 1888, CP, box 57.

9. A. A. Bode to H. W. Hill, 12 January and 30 April 1884, Hill to Bode, 20 October 1884, Bode to Hill, 3 November 1884, Adolphus A. Bode files, folder H, GNC; *St. Paul Pioneer Press*, 27 March 1884.

10. Budde to Comstock, 20 August 1887, CP, box 57, folder 5.

11. Letters to Comstock from L. E. Francis, 14 March 1887, F. E. Champlin, 15 September 1887, C. F. Anderson, 10 September 1887, L. E. Blanchard, 22 March 1887, CP, box 57, folder 4.

12. *La Follette Forum*, 6 July 1906; *Plaza Pioneer*, 26 July 1906.

13. Cavalier County, Register of Deeds, plat book; Tallman to H. H. Parkhouse, 21 June 1905, GNS–3950.

14. The Tri-State Land Company was organized by the Soo Line in January 1906. Its $25,000 capital stock was held by Edmund Pennington and other Soo officials (Minnesota, Secretary of State, articles of incorporation, book L–3, p. 176).

15. Soo Line Railroad, Industrial Department, *Dozens of New Towns* (Minneapolis, 1907).

16. *Cando Herald*, 25 May 1905.

17. D. N. Tallman to R. I. Farrington, 25 July 1906, GNS–395.

18. The Dakota & Great Northern Townsite Company was incorporated 27 July 1906, six months after the Soo had organized the Tri-State company. Its $50,000 capital stock was "owned entirely by the Great Northern;" articles of incorporation, GNS–6316.

19. GNS–3950, townsites 1904–1915, files 126, 127, 128.

20. Ibid.; Ward County, Register of Deeds, plat book; memorandum, executive committee meeting, 2 March 1915. GNS–3950; L. W. Hill to R. Budd, 13 February 1915, and Budd to Hill, 16 February 1915, J. A. Coleman to L. W. Hill, 9 and 14 April 1910, GNS–3915.

21. W. N. S. Ivins, 21 July 1930, Dakota and Great Northern Townsite Company, folder 2, GNS–6316.

Chapter 8. Merchants and Trade Centers

1. Hudson, "Migration to an American Frontier," fig. 13.

2. "Pioneer Business in Minnewaukan," MS in Benson County, HDP; *Benson County Farmers Press*, 15 June 1934; Mrs. William Plummer, biography, in Benson County questionnaires, HDP.

3. William Plummer, biography, Benson County questionnaires, HDP; *Benson County Farmers Press*, 3 May 1951; Clarence F. Plummer, biography, Benson County questionnaires, HDP.

4. Shannon to Plummer, 22 March 1911, William Plummer Papers (hereafter cited as WPP).

5. Thorstein Veblen, "The Country Town," in *Absentee Ownership and Business Enterprise in Recent Times* (New York: B. W. Huebsch, 1923), 142–65.

6. "City of Fessenden," MS in Wells County, HDP, 4–5.

7. A sample of one thousand job changes in postfrontier North Dakota was computed from the HDP questionnaires. Two-thirds of those who began as merchants in North Dakota had been merchants before they moved. About 22 percent of those who arrived as farmers eventually became merchants, and 23 percent whose first Dakota job was as a clerk eventually owned mercantile establishments. Only 13 percent of the initial merchants became farmers, however. The questionnaires reached very few Dakota pioneers who left the state, making estimates of later job changes from these data unreliable.

8. Clark, "A Brief History of Towner," MS in McHenry County, HDP; Mrs. Jennie Dysart, "Esmond Village," MS in Benson County, HDP; and Alma D. Johnson, "Glenburn," MS in Renville County, HDP.

9. See, for example, G. Myers, R. McGinnis, and G. Masnick, "The Duration of Residence Approach to a Dynamic Stochastic Model of Internal Migration: A Test of the Axiom of Cumulative Inertia," *Eugenics Quarterly* 14 (1967): 121–26; P. Morrison, "Duration of Residence and Prospective Migration: The Evaluation of a Stochastic Model," *Demography* 4 (1967): 553–61; and K. Land, "Duration of Residence and Prospective Migration: Further Evidence," *Demography* 6 (1969): 113–40.

10. Conditional probabilities are defined as follows: if the proportion remaining after the first interval is p_1 and the proportion still remaining after the second interval is p_2, then the conditional probability of surviving the entire period, given survival in the first portion, is p_2/p_1.

11. Invoices and correspondence, WPP, boxes 1 and 2.

12. Plummer to Wyman, Partridge & Company, 31 March 1905, WPP, box 2. This is a sample of one from a number of such letters that Clarence Plummer wrote to distributors who sold the same goods to competitors as they did to the Plummers. The role of brand names is

discussed at length in Lewis Atherton, *Main Street on the Middle Border* (Bloomington: Indiana University Press, 1954).

13. E. O. Gunnerud to Plummer, 9 May 1910, WPP, box 2.

14. Spokesfield called Beiseker "one of the shrewdest and most noted bankers and financiers in the entire Northwest"; Spokesfield, *History of Wells County*, 390-91. Also see Clement A. Lounsberry, *North Dakota History and People* (Chicago: S. J. Clarke Publishing Co., 1917), vol. 2, 831. Beiseker was a local agent for Northern Pacific lands in Wells County and purchased some of the acreage for himself at low prices, claiming the lands were of little value. The Northern Pacific's land commissioner later learned otherwise and abruptly informed Beiseker that "your further service in behalf of this department will be hereafter dispensed with." W. B. Phipps to Beiseker, 12 February 1896, NPL, Land Commissioner's Letterpress Books.

15. Henry A. Castle, *Minnesota, Its Story and Biography* (Chicago: Lewis Publishing Co., 1915), vol. 3, 1540. Qvale organized an average of six banks a year for Tallman between 1905 and 1912.

16. E. Johnson et al. to Tallman, 1 July 1905, L. W. Hill to A. H. Hogeland, 24 August 1905, GNS-3950.

17. Lösch, *Economics of Location*, 139-67.

18. Invoices and correspondence, WPP, box 3. Buying in carload lots was a bold act for a small town merchant: "A firm at Minnewaukan received a car load of canned fruit at one time, way last winter, and has not got through talking about it yet in the local paper;" *Jamestown Weekly Alert*, 20 May 1886. The merchant was not identified, although it was not William Plummer.

19. Plummer to Farwell, 12 October 1911, Farwell to Plummer, 30 October 1911, WPP, box. 3. Plummer's dealings with distant wholesalers are given context through a comparison with one Canadian case. The Dixon Brothers, general merchants at Maple Creek, Saskatchewan, conducted their business much like the Plummers. See Donald Kerr, "Wholesale Trade on the Canadian Plains in the Late Nineteenth Century: Winnipeg and Its Competition," in *The Settlement of the West*, ed. Howard Palmer (Calgary: University of Calgary, 1977), 130-52.

20. Individual businessmen urging branch line extensions generally emphasized the trade that could be built up in an unserved area as a result. City commercial clubs were more likely to urge a railroad to come to their town for the good of the community as a whole. Commercial clubs in Fargo and Grand Forks, N. Dak., and in Moorhead, Minn., tried to interest the Soo Line in building lines there; but Edmund Pennington was firm in expressing no interest. E. S. Tyler to Pennington, 22 April 1903, Pennington to Tyler, 24 April 1903, Alvin Robinson to Pennington, 29 September 1904, Pennington to Robinson, 30 September 1904, W. K. Nash to Pennington, 24 April 1903, Pennington to Nash, 29 April 1903, historical materials, SRR. Garrison businessmen tried to interest the Northern Pacific in building west of Turtle Lake in May 1910 by offering free right-of-way and other inducements. Railroad president Howard Elliott ordered twenty-four teams to work grading the line in June, instructing his chief engineer to "do enough work up there to hold our rights a little." In July, Elliott ordered the work to halt after Louis Hill informed him that the Great Northern was going to build such a line (which, of course, it never did). In 1925 W. G. Connors, president of the Roseglen State Bank, proposed a local bond issue to entice the Northern Pacific to build to his inland town; again, it was the Great Northern that made the weaker Northern Pacific back away from the plan. W. G. Connors to Northern Pacific Railroad, 6 April 1925, H. F. O'Hare to C. M. Levy, 7 May 1910, O'Hare to Elliott, 13 May 1910, Elliott to W. L. Darling, 21 June 1910, Elliott to Darling, 26 July 1910, Elliott to Charles Steele, 29 June 1911, NPS, box 69, folder 164-B.

21. NDR, 1909, 19-21; *McCumber Herald*, 5 October 1905.

22. The support for lower rates was voiced by the commercial clubs of Fargo, Grand Forks,

Minot, and Dickinson, all wholesaling centers; NDR, 1910, 21, 28, 95.

23. Local newspapers sometimes carried weekly "directories" of out-of-town businesses. After parcel post was inaugurated, Fargo stores advertised in newspapers at Goodrich (185 miles away), Leeds (200 miles), and York (210 miles); *Goodrich Weekly Citizen*, 25 January 1914, *York Citizen*, 22 July 1915, *Leeds News*, 14 May 1914.

24. North Dakota, 7th Session Laws, chap. 179; 8th Session Laws, sec. 2985. Towns losing railroad agencies at this time included Bartlett, Surrey, Maza, Perth, and Woburn. The commissioners ruled against the Great Northern's request to close the Landa agency. Flora, which had lost its agency in 1903, had an agent reinstated after the Regan bill passed. NDR, 1903, viii; NDR, 1908, 20.

25. Howard Elliott to McKenzie, GNS–4139. North Dakota, 7th Session Laws, 169. A $500 fine was to be levied against any railroad failing to comply. Amended to exempt one train; 9th Session Laws, 200.

26. U.S. Post Office Department, Annual Report, 1904, 558. Brinsmade's fourth-class post office was one that supported four RFD routes; U.S. Post Office Department, *List of Post Offices in the United States* (Philadelphia: George F. Lasher, 1901, 1912).

27. Fuller, *RFD*, chap. 5.

28. Anthony H. Simon, "The Battle for Parcel Post," *Journal of the West* 13, no. 4 (1974): 79–89. Opposition to parcel post centered in Chicago wholesaler and retailer organizations that wanted to prevent mail-order houses from gaining an advantage on them. As late as 1911, however, the president of Sears and Roebuck was on record as being opposed to parcel post; Ibid., 81.

29. *Devils Lake World*, 1 January 1914. Small-town merchants also began making comparisons with catalog prices; *Brinsmade Star*, 3 April 1914.

30. Jeffrey G. Williamson, *Late Nineteenth Century American Development, A General Equilibrium History* (Cambridge: Cambridge University Press, 1974), 200.

Chapter 9. Social Relations

1. John D. Hicks, "The Significance of the Small Town in American History," in *Reflections of Western Historians*, ed. John Alexander Carroll, (Tucson: University of Arizona Press, 1969), 155–66; Thorstein Veblen, "The Country Town," 147.

2. For a different view, see Robert V. Hine, *Community on the American Frontier* (Norman: University of Oklahoma Press, 1980).

3. Malin, *Grassland of North America*, 316.

4. Computed from "The Dakota Territorial Census of 1885," *Collections*, State Historical Society of North Dakota, vol. 4 (1913), 338–448.

5. Ibid. and John C. Hudson, "The Study of Western Frontier Populations," in *The American West: New Perspectives, New Dimensions*, ed. Jerome O. Steffen (Norman: University of Oklahoma Press, 1979), 35-60.

6. Hudson, "Migration to an American Frontier," 256–58.

7. Hudson, "Western Frontier Populations," 57–58.

8. Ole Hanson, Ransom County questionnaires, HDP.

9. Alam D. Johnson, "History of Truro," 1; MS in Bottineau County, HDP.

10. Paul Voisey, "Boosting the Small Prairie Town, 1904–1931," in *Town and City*, ed. Artibise, 147–76; and Gary Lucht, "Scobey's Touring Pros: Wheat, Baseball, and Illicit Booze," *Montana Magazine of Western History* 20 (Summer 1970): 88–93. Scobey's bitter rival was Plentywood, thirty-five miles away.

11. Some versions of the North Dakota Historical Data Project questionnaires asked pioneer respondents to list the most common types of social gatherings in the frontier period. The

responses were, in descending order of frequency: visiting, dances, parties (house gatherings), card playing, church socials, sports, picnics, and lodge meetings. (Summary is based on a state-wide random sample of three hundred questionnaires carrying this information).

12. An example may illustrate the point. Donnybrook, an independent townsite platted along the Soo Line northwest of Minot in 1901, had no more than twenty business houses in its early years, but it did not lack for social organizations. The Odd Fellows organized in 1905, platted the town's first cemetery in 1907, and constructed a meeting hall in 1908. The Modern Woodmen of America were organized at Donnybrook in 1901, two years before the village was incorporated. Other organizations and dates of founding were the A. O. U. W. (1902), Royal Neighbors (1907), and American Legion (1920); the Legion later added a women's auxiliary. "These orders were the chief places social contacts took place." Social life also was served by a Methodist (1903) and later a Roman Catholic church (1904); congregations of Moravians and Norwegian Baptists held services for a few years, but later disbanded. Isabel B. Jaques, "History of Donnybrook," MS in Ward County, HDP; Ward County, Register of Deeds, plat book.

13. Rural community studies of the U.S. Department of Agriculture, undertaken from the late 1930s through the early 1950s, identified "communities" (which can be roughly equated with trading areas) and "neighborhoods" (spatial groupings of people defined in terms of visiting patterns, club membership, and the like). The average community so defined contained between three and five neighborhoods.

14. Ostergren's thorough study attributes the location of churches in rural areas to a "physical limit to the distance people would travel to worship, given the travel technology of the day." From his own evidence, however, it would seem that small parishes (closely spaced churches, located wherever communicants lived) were more likely a habit, directly imported from the European past, rather than a plan based on minimizing travel. Robert C. Ostergren, "The Immigrant Church as a Symbol of Community and Place in the Upper Midwest," *Great Plains Quarterly* 1 (1981): 225–38.

15. Harriet Manly Wing (Charles K. Wing), Foster County questionnaires, HDP; C. Ross Bloomquist, "Planning and Building a Courthouse for Foster County, 1907–1912," *North Dakota History* 49, no. 2 (1982): 21.

16. Jennie Dysart, "Esmond Village," MS in Benson County, HDP.

17. Mrs. William Plummer, biography, in Benson County questionnaires, HDP.

18. Ibid.; and "Minnewaukan, Dakota—1883," MS in Benson County, HDP. Theodore Morrison, *Chautauqua* (Chicago: University of Chicago Press, 1974), 162.

19. Laura Nelson Plummer, biography, in Benson County questionnaires, HDP.

20. Milo A. Shipman, "Gooseneck Township and Colgan," MS in Divide County, HDP, 6.

21. A. H. Anderson and Glen V. Vergeront, "Rural Communities and Organizations, A Study of Group Life in Wells County, North Dakota," North Dakota Agricultural Experiment Station Bulletin, no. 351, June 1948; quotation on 74–75.

22. Ibid., 35–48.

23. Voisey, "Boosting the Small Prairie Town," 164–65.

Chapter 10. Passing the Limits

1. *Minneapolis Tribune*, 14 January 1917.

2. Soo Line Railroad, *Business Directory*, 1918, 159–237.

3. Northwest Land Company papers, box 57, folder 6, and box 72, vol. 33, CP. Old St. John was an inland town from 1882 to 1888 with perhaps half-a-dozen business houses operating at any one time. Comstock and White platted their towns of Rolla and St. John in 1888, when the railroad arrived. Rolla replaced the short-lived inland town of Boydton, about a mile

north of the present town of Rolla. Rolette County, Register of Deeds, plat book; Laura Thompson Law, *History of Rolette County, North Dakota* (Minneapolis: Lund Press, 1953), 74-75, 92.

4. Tallman's Northern Town and Land Company was the short-lived successor of his Dakota Development Company. Six towns in the study area (Hamar, Tokio, Warwick, Hong, Loraine, and Dunning) were platted under the auspices of Northern Town and Land between 1906 and 1909. Hong and Dunning were little more than elevator sites.

5. Kelly to Hill, 7 February 1905, Hill to Kelly, 14 February 1905, GNS-3982.

6. *Cando Herald*, 7 September 1905.

7. *Grand Forks Herald*, 30 November 1905.

8. H. Stene to D. N. Tallman, 24 July 1905, GNS-3950.

9. *McCumber Herald*, 5 October 1905, 8 February 1906, 23 April 1907, 19 September 1907, and 23 January 1908; *Rolette County Journal*, 1 September 1905, 20 October 1905, 2 February 1906, 9 August 1907, and 20 September 1907.

10. L. W. Hill to E. Pennington, 20 August 1907, Pennington to Hill, 21 August 1907, GNS-3950, folder 1.

11. W. D. Washburn (1831-1912), the Minneapolis miller and first president of the Soo Line Railroad, also developed the lignite mining industry near Wilton, N. Dak. His Bismarck, Washburn & Great Falls Railway line from Bismarck to Wilton was constructed in 1900, extended to Washburn in 1901, and completed to Underwood in 1903. W. D. Washburn platted the towns of Wilton (1899) and Underwood (1903) before selling his line to the Soo in 1904. McLean County, Register of Deeds, plat book; "History," MS in Lydon files-historical, SRR.

12. H. M. Blackstone to J. G. Woodworth, 8 February 1923, NPS, folder 164-B.

13. R. E. Taft to L. W. Hill, 10 April 1906, James J. Hill desk files, folder 2, GNC. Hogeland to Hill, 9 March 1906, B. Campbell to Hill, 9 May 1906, GNS-3982.

14. Joseph J. Voeller to James J. Hill, 11 May 1906, L. W. Hill to Voeller, 14 May 1906, GNS-3892.

15. James J. Hill desk files, folder 11, Rugby-Fort Stevenson extension, 1905, GNC. P. E. Thian to R. E. Taft, 20 March 1905, L. W. Hill to Howard Elliott, 30 May and 20 August, 1910, GNS-3982.

16. Louis Hill was acting on his father's orders. At the beginning of the 1905 "Wheat Line war," James J. Hill—then in New York—wired a coded message to his son in St. Paul telling him to stand up to the Soo-Canadian Pacific: "Shaughnessy [president of the CP] should understand that for every mile he builds to invade us we will make reprisal that will be most expensive to his Co. and himself;" J. J. Hill to L. W. Hill, 26 September 1904, GNS-3892. E. Pennington to L. W. Hill, 25 September 1904, L. W. Hill to J. J. Hill, 26 September 1904, GNS-3892.

17. Pennington to L. W. Hill, 5 February 1910, Hill to Pennington, 7 February 1910, Pennington to Hill, 17 February 1910, GNS-4544.

18. Pennington to Hill, 19 February 1910, GNS-4544.

19. L. W. Hill to L. C. Gilman, 23 February 1910, A. H. Hogeland to Hill, 7 June 1910, GNS-4544; *Esmond Bee*, 14 May 1910.

20. *Esmond Bee*, 7 May 1910.

21. *New Rockford Transcript*, 12 August 1910; L. W. Hill to D. N. Tallman, 30 June 1910, GNS-3982; *Esmond Bee*, 1 July 1911; J. M. Gruber to J. H. Taylor, 15 June 1911, GNS-7613.

22. Foster, Eddy, Wells, Pierce, and McHenry counties, Register of Deeds, plat books; *New Rockford Transcript*, 3 June 1910; PD, vol. 17 (1910) and vol. 18 (1912).

23. Vyzralek, "David Newton Tallman," 10-12.

24. W. H. Goeson to L. W. Hill, 24 March 1911, Edward Schatz to Hill, 4 November 1910, Arvestad to Hill, 10 October 1910, GNS-4544.

25. *Esmond Bee*, 1 April 1911; D. N. Tallman to L. W. Hill, 10 June 1910, Hill to Tallman, 20 June 1910, GNS–4544.

26. Weekly reports from Great Northern traveling agents to Geo. M. Emerson, Assistant General Manager, 19 September–25 November 1912, H. R. Mitchell to Emerson, 31 March 1913, GNS–4544.

27. General Superintendent to G. M. Emerson, 19 September 1912, GNS–4544.

28. C. H. Babcock to L. W. Hill, 30 November 1909, GNS–3950.

29. *Esmond Bee* and *New Rockford Transcript*, 6 July 1912.

30. Walsh, Ramsey, Benson, Pierce, and McHenry counties, Register of Deeds, plat books. W. H. Killen was the Soo (Tri-State) land commissioner at this time, having succeeded Cyrus A. Campbell, who had become disillusioned with the Soo's townsite efforts in marginal areas of northern Wisconsin and Minnesota. Before leaving Minneapolis for the Pacific Northwest in November 1910, Campbell offered his services to the Great Northern; the correspondence record does not contain a reply, however. Campbell to L. W. Hill, 15 November 1910, GNS–3950.

31. Walsh, Ramsey, Benson, Pierce, and McHenry counties, Register of Deeds, miscellaneous books (notices of vacation). Funston, Comstock, Tilden, Ramsey, Darby, Elmo, and Sardis were vacated wholly or partially (at least 50 percent vacation). Egan was renamed Balta.

32. *Portland Oregon Journal*, 20 February 1913, *St. Paul Dispatch*, 24 January 1913, clippings in GNS–5188.

33. L. W. Hill to C. R. Gray, 21 June 1913, A. H. Hogeland to Gray, 9 November 1912, GNS–5188.

34. Tallman to C. R. Gray, 5 February 1913, Gray to J. T. Maher, 18 April 1913, Tallman to Gray, 22 April 1913, Maher to Tallman, 23 April 1913, Gray to Maher 11 April 1913, GNS–5188.

35. H. A. Jackson to W. P. Kenny, 19 May 1913, J. T. Maher to Ralph M. Budd, 27 June 1916, GNS–5188.

36. Tallman to Ralph Budd, 19 May 1916, GNS–5188.

37. Vyzralek, "David Newton Tallman," 13.

38. *New Rockford Transcript*, 6 May 1910.

39. *Esmond Bee*, 24 February 1912.

40. *Jamestown Weekly Alert*, 19 August 1886.

41. *Bottineau Courant*, 11 December 1903.

42. *Towner Tribune*, 10 August 1905.

43. Sources used as a basis for these calculations are as follows: entries for the Farmers Grain and Shipping Company Railroad, *Poor's Manual of Railroads*, 1903, 62; 1908, 629; 1910, 1218; 1915, 98. Dakota and Great Northern Railway Company, folder 2, GNC. E. H. McHenry to C. S. Mellen, 21 May 1898, McHenry to J. W. Kendrick, 26 October 1897, NPS, folder 164–A. Northern Pacific Railway, Branch Line Data, Eastern District, 1922, NPS, folder 164–B. Edmund Pennington to Thomas G. Shaughnessy, 29 January 1903, Historical Materials, folder 1, SRR.

Bibliography

Bibliography

Manuscript Collections

The letter abbreviations are those used in notes to the text.

CP   Solomon Gilman Comstock Papers, 1872-1939. Northwest Minnesota Historical Center, Moorhead State University, Moorhead, Minn. Boxes 50–53, 57–58, 67–69, and 72 contain materials relating to the Northwest Land Company.

DBM   Dun & Bradstreet (predecessors) Credit Ledgers, 1840–1895. Baker Library, Harvard University, Cambridge, Mass. The Dakotas are included in vols. 1–3 of the Western Territorial Series.

DP   Grenville M. Dodge Papers. Iowa Historical Society, Des Moines, Iowa. Boxes 152–154, 170, 175, and 218–219 contain material on Dodge's role in townsite matters.

GNC   Great Northern Railway Collection. Minnesota Historical Society, Division of Archives and Manuscripts, St. Paul, Minn.

GNS   Great Northern Railway, Presidents Subject Files. Part of GNC, but containing historical materials arranged topically by the railroad company.

HDP   Historical Data Project Files. State Historical Society of North Dakota, Bismarck, N. Dak. Contains several thousand autobiographical sketches in questionnaire form completed during the late 1930s by pioneer residents of the state. Additional files on towns, ranching, ethnic groups, and other subjects are arranged topically and by place.

NPS   Northern Pacific Railway Collection, Presidents Subject Files. Minnesota Historical Society, Division of Archives and Manuscripts. Similar to Great Northern's subject files.

NPL   Northern Pacific Land Department Records. Part of NPS, containing correspondence and ledgers; other materials relating to townsites found in NPS.

SRR   Soo Line Railroad Company Records. Minnesota Historical Society, Division of Archives and Manuscripts. A much less complete collection than for the Great Northern or Northern Pacific companies; about ten boxes of historical materials, advertising, maps, and some correspondence.

WPP   William Plummer Papers. State Historical Society of North Dakota, Bismarck. Collection A–97. Largely uncatalogued business correspondence, invoices, and some personal papers of the Plummer family of Minnewaukan. N. Dak.

United States Government Documents

U.S. Department of Agriculture. *Farm Practices in Grain Farming in North Dakota.* Prepared by C.M. Hennis and Rex E. Willard. *Bulletin* no. 757, Washington, D.C., 1919.

U.S. Department of the Interior. Census Office. *Statistics of the Population of the United States at the Tenth Census (June 1, 1880).* Washington, D.C., 1883.

——. *Report on Population of the United States at the Eleventh Census: 1890.* Parts 1 and 2. Washington, D.C., 1895.

——. *Eleventh Census.* Report on the Statistics of Agriculture, vol. 5. Washington, D.C., 1895.

U.S. Census Office. *Twelfth Census of the United States, 1900.* Population, parts 1 and 2. Washington, D.C., 1901.

——. *Twelfth Census.* Agriculture, parts I and II. Washington, D.C., 1902.

U.S. Department of Commerce. Bureau of the Census. *Thirteenth Census of the United States, 1910.* Population, vol. 1. Washington, D.C., 1913.

——. *Thirteenth Census.* Agriculture, Reports by States, vol. 7. Washington, D.C., 1913.

——. *Fourteenth Census of the United States, 1920.* Population, vol. 2. Washington, D.C., 1922.

——. *Fourteenth Census.* Agriculture, vol. 4, Part 1. Washington, D.C., 1922.

U.S. Department of Commerce. Weather Bureau. *Maps of Seasonal Precipitation Percentages of Normal by States, 1886*–1938. Washington, D.C., 1942.

U.S. Congress. *House Executive Documents.* "Offers and Contracts for Carrying the Mails." 46th Cong., 2d sess., vol. 23.

——. *House Executive Documents.* "Offers and Contracts for Carrying the Mails." 48th Cong., 1st sess., vol. 23.

——. *House Executive Documents.* "Offers and Contracts for Carrying the Mails." 49th Cong., 1st sess., vol. 22.

——. *House Executive Documents.* "Offers and Contracts for Carrying the Mails." 50th Cong., 2d sess., vol. 23.

——. *House Executive Documents.* "Contracts for Carrying the Mails." 51st Cong., 1st sess., vol. 29.

——. *House Executive Documents.* "Offers and Contracts for Carrying the Mails." 51st Cong., 2d sess., vol. 32.

——. *House Executive Documents.* "Offers and Contracts for Carrying the Mails." 52d Cong., 1st sess., vol. 13.

——. *House Miscellaneous Documents.* "Report of the Second-Assistant Postmaster General." 54th Cong., 2d sess., vol. 11.

——. *House Executive Documents.* "Contracts for Carrying the Mails." 57th Cong., 1st sess., vol. 21.

U.S. Congress. Joint House-Senate Committee. *Investigation of the Northern Pacific Railroad Land Grant, Hearings.* 69th Cong., 2d sess., 1926.

U.S. Post Office Department. *Report of the Postmaster General.* Washington, D.C., 1896.

——. *Annual Report.* Washington, D.C., 1900–1910.

United States Statutes at Large, Vol. 13, 367–68.

——. vol. 16, 378.

State and Territorial Documents

Dakota Territory. *Annual Report of the Railroad Commissioners*, 1887–1888.

Minnesota. Secretary of State. *Articles of Incorporation Records*, 1883, 1906.

North Dakota. Agricultural Experiment Station. *Rural Communities and Organizations, A Study of Group Life in Wells County, North Dakota.* Prepared by A. H. Anderson and Glen V. Vergeront. Bulletin no. 351. Fargo, N. Dak., 1948.
——. Board of Railroad Commissioners. *Biennial Report*, 1920.
North Dakota. Commissioner of Agriculture and Labor. *Biennial Report to the Governor of North Dakota*, 1894–1912.
North Dakota. Commissioner of Railroads. *Annual Report*, 1890–1918.
North Dakota. Public Service Commission. *Biennial Report of Chief Elevator Accountant*, 1918.
North Dakota. Legislative Assembly. *Session Laws*, 1901–1912.
North Dakota. Senate. *Journal.* 1905 State Census. 10th sess., 1907.

North Dakota Local Documents

Benson County, Minnewaukan. Register of Deeds. Plat book.
Bottineau County, Bottineau. Register of Deeds. Plat book.
Cavalier County, Langdon. Register of Deeds. Plat book.
Eddy County, New Rockford. Register of Deeds. Plat book.
Foster County, Carrington. Register of Deeds. Plat book.
McHenry County, Towner. Register of Deeds. Plat book.
McLean County, Washburn. Register of Deeds. Plat book.
Mountrail County, Stanley. Register of Deeds. Plat book.
Pierce County, Rugby. Register of Deeds. Plat book.
Ramsey County, Devils Lake. Register of Deeds. Plat book.
Renville County, Mohall. Register of Deeds. Plat book.
Rolette County, Rolla. Register of Deeds. Plat book.
Sheridan County, McClusky. Register of Deeds. Plat book.
Towner County, Cando. Register of Deeds. Plat book.
Walsh County, Grafton. Register of Deeds. Plat book.
Ward County, Minot. Register of Deeds. Plat book.
Wells County, Fessenden. Register of Deeds. Plat book.

Newspapers

Balfour Messenger, 1906, 1910.
Benson County Farmers Press, 1934-1951.
Bottineau Courant, 1903–1905.
Brinsmade Star, 1914.
Cando Herald, 1905.
Devils Lake World, 1914.
Esmond Bee, 1905, 1910–12.
Fargo Forum, 1904.
Goodrich Weekly Citizen, 1914.
Grand Forks Herald, 1904–1905.
Jamestown Weekly Alert, 1886.
LaFollette Forum, 1906.
Larimore Pioneer, 1882–83.
Leeds News, 1914.
McCumber Herald, 1905–1908.

Minneapolis Tribune, 1917.
New Rockford Transcript, 1910.
Plaza Pioneer, 1906–1907.
Rolette County Journal, 1905–1908.
St. Paul Pioneer Press, 1884.
Towner Tribune, 1905.
Villard Leader, 1886–88.
York Citizen, 1915.

Directories

Polk, R. L., and Company. *North Dakota, South Dakota, Montana Gazetteer and Business Directory.* Vols. 1–21. St. Paul, Minn., 1879–80 through 1918–19.
——. *North Dakota State Gazetteer and Business Directory.* St. Paul, Minn., 1920.
Poor's Manual of Railroads. Vols. 13–53. New York: H. V. and H. W. Poor, 1880 through 1920.
Soo Line Railroad. *Business Directory.* Minneapolis, Minn., 1918.
U.S. Post Office Department. *Post Office Directory.* List of Post Offices in the United States. Washington, D.C., 1870.
——. *United States Official Postal Guide.* Philadelphia: George F. Lasher, printer; 1892, 1901–1902, 1909, 1911–20.

Maps and Atlases

Map of North Dakota. 1: 1,267,200. Buffalo, N.Y.: J. N. Matthews Co., 1908.
Minneapolis, St. Paul, and S. Ste. Marie Railway. *Soo Line Map of North Dakota.* 1: 1,267,200. Buffalo, N.Y.: J. N. Matthews Co., 1928.
North Dakota Commissioner of Agriculture and Labor. *Official Map of North Dakota.* 1: 1,267,200. Bismarck, 1902.
North Dakota Commissioner of Railroads. *Map of North Dakota.* 1: 1,330,560. Chicago: Rand, McNally & Co., 1905.
North Dakota State Geological Survey. *Geologic Highway Map of North Dakota*, by John P. Bluemle. Miscellaneous map no. 19. 1: 1,013,760. Grand Forks, 1977.
Standard Atlas of Benson County. Chicago: George Ogle & Co., 1910.
——. Chicago: George Ogle & Co., 1929.
Standard Atlas of Bottineau County. Chicago: George Ogle & Co., 1929.
Standard Atlas of Eddy County. Chicago: George Ogle & Co., 1929.
Standard Atlas of Foster County. Chicago: George Ogle & Co., 1929.
Standard Atlas of McHenry County. Chicago: George Ogle & Co., 1910.
Standard Atlas of McLean County. Chicago: George Ogle & Co., 1914.
Standard Atlas of Pierce County. Chicago: George Ogle & Co., 1910.
Standard Atlas of Ramsey County. Chicago: George Ogle & Co., 1909.
——. Chicago: George Ogle & Co., 1928.
Standard Atlas of Renville County. Chicago: George Ogle & Co., 1914.
Standard Atlas of Rolette County. Chicago: George Ogle & Co., 1910.
——. Chicago: George Ogle & Co., 1928.
Standard Atlas of Sheridan County. Chicago: George Ogle & Co., 1914.
Standard Atlas of Towner County. Chicago: George Ogle & Co., 1928.
Standard Atlas of Ward County. Chicago: George Ogle & Co., 1915.
Standard Atlas of Wells County. Chicago: George Ogle & Co., 1915.

——. Chicago: George Ogle & Co., 1929.
U.S. Department of the Interior. General Land Office. *Territory of Dakota*. 1: 1,584,000. Senate Executive Document 120, 1879.
——. *State of North Dakota*. 1: 760,320. 1889.
U.S. Department of the Interior. Geological Survey. *Western United States*. 1:250,000 series. NL 14–2: New Rockford; NL 14–1: McClusky; NM 14–11: Devils Lake; NM 14–10: Minot.

Secondary Sources

Arnold, H. V. *The Early History of the Devils Lake Country*. Privately printed, 1920.
Artibise, Alan F. J. "Boosterism and the Development of Prairie Cities." In *Town and City: Aspects of Western Canadian Urbanism*, edited by Alan F. J. Artibise, 209–35. Canadian Plains Studies, no. 10. Regina, Sask.: Canadian Plains Research Center, 1981.
Atherton, Lewis. *Main Street on the Middle Border*. Bloomington: Indiana University Press, 1954.
——. *The Frontier Merchant in Mid-America*. Columbia: University of Missouri Press, 1971.
Bannister, Turpin C. "Early Town Planning in New York State." *Journal of the Society of Architectural Historians* 3 (1943): 36–42.
Barnett, LeRoy. "The Buffalo Bone Commerce on the Northern Plains." *North Dakota History* 39 (1972): 23–42.
Barton, Bonnie. "The Creation of Centrality." *Annals*, Association of American Geographers, 68 (1978): 34–44.
Berry, Brian J. L. *Geography of Market Centers and Retail Distribution*. Englewood Cliffs, N. J.: Prentice-Hall, 1967.
Billington, Ray A. "The Origin of the Land Speculator as a Frontier Type." *Agricultural History* 19 (1945): 204–12.
Bloomquist, C. Ross. "Planning and Building a Courthouse for Foster County." *North Dakota History* 49, no. 2 (1982): 17–24.
Bryant, Keith L., Jr. *Arthur E. Stilwell: Promoter With A Hunch*. Nashville: Vanderbilt University Press, 1971.
Burdick, Usher. "Recollections and Reminiscences of Grahams Island." *North Dakota History* 16 (1949): 5–29.
Castle, Henry A. *Minnesota, Its Story and Biography*. Chicago: Lewis Publishing Co., 1915.
Christaller, Walter. *Central Places in Southern Germany*. Translated by Carlisle W. Baskin. Englewood Cliffs, N.J.: Prentice-Hall, 1966.
Cochran, Thomas C. *Railroad Leaders, 1845–1890*. New York: Russell and Russell, 1953.
Colten, Craig. "Entrepreneurs' Allurements: Grid Streets and Gift Lots in Ohio, 1788–1820." Paper presented at annual meeting, Association of American Geographers, Denver, April 1983.
Conzen, Michael P. "The American Urban System in the Nineteenth Century." In *Geography and the Urban Environment, Progress in Research and Applications*, edited by D. T. Herbert and R. J. Johnston, chap. 9. London and New York: John Wiley & Sons, 1981.
Cushing, Marshall. *The Story of Our Post Office*. Boston: A. M. Thayer & Co., 1893.
Dahms, Fredrick A. "The Evolution of Settlement Systems, A Canadian Example, 1851–1970." *Journal of Urban History* 7 (1981): 169–204.
"The Dakota Territorial Census of 1885." *Collections*, State Historical Society of North Dakota, 4 (1913): 338–448.
De Noyer, Charles. "History of Fort Totten." *Collection,*, State Historical Society of North Dakota, 3 (1910): 178–237.

Dodge, Grenville M. *How We Built the Union Pacific Railway*. Council Bluffs, Iowa: Monarch Printing Co., n.d.

Donaldson, Thomas. *The Public Domain*. Washington, D.C.: U.S. Government Printing Office, 1884.

Donovan, J. J. "The Laying Out of Cities and Additions Thereto." *Engineering News*, 26 December 1891, 605.

Dorsey, W. H. "The Laying Out of Towns." *Engineering News*, 29 August 1891, 192–93.

Farnham, Wallace D. "Grenville Dodge and the Union Pacific: A Study of Historical Legend." *Journal of American History* 51 (1965): 632–50.

Fuller, Wayne E. *RFD: The Changing Face of Rural America*. Bloomington: Indiana University Press, 1964.

Gates, Paul W. *The Illinois Central Railroad and Its Colonization Work*. Cambridge, Mass.: Harvard University Press, 1934.

Gjevre, John. *Saga of the Soo: West from Shoreham*. Privately printed, 1973.

Glaab, Charles N. "Visions of Metropolis: William Gilpin and Theories of City Growth in the American West." *Wisconsin Magazine of History* 45 (Autumn 1961): 21–31.

Glassner, Martin Ira. "The Mandan Migrations, PreContact to 1876." *Journal of the West* 13 (1974): 25–46.

Grant, H. Roger. "Iowa's New Communities: Townsite promotion Along the Chicago Great Western Railway's Omaha Extension." Paper read at Northern Great Plains History Conference, Sioux Falls, S. Dak., October 1981.

——. "Captive Corporation: The Farmers' Grain and Shipping Company, 1896–1945." *North Dakota History* 49, no. 1 (1982): 4–10.

Greever, William S. *Arid Domain: The Sante Fe Railway and Its Western Land Grant*. Stanford, Calif.: Stanford University Press, 1954.

Grodinsky, Julius. *Transcontinental Railway Strategy, 1869–1893*. Philadelphia: University of Pennsylvania Press, 1962.

Gue, B. F. *History of Iowa*. Vol. 4. New York: Century History Company, 1903.

Hamburg, James F. "Railroads and the Settlement of South Dakota during the Great Dakota Boom, 1878–1887." *South Dakota History* 5 (1975): 165–78.

——. "Paper Towns in South Dakota." *Journal of the West*. 16, no. 1 (1977): 40–42.

Hammer, Kenneth C. "Railroads and the Frontier Garrisons of Dakota Territory." *North Dakota History* 46 (Summer 1979): 24–34.

Harness, Gregory C. "Solomon Gilman Comstock: Prairie Lawyer, Legislator and Businessman." Master's thesis, Moorhead State College, 1976.

Harnsberger, John L. "Land Speculation, Promotion, and Failure, The Northern Pacific Railroad, 1870–1873." *Journal of the West* 9, no. 1 (1970): 33–45.

Harvey, Thomas W. "The Making of Railroad Towns in Minnesota's Red River Valley." Master's thesis, Pennsylvania State University, 1982.

Hedges, James B. "The Colonization Work of the Northern Pacific Railroad." *Mississippi Valley Historical Review* 13 (1926): 311–42.

Hennessey, W. B. *History of North Dakota*. Bismarck, N.D.: Bismarck Tribune, 1910.

Hicks, John D. "The Significance of the Small Town in American History." In *Reflections of Western Historians*, edited by John Alexander Carroll. Tucson: University of Arizona Press, 1969.

Hine, Robert V. *Community on the American Frontier*. Norman: University of Oklahoma Press, 1980.

Hirshson, Stanley P. *Grenville M. Dodge: Soldier, Politician, Railroad Pioneer*. Bloomington: Indiana University Press, 1967.

Hofsommer, Donovan L. "Townsite Development along Oklahoma's Beaver, Meade and Engle-
wood Railroad." *Southwest Heritage* 4 (Fall 1974): 27–32.
——. "Townsite Development on the Wichita Falls and Northwestern Railway." *Great Plains
Journal* 16 (1977): 107–22.
——. "Town Building on a Texas Short Line: The Quanah, Acme and Pacific Railway, 1909–
1929." *Arizona and the West* 21 (1979): 355–68.
Hudson, John C. "Migration to an American Frontier." *Annals*, Association of American Geo-
graphers, 66 (1976): 242–65.
——. "The Plains Country Town." In *The Great Plains: Environment and Culture*, edited by
Brian W. Blouet and Frederick C. Luebke. Lincoln: University of Nebraska Press, 1979.
——. "The Study of Western Frontier Populations." In *The American West: New Perspec-
tives, New Dimensions*, edited by Jerome O. Steffen. Norman: University of Oklahoma
Press, 1979.
——. "North Dakota's Railway War of 1905." *North Dakota History* 48, no. 1 (1981): 4–19.
——. "Towns of the Western Railroads." *Great Plains Quarterly* 2, no. 1 (1982): 41–54.
Jackson, J. B. *American Space: The Centennial Years, 1865–1876*. New York: W. W. Norton,
1972.
Jakle, John A. *The American Small Town: Twentieth Century Place Images*. Hamden, Conn.:
The Shoe String Press, 1982.
Johnson, Arthur M., and Barry E. Supple. *Boston Capitalists and Western Railroads*. Cam-
bridge, Mass.: Harvard University Press, 1967.
Jordan, Terry G. "Early Northeast Texas and the Evolution of Western Ranching." *Annals,
Association of American Geographers*, 67 (1977): 276–98.
——. *Trails to Texas, Southern Roots of Western Cattle Ranching*. Lincoln: University of
Nebraska Press, 1981.
Kerr, Donald. "Wholesale Trade on the Canadian Plains in the Late Nineteenth Century: Win-
nipeg and Its Competition." In *The Settlement of the West*, edited by Howard Palmer,
130–52. Calgary: University of Calgary, 1977.
Killie, E. S. "The Richard Sykes Ranch and Land Sales Helped Open Wells County to Settle-
ment." *Wells County History* 5 (April 1974): 1–7.
Knight, Oliver. "Toward an Understanding of the Western Town." *Western Historical Quarter-
ly* 4 (1973): 27–42.
Land, K. "Duration of Residence and Prospective Migration: Further Evidence." *Demography*
6 (1959): 113–40.
Larsen, Lawrence H. *The Urban West at the End of the Frontier*. Lawrence: Regents Press of
Kansas, 1978.
Larsen, Lawrence H., and Roger T. Johnson. "A Story That Never Was: North Dakota's Urban
Development." *North Dakota History* 47 (Fall 1980): 4–10.
Law, Laura Thompson. *History of Rolette County, North Dakota*. Minneapolis: Lund Press,
1953.
Lösch, August. *The Economics of Location*. Translated by William H. Woglom with the assis-
tance of Wolfgang F. Stolper. New Haven: Yale University Press, 1954.
Lounsberry, Clement A. *North Dakota History and People*. 3 vols. Chicago: S. J. Clarke Pub-
lishing Co., 1917.
Lucht, Gary. "Scobey's Touring Pros: Wheat, Baseball, and Illicit Booze." *Montana Magazine
of Western History* 20 (Summer 1970): 88–93.
Malin, James C. *The Grassland of North America*. Lawrence, Kans.: privately printed, 1947.
Martin, Albro S. *James J. Hill and the Opening of the Northwest*. New York: Oxford Univer-
sity Press, 1976.

Martin, J. Edward. *Railway Stations of Western Canada*. White Rock, B.C.: Studio E, 1980.
Masterson, V. V. *The Katy Railroad and the Last Frontier*. Norman: University of Oklahoma Press, 1952.
Mattison, Ray H. "Old Fort Stevenson." *North Dakota History* 18 (1951): 53–91.
McMillan, Morrison. "Early Settlement of LaCrosse and Monroe Counties." *Report and Collections*, State Historical Society of Wisconsin, 4 (1859): 383–92.
Miner, H. Craig. *The St. Louis-San Francisco Transcontinental Railroad*. Lawrence: University of Kansas Press, 1972.
Minnesota Historical Society. *Collections* 2 (1867): 180; 9 (1901): 166, 444; 14 (1912): 536, 766.
Mitchell, F. Stuart. "Railroad Townsite Promotion in a Capitalistic Setting: Herbert Sydney Duncombe and the Midland Continental Railroad, 1906–1914." Paper read at Northern Great Plains History Conference, Sioux Falls, S. Dak., October 1981.
Montgomery, David A. "The Development of Street-Pattern Orientation Systems: A Case Study in the Platte Valley of Nebraska." Master's thesis, University of Nebraska, 1972.
Morrison, P. "Duration of Residence and Prospective Migration: The Evaluation of a Stochastic Model." *Demography* 4 (1967): 553–61.
Morrison, Theodore. *Chautauqua*. Chicago: University of Chicago Press, 1974.
Myers, G. R. McGinnis, and G. Masnick. "The Duration of Residence Approach to a Dynamic Stochastic Model of Internal Migration: A Test of the Axiom of Cumulative Inertia." *Eugenics Quarterly* 14 (1967): 121–26.
Nash, Gerald D. *The American West in the Twentieth Century: A Short History of an Urban Oasis*. Englewood Cliffs, N.J.: Prentice-Hall, 1973.
Newton, Milton B., Jr. "Cultural Preadaptation and the Upland South." *Geoscience and Man* 5 (1974): 143–54.
Ostergren, Robert C. "The Immigrant Church as a Symbol of Community and Place in the Upper Midwest." *Great Plains Quarterly* 1 (1981): 225–38.
Overton, Richard C. *Burlington West: A Colonization History of the Burlington Railroad*. Cambridge, Mass.: Harvard University Press, 1941.
———. *Gulf to Rockies: The Heritage of the Fort Worth and Denver-Colorado and Southern Railways, 1861–1898*. Austin: University of Texas Press, 1953.
Price, Edward T. "The Central Courthouse Square in the American County Seat." *Geographical Review* 58 (1968): 29–60.
"Professor T. Hayter Lewis on the Laying Out of Town Areas." *American Architect and Building News* 22 (1877): 180–82.
Pulling, Hazel A. "History of the Range Cattle Industry of Dakota." *South Dakota Historical Collections* 20 (1940): 480–97.
"Recorded Town Plats." *Engineering News* 5 (1878): 361.
Rees, Ronald. "The Small Town in Saskatchewan." *Landscape* 18, no. 3 (1969): 29–33.
Reps, John W. *The Making of Urban America: A History of City Planning in the United States*. Princton, N.J.: Princeton University Press, 1965.
———. *Cities of the American West: A History of Frontier Urban Planning*. Princeton, N.J.: Princeton University Press, 1979.
Robinson, Elwyn B. *History of North Dakota*. Lincoln: University of Nebraska Press, 1966.
Schmidt, Carl B. "Reminiscences of Foreign Immigration Work for Kansas." *Transactions, Kansas State Historical Society*, 9 (1906): 485–97.
Seagraves, C. L. "Colonization as a Factor in Traffic Development." *Santa Fe Magazine* 21 (August 1927): 19–20.
"The Shaping of Towns." *American Architect and Building News* 2 (1877): 195–96.

Simon, Anthony H. "The Battle for Parcel Post." *Journal of the West* 13, no. 4 (1974): 78–89.

Smith, Page. *As a City upon a Hill: The Town in American History*. New York: Alfred A. Knopf, 1966.

Spokesfield, Walter. *History of Wells County, North Dakota, and Its Pioneers*. Privately printed, 1929.

Soo Line Railroad. Industrial Department. *Dozens of New Towns*. Minneapolis, Minn., 1907.

Thompson, Roy. "The Naming of Cando." *Collections*, State Historical Society of North Dakota, 3 (1910): 321–23.

Trewartha, Glenn T. "The Unincorporated Hamlet: One Element of the American Settlement Fabric." *Annals*, Association of American Geographers, 33 (1943): 32–81.

——. "Types of Rural Settlement in Colonial America." *Geographical Review* 36 (1946): 568–96.

Trobriand, Philippe Regis Denis de Kedern de. *Army Life in Dakota*. Translated by George F. Will. Chicago: Lakeside Press, 1941.

Vance, James E., Jr. *The Merchant's World: The Geography of Wholesaling*. Englewood Cliffs, N.J.: Prentice-Hall, 1970.

——. *This Scene of Man: The Role and Structure of the City in the Geography of Western Civilization*. New York: Harper's College Press, 1977.

Veblen, Thorstein. *Absentee Ownership and Business Enterprise in Recent Times: The Case of America*. New York: B. W. Huebsch, 1923.

Voisey, Paul. "Boosting the Small Prairie Town, 1904–1931." In *Town and City, Aspects of Western Canadian Urban Development*, edited by Alan F. J. Artibise, 147–76. Canadian Plains Studies, no. 10. Regina, Sask.: Canadian Plains Research Center, 1981.

Vyzralek, Frank E. "David Newton Tallman and the Development of Townsites Along the Great Northern Railway, 1905–1920." Paper read at Northern Plains History Conference, Sioux Falls, S. Dak., October 1981.

Warner, George E. *History of Ramsey County, Minnesota*. Minneapolis: North Star Publishing Company, 1881.

Waters, L. L. *Steel Trails to Santa Fe*. Lawrence: University of Kansas Press, 1950.

Webb, W. E. "Air Towns and Their Inhabitants." *Harper's Magazine* 51 (1875): 828–35.

White, W. Thomas. "Paris Gibson, James J. Hill & the 'New Minneapolis': The Great Falls Water Power and Townsite Company, 1882–1908." *Montana Magazine of Western History* 33 (1983): 60–69.

Wilgus, William J. *The Railway Interrelations of the United States and Canada*. New Haven: Yale University Press, 1937.

Williams, Mary Ann Barnes. *Origins of North Dakota Place Names*. Privately printed, 1966.

Williamson, Jeffrey G. *Late Nineteenth Century American Development, A General Equilibrium History*. Cambridge: Cambridge University Press, 1974.

Wood, Joseph S. "Village and Community in Early Colonial New England." *Journal of Historical Geography* 8 (1982): 333–46.

Index

Index

Ward County, N. Dak., 36, 102, 136
Warwick, N. Dak., 137
Washburn, William D., 74, 167 n11
Washburn, N. Dak., 61, 136
Wells County, N. Dak., 42, 74, 114, 122, 128–29
Wellsburg, N. Dak., 141
West End, N. Dak., 45–46
Westhope, N. Dak., 83, 86
Wheat: precipitation and yields, 58; influence of prices on production, 60; relation to town growth, 100; expansion of acreage, 143–44
Wheat Line: constructed, 61; strategies, 66–67, 83; townsites, on, 99, 101–2
White, Almond A., 74; and Northwest

Land Co., 4, 77–80, 132; difficulty with lot sales, 89
Wholesale trade, 113, 116, 120
Williamson, Jeffrey, 120
Willmar, Minn., 84, 86, 114
Willow City, N. Dak., 78
Wing, Charles K., 76–77
Wing, Harriet Manly, 126
Wise, Ransom R., 127
Wolford, N. Dak., 114

Yankee settlers: westward migration of, 8, 9; and railroads, 9; in towns, 81, 104, 126
Yellowstone River, 143
York, N. Dak., 81–82

John C. Hudson earned his B.S. in geography at the University of Wisconsin and his masters and doctoral degrees at the University of Iowa. He taught at the universities of North Dakota and Wisconsin and is now professor and chairman of the geography department at Northwestern University. Hudson was editor of the *Annals of the Association of American Geographers* from 1975 until 1981, and now serves on the Board of Advisory Editors for the *Great Plains Quarterly*. He is the author of *Geographical Diffusion Theory*.